WIRING KIDS FOR *Success*

In life

http://wiringkidsforsuccess.com

Praise for Wiring Kids for Success

"Garth is a caring mentor with a heart-felt desire to help people. He uses his life experience and all the purposeful effort he has put into learning about family, relationships, self-discipline, personal balance, and spiritual principles to motivate and testify that change is possible. He is insightful, honest, and professional in his approach. Best of all he is a friend and respected mentor."
Karen

"Garth has helped me improve my life and has helped strengthened my family through applying principles brought to light in this book. I have been through many personal development and goal-setting seminars but Garth's plan finally has incorporated the power of enduring principles to set and achieve my goals. I'm extremely grateful Garth has taught me how to draw upon the power of heaven to both seek out and then accomplish the Lord's will for my life. I'm thrilled for the direction I am headed with my family. Our unity is increasing and we are striving for charity in our home. Garth's information has helped me and my friends get our personal lives and get our families rolling on the right track- not only spiritually but in functionality. We thank him for helping me and my friends in redirecting our families; bringing us from mediocrity and less effectiveness to becoming strong effective families. Thank you Garth, we needed this!"

Jill

WIRING KIDS FOR Success

In life

Garth & Sandi Smith

TATE PUBLISHING
AND ENTERPRISES, LLC

Published by Tate Publishing & Enterprises, LLC
127 E. Trade Center Terrace | Mustang, Oklahoma 73064 USA
1.888.361.9473 | www.tatepublishing.com

Tate Publishing is committed to excellence in the publishing industry. The company reflects the philosophy established by the founders, based on Psalm 68:11,
"The Lord gave the word and great was the company of those who published it."

Book design copyright © 2014 by Tate Publishing, LLC. All rights reserved.
Cover design by Ronnel Luspoc
Interior design by Caypeeline Casas

Published in the United States of America

ISBN: 978-1-62510-932-3
1. Family & Relationships / General
2. Family & Relationships / Parenting / General
14.01.27

Acknowledgements

We could not have completed this book, a goal we've had for many years, without the helpful hands and comments of so many. All of our children and their spouses have offered well-timed encouragement, one in particular, Lyric, even provided some welcome content. It was daughter, Hilary and her husband Andy Jorgensen, who persuaded us to switch gears from one subject to this books subject matter for which we are very appreciative. Through the editing process, all the Smith kids (spouses included) sacrificed significantly for which we are most grateful. Messages from our Kids like, "Hey Mom and Dad, how is the book coming? Sure looking forward to its publication", provided outstanding moral support. Early in our efforts friends played a large part, particularly Dr. Michael Pinegar. And, throughout the process friends such as Randy McIntyre and Vee Sanford, offered more valuable encouragement than they probably realize. And our new friend, Dan Sullivan, a gifted author himself, provided timely encouragement and suggestions. My sister, Debbie Smith O'Brien, regularly helped us stay focused with her kindly boosts of reassurance. The staff at Tate Publishing has been remarkably patient with us, particularly, Tosha Powell, Curtis Winkle, and Charlotte Freeman in the final editing process; we truly appreciate all they've done for us first-timers. Although I (Garth) did most of the typing, Sandi was always there with comments and suggestions. And without her inspiring life, many of the more colorful chapters in this book would not be.

Garth & Sandi Smith

Table of Contents

Introduction

Wiring Kids for Success in Life is, in part, a memoir. It's also a how-to book. The memoir is about our family, mostly and the how-to is about tapping into our best selves regarding our highest responsibilities, marriage and parenting, and becoming successful at both. Of course, we don't claim to have all the answers to child-raising, but what we've learned from experience and what we've learned since then, we wish to pass on to you.

We believe there are many styles of parenting and that all or most of them can bring about successful children if properly applied. Our book simply shares with you how we did it and what our approach resulted in.

Although there are many parenting styles, most would agree there are some staple principles in child-raising that absolutely must be included in all child-raising approaches. This book addresses most of those staples.

Besides chapters that apply to raising successful children, we also have some chapters that apply to creating a happy marriage, after all, who can ever expect to raise happy, successful children from a marriage relationship that's seriously impaired with continual unresolved problems? Generally, these unresolved marital problems bleed into the lives of our kids.

Knowing as we do that "no success in life can compensate for failure in the home," we've designed this book to be a book of encouragement to all parents. You will see from its pages that our ten remarkable children came from a very ordinary couple. We're ordinary in every way; not rich, famous, or outstanding in any particular way, but like you, we're crazy about our kids, and from the beginning of our marriage, we concluded that we wanted to give our kids the very best start we could possibly give them. This

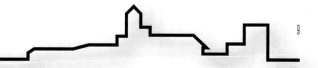

book expresses quite well, we believe, the steps we took to prepare our children for life.

All parents have the instincts to become amazing parents; all we may need is some help to connect those dots in our minds on the process of completing the task with our children. This book is intended to be a help to you in connecting those dots. It should be noted, however that parenting and marriage success is not like following a recipe to create a perfect cake since all married couples and their children have their own unique temperaments and personalities, "connecting those dots" is more a matter of divine connection than recipe reading.

We live in perilous times. Nearly half of all marriages end in divorce. Those who are impacted the most in divorce are the children. Statistics are showing children across the globe are suffering, and most studies show matters for the children will get worse before they get better. A sad commentary.

This book is designed for those parents, single or married, who desire to give their children the best start possible. Or, if your kids are older and have established some bad habits, this book can offer you some ideas and hope. We've also included some ideas for grandparents who want to make a difference in their grandchildren's lives.

This is a book for our time, troubled times. Since the core of all civilized societies is and always has been the family, and since the family unit is under such severe assault, parents across the world need not only encouragement but also some basic tools to help their children become the best they can possibly be, notwithstanding the times we live.

We are over-whelmed with the positive response our book has received. A fellow parent had this to say:

I was so excited when I heard that Garth and Sandi were putting their marriage and child rearing techniques into a book. I watched first-hand as they raised their ten (yes, ten) children

into responsible, successful, loving adults who are now parents themselves. What is so different about them is that they actually planned and strategized how they would instill the values and work ethic that was necessary for each child to become the best person he or she could be, empowering them to choose their own "roads to success." We live in a world where marriages are struggling, and where the majority of children are not "raised," they just grow up. Because of this, so many children grow up without any sense of who they are or what they are capable of accomplishing. Parents, especially young parents, will benefit from the Smiths' tried and true principles for creating an enduring marriage, as well as raising and training children from a very young age to adults.

Deborah

We don't claim to be seasoned writers. It's our hope that as you read our book you will overlook writing errors or style and concentrate on the principles taught in the book. We're confident if you do, you will come away with some helpful ideas and encouragement to strengthen your child-raising skills and enrich your marriage too.

And finally, in our book, we often refer to our children and yours, as "kids." This is an endearing term in our household and is not meant to belittle or minimize the significance of our little ones—our children of any age.

Enjoy.

Wiring Kids for Success in Life

"Lexi, it's five o'clock. Time to milk," fifteen-year-old Jesse calls to his eight-year-old sister. Lexi, with eyes still closed and in total trust, rolls off her top bunk of the bunk bed into the waiting arms of her big brother. They bundle up for the dark and cold winter weather and walk the hundred yards to the small barn. Toto, the jersey milk cow and family pet, knows it's time to milk and leads the way through the corral into the small barn sticking her head into the stanchion. Jesse gives Toto some yummy grain to eat while Lexi positions the two stools; then, they both sit down and each begin to milk their side of the cow.

After the milking, they remove Toto from the stanchion, take the milk into the house and strain it, putting it into the refrigerator to cool. After they clean and wash everything up, they both prepare themselves for another day of school. This same process is followed by a different set of siblings later in the afternoon.

You don't need to buy a jersey milk cow or own a small farm to raise good kids or to teach them responsibility and industriousness. But there are certain fundamental principles kids must learn if they are to be successful in life, and the good part is this: most of it can be accomplished within the walls of your own home.

The purpose of this book is to provide helpful information to those with children and those who hope to have children to provide information to arm you with knowledge on the subject of wiring your kids for success in life, a life of achievement, a life of happiness. Raising kids in any era is a challenge, but in these modern, troubled times, the threat to our children's moral, spiritual, emotional, and physical welfare may be more severe than at any previous time, at least over the past century. So subtle is the threat, many parents don't even know what's hit their family until it's almost too late. We need all the encouragement and direction we can get.

Note: This book is not for those who are expecting no more than mediocrity from their kids. We wrote this book to help parents wire kids for **success** in life. Our definition of "success" is to help them become the best they can possibly be, which we're confident will bring them their highest form of happiness in life. What many call ordinary could be greatness, but let's be sure that we teach and support our kids to fulfill their greatest potential, whatever that might be. As parents, we're always in the mode of teaching, training, and loving our kids in the direction of becoming—becoming who they were created to become. No doubt about it, our kids and even we ourselves were created for success in life. If you're reading this, it's not too late for you and your kids to be successful and achieve a life of happiness.

Having raised ten kids (amazing kids, if we may say so, and with twenty-nine grandchildren and more on the way), we're sure you can imagine we have had many varied experiences in raising kids—some sad times, many happy times, some stressful times, and many serene times. Lots of laughter and some tears. We have six daughters and four sons, and though we don't claim to have all the answers, we do have some, and what we have learned from others and through our own experience, we wish to pass on to you.

When we were first married, we both agreed to have as many children as Sandi's health would allow—she would be the judge of that. As a child, she always wanted to have a large family. (Sandi) As early as my grade school years, I wanted to have many children but never settled on a particular number. But when I read the book *Cheaper by the Dozen*, my mind was set. I loved that book and thought how wonderful it would be to have a large family. I said to myself then that I can do that, but rather than

twelve kids, I want thirteen—a baker's dozen. We did have thirteen pregnancies, but three were miscarriages.

I (Garth) wanted a large family, too. As a young boy, I recall thinking to myself how much I wanted to be a father of a large family with many children.

When we met at college and began growing together, we marveled how remarkable it was for two people to meet in these modern days, both desiring a large family. We married and began our dream.

After our first child was born, it occurred to us that we needed to establish a model we could use as a guide in raising well-adjusted, obedient children. We observed older, more experienced parents, parents who had shown success in raising kids. We found several parents who we felt we could use as our model, and from there, we selected one couple and family who more closely filled our purpose. We chose this family because we knew how their kids had turned out, at least to that point in their lives. We liked what we saw. We had come to know all their children prior to interviewing their parents. We knew them to be hardworking, obedient, and well adjusted. Most impressive, however, was how respectful they were to their parents.

We boldly asked them if we could visit with them for the purpose of asking questions about parenting to determine how they raised a large and very outstanding family. They were humbled and honored we asked, and they gladly consented. Our interview with them was thrilling, to say the least. We asked them pointed questions that required more than a yes or no answer. Our questions covered such topics as obedience, discipline, honesty, work habits, honoring parents, and many more. The interview lasted an hour or so and resulted in giving us a much clearer view of what lay ahead for us if we sincerely desired to teach and train our children to be the best they could possibly be. It was a wonderful interview which forever changed our perspective of how to raise great kids. We walked away from that interview with greater enthusiasm but also with some feelings of trepidation. We would later meet again with more questions. It became perfectly clear that to raise the quality of kids we desired, it would require our best effort, our best planning. We realized their kids turned out well not by accident but, rather, by design and calculated effort on their part. We got a glimpse of what lay ahead for us, well, if we wanted great kids like theirs, and we did. (You can read more details of that interview in the chapter entitled: Lessons from our First Tutors).

We would suggest that all young parents and those who hope to be parents begin your quest for good family life by finding a successful family you could use as a model, and interview the parents, get into their heads, and learn from them. We find that most young parents make far too many assumptions regarding parenting. We've gained the perspective that most young parents have no plan, no strategy, only to do with their children what their parents did with them, which may not always be the best way to go. Parental education is crucial for family success. A solid family with well-adjusted and well-prepared kids does not happen by accident.

After all, what parent doesn't want the best for their children? Yet most often, we leave their training and development in the hands of their school teachers, their friends, the TV, video games or an iPod blasting in their ears. If we truly desire our children to be successful in life, we must be willing and deeply desirous to give them the training and experiences they will need for success. Well-adjusted, successful children do not come by accident; there are cause-and-effect principles that come into play.

Imagine beginning a business without a plan, yet how much more significant is a living child, your child, than a business that could be operational today and gone tomorrow?

You may be thinking your children are past the childhood stage and that their habits are already set, that it's impossible now to make the needed changes to ensure their success. Don't

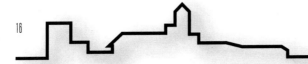

fall into that trap of failure thinking. Your children are worth the effort to never stop trying. And there are plenty of examples of parents who started late and still had success. This includes our married children. Granted, they are out of our direct care—very much on their own. But they are still our children, and their overall success never leaves our hearts and minds.

How then does a parent wire a child for success in life?

The first step starts with you, the parent. A parent must have a vision, a perspective, or a dream of how you want your children to turnout. Don't get us wrong, we don't mean to suggest you force them into success; that would be quite impossible to do. We all know kids come to us with their own unique temperaments, personalities, strengths, and weaknesses. Yet we, the parents, do have a tremendous influence on their final outcome. So with what influence we do have, we'll want to get it right or as right as we possibly can.

To have a vision of your child's life is simply to have a feeling of hope, a dream, and yes, even faith that your child is going to become a meaningful contributor to society. To gain a mental vision, you will likely need a model to follow, someone you admire and look up to, someone who has had the kind of child-raising success you desire to duplicate. We would suggest you follow the same approach we used, that you can actually observe your mentors in action as they continue to mold their children to greatness.

Your mentor may be someone living or deceased, who has already proven they have or had the qualities you want your children to have. Ideally, it is someone you actually know or have known or know of, often a family member. Or choose someone whose life has been well documented—Abraham Lincoln, for instance.

Vision of your children's successful outcome is crucial because when you slip off your desired path and feel like a failure as a parent (and those days do occur), thinking upon your vision, your

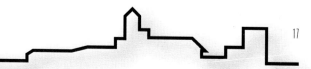

model mentor , will give you encouragement to get back on track. Vision is absolutely essential, so please don't miss that step.

Modern studies have proven the invaluable benefits of having a *mentor* to guide one through life. We all should have a mentor or mentors in life. Most great people have expressed their appreciation for someone who mentored them.

Consider the life of Abraham Lincoln as mentioned earlier. Young Abraham was influenced primarily by his stepmother, Sarah Bush Johnson, who nurtured him after the passing of his natural mother when he was ten. She filled the gap and gave him the feelings of security and peace he needed in his life at that turbulent time. Sarah also gave young Abraham and the family the needed structure and order in their lives. And she accomplished all this with a loving hand. She always spoke kindly of Abraham and him of her.

At least in part of her caring attention to him, he would later become a loving, compassionate father himself, even though his own father's influence seemed to have withered (Abraham was even absent from his father's funeral). Lincoln's own writings clearly point to the incredible caring effect his stepmother had on him in his own parental role.

As a parent, do you have a mentor, a model to follow? If not, we encourage you to choose at least one. Choose carefully because your mentor will have great influence in your life. Who do you know who has raised good, well-adjusted children? Who do you know who has done so under the same or similar circumstances as your own? They are out there, you know. You simply need to find them—at least one.

When you carefully and thoughtfully select your mentor and model, we admonish you to be a careful student of your mentor's ways and means of accomplishing their parental tasks and forming the lives of their children. Be a student of that select person or couple.

We've chosen to focus on this part of parenting in this first chapter primarily because we, the parents, will have the greatest impact upon our children, and therefore, we need to try the best we can to learn and follow tried and proven practices in raising our kids to success. As we said earlier, good kids seldom come by accident, but rather, they are taught and influenced by a loving parent or parents (and sometimes grandparents) who taught them correct principles to live by.

Mission Statements: Parents with Vision

Most of us can relate to the conversation I had with a mother whose children were raised on their own, but in each case, the children experienced severe moral and marriage challenges in their lives. Most of her children were struggling with the effects of no direction or goals for their lives. Their children—her grandchildren—were beginning another generation of no goals and no dreams for their futures and signs of little hope for their lives.

It was a sad but all too common story of how young couples begin their marriage with great hope for their family future but end up with little or no hope and the effects no hope has on individuals and families.

She came to me in tears over the kind of lifestyle her children and grandchildren were choosing. Alcoholism, drugs, broken marriages, and more were plaguing her immediate and extended family and breaking her heart.

She was sorrowful over the decisions she and her husband made when her children were young. Again and again, she told me how she wished she could turn the clock back; back to the days when she and her husband were young, when they were just beginning their family, and the many changes she would make to assure a brighter future for her children and grandchildren.

She blamed herself and her husband for not being more visionary regarding their children's futures. She said, "It's like we forgot the kids would grow up some day and be on their own. Had we been more aware of that fact, we'd have prepared them better. As it is now, nearly every one of our children and grandchildren are having overwhelming, painful struggles in their lives—mostly self-inflicted. We began with great hopes. We just took our eyes off the biggest goal, our children. We were distracted and preoccupied with lesser things."

She was almost inconsolable. All I could do was to remind her that as long as she and her husband are living, they have some influence over their children and grandchildren and that with that influence, they could begin anew to show and teach their posterity how to live their lives—how to change their lives. I tried to give her hope.

That conversation with that sweet mother is the story of far too many in our day. Most of those stories could have turned out much differently had the parents recognized their divine role to prepare their children for life, for the day when they would be on their own to fight against the normal and common struggles of life.

Following this chapter are two successive chapters on goals. But this chapter is about a process that should always precede our goals; we're speaking of mission statements.

Personal and family mission statements are like goals but more general in scope. Don't be confused by titles. Some prefer the title mission objective or vision statement, yet they are all the same.

What is a mission statement? It is a brief statement—often two or three sentences or less—*describing what you stand for as a parent*, what you are about, and *what you expect from yourself and your children*. Your mission statement *will describe what your most fundamental goal is and what you desire as an end result*, so you'll know when you've reached your goal. It will describe your *purpose* as a parent or caregiver. A mission statement allows you to glance at a written statement and be reminded of your purpose and mission in life as it applies to your life, your marriage, and your family.

Your goals will always propel you in the direction of your ultimate purpose—your mission statement. Your mission statement will always give you a brief description of your ultimate purpose,

WIRING KIDS FOR SUCCESS IN LIFE

they work in concert. So then, to get a general view of what you wish to accomplish as a parent with your children, thoughtfully write your mission statement, and read it often. However, to accomplish the daily, weekly, and monthly tasks to fulfill your mission statement, follow your written, detailed goals. First your mission statement, followed by your goals.

We know what some might be thinking: "My parents didn't have a mission statement or goals, and I turned out fine." True, and the fact of the matter is most parents do not have a family or parent mission statement to guide them in raising their kids. However, we're living in different times unlike any we've seen in the world, threatening times, times filled of moral pressure heaped upon parents and children. Added to that, we should understand that no matter what the conditions and environment we live in, we should, as parents, strive to implement any and all *tools* that will help us be *more directed* and *on track* to help our children become the best they can be. Moreover, when we have systems or programs in place to help our family do their best, we begin to feel the benefits of organization. As we've stated earlier, if we don't know the direction we're going as parents, our children are the likely ones to suffer the most. Who among us doesn't want our children to become better than we are? That's a given for most parents.

A mission statement is a simple tool, the kind of tool that is designed to help us stay on track with our ultimate desires. For the Christian believer, you will be comforted to know that "God is not a god of disorder, but of peace" (1 Cor. 14:33). You can find similar verses in the Old Testament. Order in our lives does, in fact, bring peace, and who among us doesn't appreciate peace in our lives, especially in child-raising? Peace in our lives is a signal we're moving in a good direction. To bring about such peace through order (organization and direction) in our lives, we should institute programs, systems, and tools to order our household, including systems and programs that help us stay on track with the teaching and training of our children. We do that by establishing standards to live by and by monitoring our progress as a family against our standards to determine our progress.

Before we go any further, let us share with you a couple of examples of mission statements that show how simple the process can be:

> To use every resource and strength within our power and influence to help our children become the best that they can possibly be that in the end, *there will be no empty chairs.* ("No empty chairs" makes mention of our family being a forever family and that we, as parents, would do everything in our power and influence to make sure all our children would be with us forever).

We particularly liked this mission statement:

> To be as one, united, one with God, spouse, children, and community; to invite the spirit of union and harmony within our family.

Or, how about this one from a little man who changed the world,

> *Let the first act of every morning be to make the following resolve for the day:*
>
> ** I shall not fear anyone on Earth.*
> ** I shall fear only God.*
> ** I shall not bear ill will toward anyone.*
> ** I shall not submit to injustice from anyone.*
> ** I shall conquer untruth by truth. And in resisting untruth, I shall put up with all suffering.*
>
> —Mahatma Gandhi

Some parents write their mission statement to emphasize education, while others place greater emphasis on social devel-

opment, yet others, on spiritual matters. Still, others include all three as well as other desires.

As you can imagine, every family's mission statement will be different, written to meet the respective families ultimate dreams and goals. Our mission statement has been a guide to help us stay on track, particularly when times were difficult, when challenges had a tendency to muddle our minds and move us away from our mission statement and goals. A family mission statement is intended to help us read a single phrase or two to be reminded what we desire our family to be—**the final outcome**.

We have chosen to frame our mission statement and hang it on our living room wall. As a family, when times got tough, it was not uncommon for us to walk through the living room only to glance at our mission statement on the wall, which offered us direction and hope. Reading it on the wall provided encouragement and had a tendency to help us see our circumstances more clearly and to remind us that no matter what the present circumstances may be, they can become better as we refocus our efforts toward our ultimate target. I'm sure you can imagine that when marriage and parenting gets tough, any amount of added clarity and hope is most welcome. You may wish to frame your mission statement and place it on one of your most prominent walls.

I recall, on more than one occasion, feelings were not good in our home; tempers were raised, and arguments ensued, causing misunderstanding and hurt feelings. I would be feeling bad or disappointed in myself. I would either walk past our mission statement mounted on the wall, or I would simply recall it in my mind. In each case, our mission brought me to my senses which resulted in sincere apology and improved relationships. You see, whatever tools we can use to help us do better and stay on track, we should implement. But again we remind you: *We can't stay on track if we do not have a preferred track to run on.* Make your mission statement clear and concise, you'll never be sorry you did.

Once a mission statement is crafted, we can work on our goals, each goal written to direct us toward the fulfillment of our overall mission statement.

There is purpose in life, and each one of us has purpose and meaning in this frail existence. We can't afford to leave our outcome or that of our kids up to society, friends, television, school, or anyone or anything else. Parents, for our kids' sake and the sake of our marriage, we must take charge!

We hope you will take the time to ponder deeply the ultimate mission you have for your family. And with that mission statement, design goals that will help you fulfill your mission. *Kids Wired For Success* in life didn't happen by accident. It was intentional, well thought-out, and strategized by parents.

Using Goals to Wire Kids for Success

In Lewis Carroll's *Alice in Wonderland*, Alice, when at a fork in the road, asks Cheshire Cat, "I was just wondering if you could help me find my way."

Cheshire Cat responded, "Well, that depends on where you want to go."

Alice responded, "Oh, it really doesn't matter."

Cheshire Cat said, "Then it really doesn't matter which way you go."

Wiring kids for success in life cannot be dependent upon a no-plan plan. That's an oxymoron, we know. We use that foolish phrase because nothing could be more foolish than trying to raise our greatest treasure without a plan.

Wiring kids for success begins with the parent(s) and is an inside-out job. Such success requires our best effort and will not likely occur without parents being at the top of their game or *striving* to be so. It doesn't require perfection, but it does take a *fixed* and *determined desire* to see your child through to success. And as you can imagine, much depends on your definition of "success."

This chapter is about how goals can help us to raise happy, well-adjusted children who reach their full potential. After all, "The greatest work we will ever do will be within the walls of our own home." That is not just a catchy quote; it is time-tested.

What are goals? Goals are objectives, a target we individually select to try to achieve. Goals determine the direction in life we desire. Clearly defined goals with plans to achieve them fulfill

our mission statement. We can and should establish short-term goals (daily, weekly, or monthly), intermediate goals (quarterly or yearly), long-term goals (five years or more), and lifetime goals.

If, like Alice, it doesn't matter which direction we're going in relation to our child's development, any way will likely be the wrong way. Without a mental vision and a goal, we're likely to be led by an unruly society, and our children will feel the major brunt of it. And we, the parents, will be left with heavy hearts.

How pleasant and rewarding it is for a husband and wife to have agreed upon goals and agreed upon ways and means to reach those goals, particularly as it applies to raising our kids. The time it takes to establish common goals is well worth the time and effort. Work on your *desired outcomes* (goals) as they apply to matters that will affect your children; ponder what you want as goals. Write your goals down, and read them often. Value that time, for it will prove to be key in the overall welfare of your children and the family as a whole.

Once the goals are clear in both your minds, simply put the goals into practice. This is easier said than done. You will likely find that reaching your lofty, united goals will be some of the hardest work you will ever do. The task of raising good, well-adjusted kids requires mental determination from both of you. These goals are more substantial than so called New Year's resolutions. And since so much is at stake (our children's overall welfare), our goals must be considerably more serious in our minds than easily broken resolutions. Because the kids are worth it, both parents should be solidly engaged in the pre-established goals. The chances of success with your children will expand considerably when both husband and wife are united in this effort. And besides, it has a tendency to draw married couples together in a common interest.

This united effort will show its brilliance once the going gets tough. It's not uncommon for either husband or wife to fall off

the wagon, so to speak, and get away from the goals you've set. But if the other spouse is still engaged in them, he or she can hold up both ends until the other gets a grip and picks up his or her end once again. Later on, roles may be reversed. Remember, you're a team, and the end goal is to help sons and daughters become well-adjusted, happy, and prepared for the world we live in and to be the best they can possibly be. No need to criticize the spouse who dropped the ball for a time because the other will most likely drop the ball at some point. Tolerance and patience are critical virtues in parenting and marriage—not just toward the kids but toward each other.

As mentioned, having a model and mentor whom you can look to for a path to follow will offer tremendous encouragement as you strive to stay engaged in your goals. You would be wise to think often of the example your model set, and then work each day to mimic it. When times become challenging, thinking upon your model can supply extra energy and resolve to work through your challenges of raising your kids according to your desired goals.

A united team effort between husband and wife could well be the single most important thing parents can do for their kids and the family. Why? Because unity brings peace—peace of mind, peace in our relationships, and peace in our home. Peace in the home brings genuine concern for others, calmness, and gentleness. These are wonderful traits parents want their children to recognize and embrace. The truth is, the single most important thing you can show and tell your children is how much you love their mother, and vice versa.

As a reminder, your goals for your kids' sake, are designed to help your children BECOME all they are capable of becoming. Your goals are not simply tasks to do and accomplish regularly, they are intended to help your child become their best self. "Becoming" and not just doing is the point we need always

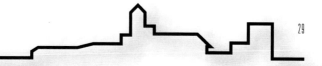

remember as we're striving to stay engaged in our goals. Imagine in your mind's eye your child becoming a remarkable human being. This simple mind game helped us stay on track regarding our goals; hopefully it will work for you, too. If you are a single parent, who do you unite with to gain strength and support to help you achieve your goals for your kids? As we all know or can imagine, your task is one of the most challenging tasks of all, but that's ever more reason to establish goals.

Do you have a reliable social circle? Do you have parents, siblings, grandparents, or trustworthy friends? Rely on them if possible for support and encouragement. They need not live nearby necessarily. As long as you can reach them by phone when emotional support is needed, they can be a tremendous help to you.

Whether family support is available or not, we admonish you (as well as couples) to embrace a religion of your choice. Many churches have programs for children, youth, and adults. Boy Scouts of America is a tried and tested program for boys. Similar programs are available for girls. Develop close relationships with the strongest and most faithful of the church. Get close to the church leadership, close enough that a trusting relationship is developed. Try your best to not only get in the church but most importantly to *get the church in you*. Find a church you can put your trust in, a church that will lead you and your children to a higher power. For your children's sake as well as your own, seek for *truth*. Whether you are Christian, Jewish, or agnostic, we state to you in the plainest language we can, that there are many absolutes, things we can count on again and again and again, for they never change—ever!

Seek those absolutes, and share them with your children. Make them part of your goals for desired achievement for yourself and your kids. They are the principles that will provide an *anchor* for you and your children, particularly when times are tough. We have found as parents there are certain universal absolutes that must be instilled in every child if we want them to be the best they can be —wired for success. Here is a fundamental list:

- obedience to law
- moral, principle-based life
- honesty with self and others
- industriousness: willingness to work hard
- cooperation: willingness to be a good team member
- faith: a fundamental trust in a higher power
- thriftiness
- goal-oriented (setting targets in every aspect of life and working to reach them)

These represent but a few of a much larger list, but if we at least begin with these, we will be well on our way.

These are absolutes we can trust and have been proven over all time to bring about success at any level. The sooner we begin to instill these principles into our children, the sooner they will become hardwired for success.

You may ask what kind of goals we set as parents. The answer to that question is answered as you read the following chapter in conjunction with this one. Our goals were based and focused on the list above: obedience, honesty, morality, work ethic, thriftiness, and faith in God. We had a vision in our minds how we wanted our children to turn out; we then fashioned our teachings at home and work duties we assigned to them to help them gain or buy into those character traits. Little by little, we could see their character being formed in each of their lives. We would be amiss if we failed to add how helpful our religion was in molding our kids—Sunday school classes, Boy Scouts, young women's organization, and many more. Leading our children to a higher power is most significant. The church became, in a sense, part of our family.

You may feel uncomfortable about setting goals at first; maybe you have no experience in goal-setting. That's okay, no problem. As long as you have the *vision* mentioned in the chapter regarding mission statements, you can write down those thoughts—those *dreams*. Read them often to keep that dream alive; *they become your goals!*

We believe the best way to establish goals is to determine what you want the end result of your kids to look like—*to be*, more particularly, to become. In this case, we desired children wired for success. Remember, when we say "wired" we mean that the child eventually comes to that point where he begins to pull his own self-driven weight. He comes to agree with what you've taught him, and he uses his own strength and vision to move in that direction.

When he accepts it, there is no more parental pulling or coaxing, and he is a convert to what it takes to become solid and true in the direction of his goals. If that becomes your goal, then determine in your mind what your children's lives will look like when your goal is reached (example: self-assured, content, well adjusted, living by moral standards, love for all mankind, etc.).

Once the end result is seen in your mind, simply determine what your children must *feel, experience,* and *know* to fulfill your vision—your goal for them. When the "*feel, experience, and know*" exercise is thoughtfully completed in your mind and then on paper, determine what you can do as parents to help him gain those *feelings, experiences,* and *knowledge.* Once you've connected in your mind the predetermined vision, it's simply a matter of designing daily and weekly activities and projects that will help your child receive the *feelings, experiences,* and *knowledge* that he can make them his own, so to speak. And then, it becomes his vision and not just yours for

him. At that point, the reward for parents becomes more visible. It's all worth the effort, we promise.

The best place to start creating your future or that of your children is by making the most of your present. Let's not allow another day to pass without some serious thought on what we want for our children's futures and how we plan to help them be their best selves.

Goal #2

If you read the previous chapter, "Using Goals to Wire Kids for Success in Life," hopefully you've gained the belief that goal-setting, or we should say, goal achievement, is essential to raising kids to be wired for success. This chapter is the second installment on goals but with more emphasis on implementing goals in raising your children to become all they can be. One of our duties as parents is to teach our children they are to "act" and not be "acted upon." If we individually fail to have a plan for life and see purpose in life, we will be "acted upon" by forces outside ourselves like society and all its whims and fashions. We should desire for our kids to take action and "act" rather than be "acted upon" by others.

The following is a story about our daughter Hilary and how she used goals to help her through a particularly difficult time of her life. Although this is her experience, the process she used to reach her goal—to solve her problem—can be applied in anyone's life and under most circumstances. We will tell her story in our own words as Hilary shared it with us. We highly encourage you to apply this goal-achievement process in your own life and to teach it to your children as quickly as they come of age to understand it.

Hilary was getting to the age where she was concerned about whether she would ever get married. She spoke with us and shared with us her doubts and fears. We encouraged her to establish a specific goal to get married. It was her dream to be married to a fine man and to raise a family of her own—this dream she carried in her heart since childhood. Yet writing the goal down and placing special emphasis upon it, she had never done, specifically at least.

She took our counsel and began the process. She began by pondering deeply about the matter. She then determined she would, in fact, set it as a written goal. Finally, she wrote down a goal. It went something like this: "To meet the guy I should marry and to see his qualities." This was intended as a one-year goal—to be fulfilled within a year.

Because effective goals generally require something from us—a *sacrifice* of some sort—she determined to put forth her best effort to show she really meant what she wrote on paper. In her case, the sacrifice she chose was to better educate her mind that she would become her best self when she met her future husband. It was her desire to bring to the marriage her best self.

She set the goal at the beginning of the year and put the deadline at the end of the year. For twelve months, she kept her commitment to herself to better educate and prepare herself. She did this by reading specific, handpicked books that challenged her mind and spirit—one book per month. This was an honorable *sacrifice* for her, and it truly did require effort because of her already busy schedule as a new dental hygienist.

Before the year ended, a friend of hers introduced her to one of his friends. This friend (her future husband) was quite smitten by her, but she was more cautious. She recognized his goodness and his fine qualities—everything she had desired in her goal, yet she wanted to be sure. So she set another goal: "to find out if he was the one I should marry and, if so, to marry the man who could make me fulfilled and I make him fulfilled."

This goal had a much shorter deadline, just a few months. Within a couple of months of dating, she could plainly see he was the man for her. They were married shortly thereafter. From this union we have two more gorgeous granddaughters.

Goals work. Or we should say, clearly defined goals, sincerely set in written form, with a clear set of plans to achieve them, work.

The following is a simple and basic step-by-step approach to goal-setting and achievement.

Steps to Goal Achievement

1. Get a statement of your goals on paper. This represents you're "what," meaning, what you want. It should be stated with verbiage to show what the *end result* will be like when the goal is reached, so be descriptive, as well as optimistic and positive. This represents clearly defined goals.
2. Determine your "why." Why do you want this goal? A solid "why" is essential to success. The "what" informs. The "why" transforms. A clear "why" keeps us enthused and motivated.
3. Determine "how" you plan to achieve this goal—action steps. This can be one or more strategies you plan to follow to reach your goal. Action steps are steps that will point you and advance you directly toward your goal. Typically they are logical actions that as you complete them you will end up with a completed goal.
4. Be willing to sacrifice your time, efforts, and sometimes even money to reach your goal. A willingness to sacrifice your efforts is the part often left out of most traditional goal programs. To sacrifice is intended to stretch you and also to apply a sort of earnest money, good faith effort, testifying to yourself you are deeply serious about this goal. *Then do it!* This will be a sacrifice on your part, something you normally would not do. It could be giving up something you know you should not be doing—a vice. Or it could be to apply yourself more diligently in a path you know you should be following. Interestingly, your sacrifice may not even relate to your goal, directly.

    Your sacrifice can be such things as taking the needed time to read to each child each day, if that's something

you've not been doing. Another could be to place your child's happiness and welfare above your own (if that is a weakness for you). Or you may consider accelerating your child's education by having your own little school each day to prepare them better for formal education, and more (read chapter entitled, "Ready, Aim, Fire," for more on this). Each of these could be *sacrifices* to you. Stretching ourselves for the sake of our children's overall development is an honorable pursuit, one which we will always look back on with tenderness.

In Hilary's case, she stretched her mind with additional, focused reading. Already an avid reader, this extended her beyond her normal reading output. Her selected books were not about dating, relationships, or marriage, but they stretched her mind nonetheless, and they helped her gain new knowledge at the same time keeping her mentally engaged in her goal.

Some people confuse their "how" action steps with sacrifice; they are two different aspects of the process. Again, action steps are specific to your goal, and as you pursue them one by one, the end result should be your goal. But sacrifice is another aspect of goal achievement that will turn your goals into "serious business," so much so you are willing to give of yourself in more significant ways.

In Hilary's case, her sacrifice was designed to include the Lord in her goals. The books she read increased her understanding of God and helped her learn to trust God's timing and his love for her. It worked.

5. Review your goals and visualize them each day. Some goal specialists suggest rewriting your goals each morning to fortify them in our mind. Whatever approach you use to review and visualize your goals each morning, we highly encourage it. If goals are worthwhile to you, they are worth doing right.

Our goals for our children's success can follow the same pattern as our daughter, Hilary. All five parts of the goal process are significant and are designed to help us achieve our highest, most noble desires.

In the chapter entitled "Wired for Success: 'How To,'" we introduce you to how our children's minds develop from their earliest beginnings at birth. Of course this applies to all of us. As one examines carefully the workings of their God-given mind, they will quickly realize how significant, how powerful learning is to our mind's development. We've all got to *learn to love to learn*; otherwise our minds begin to atrophy ever so slowly. For this reason, we would like to share some final thoughts of how goals in our lives affect our minds. We don't claim to have any deep scientific knowledge nor do we have degrees in this area. So you can be assured our explanation will be basic, easy for all to understand.

We are absolutely convinced, as said before, our minds are designed for advancement, regular development, and learning. What's more, they light up like light bulbs when we apply goals for personal growth into our minds.

Our minds are fashioned for happiness and joy. Aristotle agreed, he said, "Happiness is the meaning and purpose of life, the whole aim and end of human existence." (Thinkexist.com) If we're not feeling happiness and joy in our lives, we can look at how we're treating our minds, the quality of our thoughts. Are we working them like the muscle they are, or do we largely forget how amazing they are? Consider this: It is our thoughts and the way we apply our thoughts that determine all our success whether it be with diets, marriage, and education, whatever. It all begins in our mind.

Our minds work like robots. Imagine having your own electronic butler, designed to help you with whatever task you give it. That is what each one of us have, pretty amazing don't you think?

Our mind does not think on its own. It simply receives instructions from us, and then it puts all its muscle and influence into

the achievement of our desires. But (and that's a big "but," no pun intended), if we fail to instruct our mind, or if our instructions are vague and unclear, our mind does not know which direction to search. Remember, all it can do is what we tell it. So when we form our goals or desires, we will want to create them in simple and clear, easily understood language, not because our mind is stupid and needs clearer instructions, but rather, because of the way our mind is designed. It is designed like a robot, with the most incredible computer to work from. We simply must be specific when we instruct our mind what we want.

Like a thermostat, our mind, when clearly instructed, becomes like a set point, so to speak, which will use all available resources to achieve the instructions we give it. If we clearly instruct it, it will not allow us to go beyond our thermostat set point.

Next, at the base of our brain stem is a piece of equipment God gave us to filter out all other data. We can focus our efforts more directly on what we want and desire. Ever more reason to make our goals crystal clear. This is important because, through our five senses, our mind computes billions of info daily. With the help of our God-given filter, the **reticular activating system,** our mind operates with the law of attraction, and like a guided missile, it moves us toward our clearly defined goals. Can we see why our daily marching orders to our mind must be written and thought in ways that cannot be misconstrued?

In addition, our mind only takes instructions (thoughts and goals) that are optimistic and positive. Many have learned that for best results with their goals, they write down their goals and instruct their mind—with language as though they've already received the goal—in a language of gratitude for already receiving what they have not yet received. Pretty amazing, huh?

Imagine a wise parent who knows these incredible truths, and who gives to their children the kind of start that will take full advantage of this amazing equipment that sits above our shoulders. This "wise parent" can be you.

Our children are God-given. We have a divine duty and responsibility to give them our best effort. Establishing goals for each child and the family is a special way to keep ourselves engaged in the role of parenting. In so doing, and in concert with the knowledge of our powerful mind, we can learn to be happy and joyful each and every day, and teach our children to do the same.

Wired for Success: "How To"

How do we wire our kids for success? To answer that question, we need to rub against one of the greatest mysteries of all time, the mind. In this chapter, we get to learn more about the workings of the mortal brain, particularly as it applies to its early development, and the role of parents in helping the child become wired, that he may become the best he can be.

This is fun stuff. Don't be intimidated. It is within your ability to understand. We have simplified it with the following article which we obtained from the United Way website under the section entitled "Help Wire Child's Brain." It comes from a scientific article but has been condensed by LeAnn Simmons. This article can literally change the way we see our parental role as it pertains to our duty to nurture and teach our little children. Actually, it is the process we use for all of us whatever our age.

Here is the condensed article:

> Neuroscientists tell us that the experiences that fill babies first days, months and years have a decisive impact on the architecture of their brains and on the nature and extent of adult capacities.
>
> Did you know the brain is the least developed organ at birth, that 90 percent of the brain's growth occurs from birth until age 5, and that a baby's brain doubles in weight from birth to age 3?
>
> At birth, the human brain has about a 100 billion nerve cells called neurons, most of them unconnected. Forming

and reinforcing these connections are the key tasks of early brain development.

As the infant sees, hears, smells and feels, the neurons form trillions of connections known as synapses. A neuron may connect to as many as 15,000 other neurons, forming an intricate network of neural pathways.

This immensely complex network is the brain's "wiring." The patterns in which connections are formed lay the groundwork for future learning. The circuits created and reinforced will dramatically affect the child later in life-for better or worse.

In the early years, children's brains form twice as many synapses as they will eventually need. If these synapses are used repeatedly in a child's day-to-day life, they are reinforced and become part of the brain's permanent circuitry. If they are not used repeatedly, or often enough, they are eliminated.

In this way experience plays a crucial role in "wiring" a young child's brain. Our responsibility is to nurture young children and provide the stimulation that will give them the best possible start in life (emphasis added).

Did you catch that? "Forming and reinforcing these connections are the key tasks of early brain development." So, the key to our kids' mental wiring (for future success) requires frequent use of the five senses and repetition, repetition, and more repetition. These repetitive experiences give our child the wherewithal to connect brain cells until they become permanent connections in the brain. So, this becomes (or should become) our parental marching orders, to determine what we want our kids wired for and to become, and then we expose them to it so often it becomes part of their human system, likely never to be erased.

So what permanent connections do you want for your children? You, the parent, can choose them, and once you do, let them experience them with the five senses again and again and again. In this way, solid circuitry is set in the brain. Do we want

them to feel loved, tender toward others, kind, and patient? Then let them feel and see that love multiple times each day.

What about their ability and desire to learn? Who doesn't want their child to have a head start in his learning process? If that's what you want, then introduce him early and often to the love of books and the love of learning. We have within our control the ability to largely determine the success or failure of our children. Granted, in the end result, our kids will become who they choose to become. However, their road to become who they choose to become can be enhanced and better prepared by the way we nurture them in their early years, particularly. Yes, they will be who they wish to be, but through our parental efforts, we can set them on a good path that will make their lives much happier and more fulfilled, more optimistic, and in most cases, less stressful.

James Allen, author of the world famous book *As a Man Thinketh*, said the following:

> A man's mind may be likened to a garden, which may be intelligently cultivated or allowed to run wild; but whether cultivated or neglected, it must, and will bring forth. If no useful seeds are put into it, then an abundance of useless weed-seeds will fall therein, and will continue to produce their kind.

From his wisdom, we add how much more beneficial it is to the man-child when we begin the cultivating process of the mind in the infant and childhood stage.

The question some of us might ask has to do with the "how to." From a practical perspective, how do we wire our kids' brains for success that we may take full advantage of our children's God-given brain cells? The answers you'll find quite simple; we simply have to implement the concepts into our daily life as we interact with our kids and do so until it is a daily habit. Here are some of the simple to-dos parents should do to lay the groundwork for your child's brain to begin the wiring process:

1. Hold your babies and young children close, and cuddle them often. This wires their brain with an assurance they are in a safe place and with safe, loving caretakers. Feelings of security are essential to their growth. When they are wired for security and safety, they are much more likely to blossom in every other way. You cannot spoil a newborn, and it's nearly impossible to cuddle them too much in their earliest years.

2. Speak to them—yes, even (and especially) the newborns and babies—and do so with a soft, gentle voice, and do so often. The more we speak to our children, the more data they have to begin the wiring process with. Read to them—even the newborns. Sing to them some mild, gentle songs. Introduce them early on to pictures and images that will enhance their learning: pictures of people, places, animals, and other images that you choose to direct their lives toward.

3. As soon as their age permits, teach them to hold a crayon and to write or scribble whatever they desire. Let them see your pleasure with every small step of progress.

4. When age permits (and for some, this can begin as quickly as they learn to walk), give them work assignments: clean up their own messes, make their own bed (or try to), and pick up their own clothes and toys, etc. This wires them in many, many areas, not the least of which is the following: industriousness (good old-fashion hard work), cooperation (teamwork), and obedience to authority—to parents. Wiring your children in this way will do more for your child and yourselves than most would believe. So don't miss this step.

5. As soon as they begin to learn to speak and from that age to age five or six, introduce them to other selected languages such as Spanish, French, German, or whatever you choose. If you know another language, speak it to them

daily, along with your native language. Allow them to hear those languages multiple times, the tones and inflections of the words spoken. Why, you might ask? Recent studies show that children who have been exposed to other languages early in their lives are much more capable of learning and embracing those languages later in life. In doing so, you've wired your child's brain with the sounds and inflections of that respective language. What a great opportunity for them to have their brains wired for success in learning other languages. Wiring our children's brain cells in this way early in their lives creates greater *capacity* for their achievement.

6. Isolate them as best you can from loud, harsh sounds. Try to let them see only those images and movies that will give them the impression of a gentle, kind family, a gentle world. Allow them to gradually see the world for what it is. But in his beginning years, give him pure gentleness, love, loving touches, and a kind, tender voice.

7. As soon as they are able to understand instruction, introduce them to goals and goal achievement. Progress is the name of the game in this life, so as parents, we should, as soon as reasonably possible with each child, guide them through the time-tested steps of advancement—achievement. As we persist, always coaching and guiding them to the fulfillment of their chosen goals, they not only become wired goal achievers, but they also begin to see life long-term rather than simply one day at a time. They try to look into their futures, which is exactly what we should hope they will do.

As wired goal achievers, they are no longer doing as most do—play checkers with their lives, one move at a time. Rather, their lives are created more like a chess match, always trying to look a few moves ahead as best as possible. This kind of life strat-

egy builds self-confidence, but it also creates a sort of visionary perspective. Simply said, they are trained to not only look
at the here and now of their lives, but they become trained to
connect their "here and now" decisions to their long-term goals
and aspirations.

As we apply these techniques to wire our children's brain cells,
we are applying the law of increased capacity. The law of increased
capacity simply means, as it applies to developing our children's
brain cells, that as our child develops and enhances brains cells,
their capacity to understand more increases, thus enabling them
to learn more and accomplish more. In many cases, more quickly
than they otherwise would. Parents can aid their children while
they are babies to become far more ready and able to achieve their
life's mission and desires. More on this in the chapter entitled,
"The Law of Increased Capacity."

We should apply these methods many times each day, especially for the newborn and the little children. If, by chance, we
failed to effectively wire our children when they were young, is
it too late? Granted, the best time to apply these principles is for
the newborn and the little children. However, it is never too late
to build and nurture brain cells. We all know that even adults
can change, and to change our minds from one perspective to
another requires a new neural pathway to be connected in the
brain. So yes, even youth, young adults, and adults can be wired
and rewired.

If, by chance, you missed out on using these techniques with
your little ones and your little ones are now older children, teenagers, or adults, how do you apply the same techniques?

Let's make an assumption. Let's assume you are a single parent with teenagers that were not raised with these loving, tender,
"wiring" techniques yet desire now to help them become the best
they can be. Here are some suggestions:

1. Make the inner commitment that you, the parent, will begin a new approach to life; an approach that will exude love and kindness to your children and other's. This approach to change self creates an excellent *example* for your children to see. Your example helps them see how change can be possible.

2. Show and tell your children things will be different in the home from now on. There will be more kind words and less harshness. *Show* and *tell* them there will be more patience and tolerance with each other, beginning with you. Remind them of your devotion to this new change by allowing them to see your willingness to apologize to them when you forget your commitment (that day will surely come).

3. Begin the practice of *showing* them and *telling* them how loved they are to you; embrace them warmly, and tell them daily your love for them.

4. Institute the habit of some small kindnesses for them you otherwise would not do. That can be as small as sending little notes in their school lunch sack or taking them individually to lunch periodically. Ask them questions about their lives, and sincerely show interest in their responses.

5. If you are not a religious person, you may wish to begin to be so for your sake as well as theirs. Few habits have as much positive impact upon a family like personal and family prayer. Kneel in a circle, all holding hands. This may seem uncomfortable at first, but stay with it. Speak to God, open your heart to him in prayer, allowing your children to hear it.

6. Make these habits permanent. Permanent, heartfelt changes will prove to your children dedication to their well-being. Over time, these personal and family changes will replace feelings of insecurity and fear with feelings of love, trust, and unity in the home.

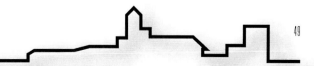

Does all this sound too simplistic, too easy? We know, personally, of hundreds of success stories of those who have used the patterns above to change their own lives and those of their children. Does it always work; does success always result? Yes. However, not all success is seen immediately. There are some youth who will not allow change in their lives now, but later in life they will begin to embrace it. For those, we encourage a hopeful attitude.

Let me share with you part of my story regarding wiring kids.

I (Garth) was born into a challenged family. My father was a kindly man but an alcoholic and very insecure and continued to party like a wild teenager until the last year of his life. He died in an industrial accident when I was seven. Mother was also a kindly, loving person but struggled as a single mother to control or teach her four young children, ages three to thirteen. There was no religion in the home, and except for a blessing on the food periodically, there was no family prayer. My mother had a special gift regarding budgeting money, so we fared well in that regard. But what we kids needed the most were feelings of emotional and spiritual security; we needed to begin to feel good about ourselves. She tried the best she knew how, and we all knew she loved us very much.

Not long after my father died (at age thirty-eight), I recall myself sitting outside my home worried about my mother, who was still weeping over the loss of her husband. While sitting there, I thought to myself in my young seven-year-old mind, *God is bad. If God were good,* I thought, *he wouldn't have allowed this to happen to our family.*

It was at this time of my life that my mother came to my room one evening and knelt next to my bed and asked if I'd like to have prayer with her. She and I entered into that habit, which we continued for many years. It provided a special feeling of security and strength I needed in my life especially at that time. It also helped bond my mother and me together all the more. It was a simple

parental act that took only about five minutes out of her every evening, yet it began a wiring process in my mind that would prove to be a building block, which would help form the remainder of my life. I shall forever be grateful for her wisdom and love.

Let me remind you, this new habit of prayer at my bedside was a new habit being formed. As I said above, we were not a praying family. This, then, was a new commitment formed by my mother because it had not been formed in our family prior. We didn't begin attending church or anything of the like. My mother simply began the evening ritual of prayer at my bedside.

We should remind you, it doesn't matter how old your children are to implement prayer. Wherever we are in the stages of parenting, now is the time to begin prayer with our children, yes, even teenagers, young adults or if you have adult children in your home, begin there. Let's make sure we begin now.

This habit, if done sincerely, boosts confidence in children's minds. Years ago, when all or most of the ten kids were still living at home, Sandi and I noticed the incredible effects of a parental teaching technique we literally stumbled into somewhat by accident.

While Sandi and I were sitting in our living room in our home, one of our grade-school daughters was walking from one room to another, passing through the living room we were in. And now while she was in the kitchen but within earshot of our conversation, Sandi said to me as in a whisper but loud enough she could hear, "You know, Garth, our daughter (called her by name) is a girl we can trust to do what she says and to get her assignments done. She's a trustworthy daughter."

We knew she heard it because we saw it in her attitude and behavior for several days to come. She had a boost of confidence because she overheard a vote of confidence for her.

Everyone including children need regular feedback regarding how much they are appreciated and loved. To feel and hear such appreciation boosts confidence and grows relationships.

Confidence in relationships is a must if we expect them to grow and develop.

You can do the same with your children. Begin now!

Wiring our kids for success is the single most important thing we can do to show our love for our children. Your new daily ritual might be reading to your children or introducing to them educational channels on television or the computer. Maybe it could be spending time at the library finding and checking out books. Whatever it is, whatever would be best for your child, begin it now. You will look back on that decision as a turning point in your child's life, a benchmark time where momentum shifted to more progress, more optimism, and more hope for your future and that of your kids.

Lessons from Our First Tutors

As mentioned in the chapter "Wiring Kids For Success in Life," when we were first married, we met with a middle-aged husband and wife (hereafter in this chapter, we will refer to them as "first tutors") who had had tremendous success in raising their kids, and we were allowed to ask them questions about their child-raising techniques. Their answers to our questions proved to be a sort of basis or foundation for how we've raised our kids. Their answers helped us connect some mental dots, which gave us confidence in the direction and *style* of child-raising methods and practices we chose to follow. Over the years, we've tried our best to put into practice their counsel, and their counsel proved a great help.

They reminded us that nurturing and training children is more a matter of becoming rather than simply doing. Teaching children is not just going through the motions, checking off a step and then going to the next. Instead, it's a matter of complete development for the purpose of helping our children become all they can potentially be. A thrilling and very serious ride.

They shared many principles and ideas with us, but they specifically focused on four principles, each one, they told us, proved to be the most significant in molding their children. We begin with a principle, which they said, "If children do not learn this lesson, it will prevent them from learning most other lessons in life." We've gained the opinion that if a parent fails to obtain this from their kids, they will likely fail in their parenting responsibilities.

What is that principle? ***Expect respect***. After all, when kids get to a certain age of reason, if they do not respect us as their parents, they will not likely obey us either.

In that interview years ago, while sitting in their kitchen and then later shifting to their living room, they emphasized heavily how important *respect* is to *obedience* of children. They taught us that if kids don't respect their parents, it will take a whip and harsh language to get their attention, let alone obedience to the parent's requests. They told us that to gain that respect, kids will respond more to *love* and *tenderness* than to threat and tough language. They told us that gaining their children's respect was done not out of fear (though there could be a few exceptions to this, but they are very rare) but rather, out of love. The kind of love that we feel when we want to make someone happy and pleased for what we've done for them—an inner desire to gain parents look and voice of approval. They said it was a sort of high regard at first which eventually turns into a deep respect then to genuine, enduring love.

Sandi and I have noticed that as we sincerely give of ourselves to our kids, it is most common for them to reciprocate that giving nature. As we continue to give and to do for them, to love and teach them along the way, their softer, more loving side comes out. "We loved him because he first loved us" sort of thing begins to take place. The giving to our children we speak of is not toys or anything of the like. It is the giving of self, time, and attention to their needs and wants.

Regarding our time, we've read from some who have spoken of quality time and how valuable quality time is to raising kids. We've found, however, that when we pack our schedules so tight that we have to carve out time for our children, we've relegated our children to a lower place on our list of priorities. Our kids can sense it and feel it. Often disrespect from our kids begins when they are calling out for our attention, our love, our time.

We've all seen kids who were disrespectful to a parent or parents before. The counsel of our first tutors was this: "Don't let that happen. Nip it in the bud as quickly as possible." The long-term problem disrespect brings upon the kids is far more detrimen-

tal than kids (even many parents) realize. For kids to be allowed to speak or act disrespectfully to their parents, grandparents, or others creates a form of *selfishness*, *conceit*, and *arrogance*, which becomes more difficult to fix the longer it is ignored.

We've found that kids must—yes, they must—learn respect for parents and others. The reason for that, primarily, is that they need order and structure in every aspect of their lives. They are wired that way—we all are. Even though we're wired that way, we need, as children or at some point in our life, to learn to unlock that gift, to empower it. And without that social, disciplined structure we call respect, order falls apart in their lives and confusion fills the void. A confused child is basically a child out of control and often disgruntled. Their very system cries for order and structure, including the social order we call respect.

On one occasion, we were recreating with several families— parents and their kids, including our own. It didn't take but a few minutes to spot the kids who were taught to be respectful by their parents and those who were not. The kids who were disrespectful –the grade school kids and teens—were mostly obnoxious and sarcastic. Their rudeness to their parents and siblings was almost unbearable to allow continuing. Not all the disrespectful kids were loud and overbearing; some were quieter yet still had a subtle form of the same problems. It comes in different forms, but the end result seems to be the same for all who are left without correction. While at that social, I overheard one father interject when he heard a teen speak disrespectfully to his mother, he said, "Young man, please don't speak that way to your mother." I knew how he felt, but I chose to remain silent.

Our first tutors explained and showed us *how* respect is taught in the home. We were in their home on several occasions, and we saw firsthand how each one, husband and wife, modeled sincere love and respect for each other. He honored his wife, and she honored him, and you could easily see it in the tones of love as they spoke to each other. This honor was easily interpreted as deep respect. Their kids were shown daily how to act respect-fully by the way their parents respected each other as well as each of their children. That is where we all must begin if we are to *expect respect* from our kids in the home, showing sincere respect to each family member, beginning with the parents. In fact, to expect respect from the kids without *modeling* it in our marriage relationship could send a confusing signal to the kids creating some feelings of resentment toward the parent or parents. "Do as I say, not as I do" is not an effective teacher as it applies to teach-ing respect.

Single parents are not able to model respect with a spouse, which is all the more reason for single parents to show deep respect for each child, also other adults in your life and to take occasion often to teach the principle to your children.

Our first tutors counseled us to never argue with the kids and that once an argument begins, the parent has already lost. They said to argue with them creates the opposite message you want to send and teach. Discussion and sharing differences of opinion is healthy, but argument—rising of voices—is counterproductive. This means that when the parent hears kids' thoughts or opinions on family issues and the kids hear the parents and then when the parent puts his or her final stamp of approval on a decision, it is finished! The kids may not agree with the final answer, but the kids' obligation to respect the answer is crucial to their social and moral growth. As they learn to accept decisions from authority, they will begin to learn how to fit into society.

There are many significant reasons why this lesson of respect must be learned. The sooner our kids learn it, the better. But notice the importance of first "sharing differences of opinion." If we fail to listen to our kids' perspective respectfully on any given subject of concern to them is to send the clear message: "my par-ents do not value my opinion." It is just the opposite relationship we should want with our kids. When we listen with interest, then make a parental decision, they are far more likely to appreciate

the answer even if they disagree. They want to be heard, respected, and appreciated. Bottom line though is that they learn to respect and obey your final decision.

The most ideal is for them to not only obey your final decision but to respect and even honor it. Yes, they may even disagree with the final parental decision, but if they can learn to obey, honor, and even come to unite behind you as though it were their idea, you've got a child who is maturing quickly—one who will carry that wonderful ability to unite with others into his or her adult life and will see wonderful remarkable fruit from it. But if all you can get is obedience and respect, that is good for now.

Your decision you expect them to follow may even prove to be wrong. That's okay, and the point here is that we want our kids to learn to follow leadership respectfully. For them, at such a young age, to learn "it is better to unite than to be right" is to teach them the value of unity at almost any cost.

From time to time, we hear so-called specialists teach the importance of being a "friend" to your child. From our first tutors, we gained the perspective that more than anything else, *children need parents to be parents and not just friends.* Of course having a good relationship with our children is essential. But to exchange parenting for friendship is to change the playing field significantly. It can make it more difficult for some parents to parent and discipline when necessary. After all, when was the last time your "friend" disciplined you when you really needed it?

I lived down South for a couple of years back in the late sixties. It was impressive to hear many adults, children, and youth speak to parents and other adults with respectful language: "Yes, sir," "Yes, ma'am," etc. What a wonderful thing it is for kids to learn to respect parents, leaders, and all people and to speak respectfully to them. I'm sure these kids were taught this habit from their mother's knee.

To speak respectfully to parents and others does not necessarily mean they do, in fact, respect their parents, but it's a good

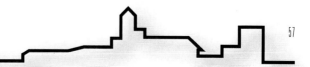

habit nonetheless. It's like dress standards for youth. Kids (probably parents as well) often tend to act to the level of their dress. Dress up nicely and the youth have a tendency to improve their behavior, to rise to that level. Likewise with language, when they speak with respect, true respect is likely to follow.

Most Americans can spot a man or woman who has served in the US Armed Services even without their uniform. "Yes, sir" or "yes, ma'am" is what you most often hear as they speak to you, and you can feel they are earnest in their respect. Respect is part of the army code, along with loyalty, duty, selfless service, honor, integrity, and personal courage. We need not send our kids off to the army to learn this code; we can and should teach them in the home. And, of course, we should model this code in our own lives for our kids to see.

As our children model our behavior, they will learn to respect all people—they will learn the difference between tolerance and respect. Let us explain.

We believe we should teach our children to respect other people no matter the language they speak, color of skin, dress standard, habits, or other traits. Our job as parents is to teach them to accept people for whom they are and what they are. That respect remains in place indefinitely or until that person does something to lose our respect—like, tries to harm us, lie to us, cheat us, etc. Our level of respect for others will grow to the level we learn to know them and understand them.

Tolerance is a valuable part of respect. Often, we tolerate certain behaviors contrary to our own in order to unite with others and show respect to them. Yet it is important to know that of all virtues, tolerance is the weakest of all. As parents, we must beware and teach our children the same—tolerance does not mean acceptance of other's views, life standards, or practices. We should be friends and friendly to all no matter what their views or life standards, yet we need not and should not embrace their views if they are contrary to our standards. Obviously, we wouldn't

encourage our kids to become bosom buddies with severely troubled kids, yet they can learn to show respect for them without embracing their lifestyles.

One of our greatest heroes said, "I don't care what a man's character is. If he's my friend—a true friend—I will be a friend to him."

And of course, a "true friend" would never try to talk us away from our revered principles. So as we teach and train our kids in these thoughts, we will want them to be accepting, respectful, and kind to one and all, and be a faithful friend to all, yet always hold true to chosen standards and beliefs.

We agree with Martin Luther King Jr. who said, "I look to a day when people will not be judged by the color of their skin but by the content of their character."

As we strive to wire our kids for success in life, we will want to be sure that one of the first lessons we teach and show them is sincere respect for parents, other adults, and all people. In so doing, they will have many friends, and they will find life's journey much more peaceful and their road to success in life much smoother.

Expecting respect from our children carries such an enormous range of benefits to the child and the family that we should do, as parents, our best to

- understand it,
- reinforce it,
- model it,
- expect it,
- teach it,
- praise it,
- discuss it,
- correct it, and
- reward it.

Associated with *respect*, our first tutors then taught us how important *obedience* is to a young child. They reminded us that respect leads to obedience and that they go hand in hand. They also reminded us that a respectful, obedient child is a happier child.

The more obedient children are to rules and laws set down by parents and authorities, the happier they will be. For that reason alone, we should work with our children to become obedient to us as parents. You might think this is too obvious to even mention, but we've noticed many parents who have given up on expecting obedience from their children. "I give up," some have said, feeling overwhelmed with the effort to bring their kids to a point of obedience. The parents still want obedience, but they've lost sight of consistency. They've learned how hard that part of parenting is and how much attention must be paid to consistency. With that difficult challenge, they often give in to the child.

If we can be consistent with our children as we teach principles, they will catch on. For a child to learn obedience, it takes time, lots of repetition, and determined parents to last through the initial struggle. All who have had children know the early life of a child can be explained in one word: struggle. They struggle to learn every single thing they do. If the child struggles, the parent, to a lesser degree, struggles also. We must stay with them, protect them, coach them and love them. All these require our best efforts of consistency. It seems logical, doesn't it, that if we're going to struggle any way, why not struggle a little longer, long enough to bring about habits in the child's life that will bless the child the most. As long as the struggle takes to help them obtain the habit of obedience, we must be willing to stay with it to the end.

We have noticed with our own kids when they were obedient to us, they were more happy and confident children overall. If you're a parent, we're sure you can imagine the struggles we went through trying to get the kids to obey. There were times with a few of the kids particularly, who really tried to test our resolve as well as our patience. In fact, had we not been so firmly determined to

endure through the struggles, we could easily have given up and given in to the kids' wishes over our own best judgment.

However, we determined we cannot give up on such a noble cause; a cause that when the fruits of our labors are realized, will bring some of the highest levels of achievement and happiness to our children and ourselves. So we persevered day by day, one child after the other, one battle after another, until one day the battles disappeared and what remained were self-reliant, more confident, more trustworthy, happier children, and more grateful parents for the end result. The battle with children is worth it if the end result is worth it, and for us, it most definitely was.

We say "battle", but what we mean is the contest between wills—our will versus the child's will. How often have you heard, "I don't want to do that," "I don't want to. I hate cleaning the toilet," "I cleaned the dishes yesterday," "I can't. My friends are waiting for me," "I took the garbage out yesterday. It's someone else's turn," etc.

We don't want to be considered bullies by our children, yet we want our kids to complete the assignments given them for the sake of obedience, for their sake. We don't want to harp at them, nor do we want to get to the point of begging them to complete their task—to be obedient. How do we do that?

Start when they are young as mentioned in a prior chapter. If you begin the process of jobs, duties, and follow-throughs to completion (obedience) and if you begin it when they are little children, it becomes second nature to them. This "second nature" is the parent's best and most effective tool. When we organize the little child's life around tasks and obedience to follow our will, and when we add a smile to it, the child's nature is to be obedient—to make us happy. It's important to know that our babies are wired to be obedient (for some of you that may seem a stretch to say, but we assure you, it is true). Granted, there are some children who challenge you more than others. From our experience, children who are consistently unwilling to be obedi-

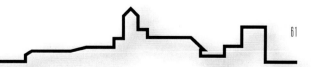

ent or to please their parents *were raised that way.* We often wire our kids to act contrary to their nature. We rewire them through our *negligence* or our *unwillingness to stay engaged in the battle of wills—to be consistent.*

So then, begin when they are very young, if possible. For those of you who didn't begin when they were young, whose kids are now disrespectful and disobedient, yet now, more than ever, you are desirous of teaching them obedience for their own sake before they leave the nest, you might consider this method.

Sit down and take stock of the whole picture—the big picture relating to your problem. Spell out on paper what you see as the biggest obstacles to reaching your goal of having obedient children. This could include your *time,* your level of *resolve,* and the *temperament* of each child, or anything else that might, or anything else that might get in the way or appear as an obstacle of you fulfilling this goal.

Now that you see more clearly the challenges before you, you can write down all the *resources* and helps you have, which would also include your *parents,* your *siblings, friends, school teachers,* or *church leaders.* This is not a time to be shy or to hide your problem; after all, your children are worth the effort and the possible humiliation you may feel at first as you engage the help of others.

As you meet with some of your resources requesting their help in your cause, consider being very open with them—very honest and forthright. Share with them what you want your kids to learn and why. Ask for their support and then work with them to spell out a strategy of ways and means in which they can be helpful, using their gifts and talents and influence.

Of course you don't want them to feel as though you are transferring your problem on to their shoulders but simply to receive their influence on your child as best they can. We can only suppose they will be honored and flattered you have such respect and confidence in them.

It's not uncommon for a grandparent, brother, sister, or friend to have a special relationship with your child. That closeness and trust can be a way to help your child through this phase of his life.

A friend of ours shared this story of their older, teenage son, but it could just as well been a younger teenager or a child. This same principle can apply with any of our children at any age.

> My son was dating this girl. They were considering getting engaged. My wife and I could see this was not a good match. In fact, from our perspective, it appeared to be a disaster waiting to happen. Even our other children could see how wrong this looked. The girl was sweet and kind but didn't have some of the key aspirations and goals our son had, and everyone could see it but our son.
>
> Our son informed us he was about to propose to her. Our relationship with our son was good, but he was not in an emotional position to take our suggestions or counsel at that time. So we went to plan B. We called upon our oldest daughter, his oldest, married sibling, the daughter all our children looked up to and especially our son.
>
> We invited that daughter and her husband to visit with our son and to see if they could offer some guidance and help. Our daughter and her husband were as concerned as any for the apparent mistake that was about to happen.
>
> They invited our son out to lunch at a local restaurant, where they got right to the point. They spoke respectfully and lovingly, yet directly. They asked pointed questions and asked our son to ponder them. They spoke logically with him inviting him to try and look down the road a few years to see how he thought things might be if he married that particular girl, particularly as they applied to his highest goals, values, and aspirations.
>
> While in the restaurant with our daughter and son-in-law, our son began to examine his future more carefully and to try and see if this girl could help him reach his highest goals and to remain true to all he holds dear.

He began to tear up, realizing his eldest sister was right, that the direction he was going could well sidetrack his most noble dreams of family. After the lunch meeting with his sister, he walked the streets of his city most of the night in the deepest thought, pondering and praying. He concluded that his sister and brother-in-law were right, so he called off the engagement. About two years later, he met the girl that would prove to be the girl of his dreams. He has stayed true to all his values and goals, which has been much easier because his wife and he hold the same values and dreams.

This leads to another principle our first tutors shared with us: *industriousness—good, old-fashioned work habits.*

We all want successful children, and for them to be the best they can be. History is clear on this point: industrious, hardworking children are far more likely to find success in their lives, will endure through trials until they find it, and will pay the price of effort that is always needed to achieve success.

On the other hand, children who never learn how to stay engaged in a project to the end, who easily give up or are easily discouraged because of the long intensiveness of what they would like to have, are more likely to let success pass by them. That level of work will discourage the child and break their parents's hearts. This will especially hurt if the give-up-ites, involves the kids' future marriage. Anyone who has been married realizes a successful marriage requires work, focus, and determination.

Obviously, failing to teach our kids how to work and how to stay engaged in a responsibility to completion will harm the child far more than many parents realize. The total impact of laziness and lack of vision and focus can be measured in heartache, disappointment, discouragement, depression, and even in dollars and cents. It can break up a marriage and, in general, makes every phase of life harder for the kids. If left unchecked, it could well extend to the next generation and beyond.

Teaching our kids to appreciate a good work ethic and to stay engaged in a work project to its completion offers many benefits, not the least of which is the blessing of having a *trained and disciplined mind*. We've discovered for ourselves that kids with a disciplined mind are far more likely to endure through the tough challenges life gives us all. Also, they are more able to endure through the educational process allowing them to go on to college education and advanced education with all the advantages that offers.

Alexis de Tocqueville was a gentleman-scholar who emerged as one of the great historians of his day said, "*Given love of work, [a man's] future is certain.*" (*www.thefreemanonline.org*).

Our first tutors owned a small farm, and the father was a plumber by trade. They always had jobs for the kids to do. When his sons were very young, he gave them many odd jobs. If he ran out of jobs, he gave them the task of straightening old, bent nails (no kidding). He knew the importance of keeping them busy as it applied to industriousness, but he also realized the importance of causing them to feel their jobs were meaningful. Because kids' radar is so in-tune, we don't want to give our kids a chore just to get them out of our hair. For that reason, when he gave the chore to his sons, he told them how helpful the chore was to him and why.

Each summer day morning, the father would take each child aside one by one, offer them the jobs that had to be accomplished, and would allow him or her to choose, each job suited for the age and ability of each child. Often, they would work in teams, two by two, an older child with a younger. This strengthened their ability to make choices; it also allowed an older child to help train a younger. The father learned that point early while raising his kids, that by giving them options when possible, they would strengthen their decision making abilities. The mother was an old-fashioned housewife. She stayed home and made home a little bit of heaven for the family. She did this by beautifying

the home in the traditional female fashion. She also had many projects every day for her daughters and sons to help with, such as helping in the large, family garden, canning and bottling fruit and vegetables, cleaning house both straightening up as well as deep cleaning, washing clothes, and a dozen other similar chores. She never (at least, as long as we knew her) owned a clothes dryer, so the children were daily hanging the family washing on the outside clothes line, and once dried and folded, the clothes were put away in their proper places. Both the girls and the boys learned how to do housework, deep cleaning, yard work, basic maintenance of a car, and much more.

They owned a milk cow which gave the kids morning and evening chores with milking and all that goes with it. It was obvious to see in their family, that good old-fashioned work was a key element to the kids' daily activities. They worked hard, but when it was time to play, they played hard.

The babies and little children were raised watching older siblings and parents work and with a smile—usually, depending on the chore. The little ones were given things to do so they felt like contributors. Family projects and work was such a central part of their daily family living, that whenever we went to visit them, they were always involved in a family work project of some sort, something that involved many or most of the children. Common in their work projects was laughter; the kids were actually having fun being together with the family working and sweating, all involved in the common cause. With all their family chores, the kids were still expected to keep up good grades at school during the school year.

Obviously, our first tutors' kids learned to love to work, and they learned the value and benefits of industriousness. It was a thrilling thing to observe. Had it been a once or twice sort of observance, we might have been tempted to think it was a quirk. But we found just the opposite; the kids and family were always engaged in work, pleasure, and laughter every time we were privi-

leged to visit their home. Those visits were often unannounced, as we just dropped in. Wow, what a concept! Teach kids not only to work but to enjoy it!

The question again is, how do parents teach their kids to work: and even learn to enjoy the work?

The answer (like a broken record) is the answer to most children's learning process: start when they are young, very young. Our first tutors began the momentum with their large family by working diligently with their first child, a son. Our first tutors told us how they worked with their son as soon as he could walk. They expected him to clean up his messes under his high chair after each meal. At first, they worked with him to learn what to do and how to do it. After several days of practice with him, he began to take the lead picking up the food and throwing it in the chicken bucket (yes, they raised chickens too for eggs so no food was ever wasted). After a while, he was in the habit of picking up his own messes, and they praised him along the way. They did the same with toys he played with and clothes he wore; everything had its place, and he learned that when he was through with it, it was put away in its designated place.

The older he got, the more responsibility he received. All he knew was work, play, family, church, and neighbor friends to play with. When the next child came along, she grew up watching her older brother doing jobs, so it came more automatic for her and the later children. As you might imagine, the parents were dogged determined, which is what kept them solidly engaged in the children's work habits. And because they remained focused on their children's development of work habits, all their children grew up in the same way. Industriousness was a central family theme.

We've noticed that at a particular age, each child desires to feel like he or she has some degree of authority, allowing him or her to make decisions on their own. These are natural feelings, and it is good for us to nurture those feelings within them. We can easily accomplish that within the work responsibilities we give them

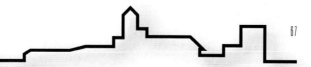

each day. We can allow them to make small decisions that allow them to feel responsible and grown up. This can begin with very small decisions like what to wear each day or how to complete a work assignment. We can always stay in complete control if necessary yet allow them to feel they are the boss of a project. Those grownup feelings foster the character trait of responsibility we all want for our children. Each morning, the mother would hold up two or three sets of clothes to wear and give the little kids the choice of what to wear. In this way and dozens of similar examples, the kids felt they were the boss, so to speak.

As their ability to do increases and as their level of responsibility grows, more can be placed on their shoulders. As we combine their developing work ethic with their growing responsibility, we begin to see a new, mature young man or woman burst forth in your home.

The last point of emphasis our first tutors gave us was *love*, *compassion*, and *empathy* for each child and for each other.

You couldn't walk in their home but what you felt the love present there. One of our friends commented on the same when he said, "The love in their home is so thick, you could cut it with a knife." How did they generate that much love in one family with so many mouths to feed, demands to meet, and noises coming from each and every child?

As stated before, we noticed the love and respect between the two parents, for each other, and the kids. I asked them once how it was they had such a sweet, loving relationship between them and in their home. They both responded, but she led the way. She spoke of *common goals* and *interests*. She said they both shared the same belief in God—the same religion. She told me how helpful that has been to their marriage and their family. She went on to say how each night before bedtime, the whole family would gather in the living room, where they would read a few verses of Scripture, and then discuss their meaning in language the kids could understand often using pictures to help explain, and then,

they would kneel in a circle, all holding hands, and have family prayer.

Regarding prayer, the wife said, "Each morning and night, my husband and I kneel next to each other at our bed and offer a couple prayer, hand in hand, shoulder to shoulder, and hip to hip, tightly knit together in the posture and spirit of prayer. Our habit of couple prayer has probably been the single most important thing we've done in our marriage to foster a feeling of love and unity."

Upon hearing this from her, my mind thought of the old saying, "A family that prays together stays together." Maybe we could also say, "A couple who prays together stays together."

The husband chipped in with this comment, "Our feelings are so deep and tender for each other and our kids, we would never think of intentionally offending any of them." He went on to say regarding the children, "We love them so much we simply had to give them the best we both had to offer, and it all seemed to land on these four principles: *respect* for *authority, obedience, work ethic,* and *love.*"

Regarding their children they added: "Our kids need to know that anything they say or do will never cause them to be unworthy of our deepest love and devotion. Some of their decisions or actions may disappoint us even anger us, but never will they be out of reach of our love. In other words, they are always worthy of our love and deepest feelings of compassion." These are thoughts and feelings parents will want to place in their children's hearts and minds early and often, even when they are adults.

I asked him, "Certainly there were times, weren't there, when your patience between the two of you or your kids wore so thin, you exploded"?

He said something like this, "Listen Garth, we're just ordinary people just like everyone else. We're not super human or anything of the kind. We've had our days and moments we wish we had done things differently. We've said and done things we wished

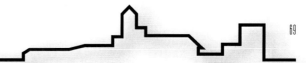

we wouldn't have, things that have caused great hurt. But because our feelings were so tender for each other, we would quickly repair our damage with sincere apology, commit to do better, and try to show our love all the more, and then go on to the next day."

She added, "Whenever times got tense, which happened from time to time, I would try to lighten up my mind by recalling a statement by one of my most favorite people, Emma Rae McKay, who was the wife of a great leader and the mother of nine children. She is reported to have said, 'I was once asked, when all the kids were home and disagreements came between you and your husband, did you ever consider divorce? I responded, Divorce? No. Murder? Yes.' I've learned that stress and trials are temporary, but my relationship with my husband is forever. Keeping things in their proper perspective and adding a little humor saves lots of heartache."

He explained how when things were at their worst, they would be driven to their knees in prayer. He said, "We knew no other way to get over that trial." He emphasized how helpful sincere apology has been to him and their marriage. He told us, "At the beginning of our marriage, we promised each other we would diligently strive to never hold a grudge against the other." He emphasized how that promise alone has really blessed their marriage and family. He went on to say, "Over time, we simply became mellower, more patient, and less stringent with each other and the kids, which made life far more enjoyable for us all."

She added, "We both made the habit of doing little kindnesses for each other. I don't know who started that habit, but it caught on for the both of us. It has had a tendency to draw us closer. We've tried to pass it on to the kids, and it's been fun watching them care for each other in tender, kind ways." They both expressed how unselfish service to the other has drawn them both together.

She mentioned how he would often be found doing household chores to make life easier for her. She said, "I couldn't do much of his hard work, but I could act as a secretary when he needed me. I knew he appreciated that."

They both mentioned how important it was to their marriage, that they strive to find common interests they could each share. They learned to enjoy the same kind of entertainment, and they learned to enjoy reading to each other each evening books that interested both of them. They would discuss what they read, and in that way, they grew together.

It became obvious to us why love permeated throughout their home. They had made love the highest priority in their marriage, with their children and in the home in general. They both made mention how some days one or both would awake in the morning not feeling very lovable or worthy of love. He said, "On days like that, we both have made the habit of going to a private place, maybe the bedroom, and kneel in prayer. On some occasions when things got tense between us, we would kneel together in prayer to God, pleading for the spirit of love to enter into our hearts. Our prayers were always answered."

She mentioned how important it has been for their marriage "to be quick to apologize. We've learned to avoid contention like we would an awful plague." She added, "There were times earlier in our marriage, when I felt I should teach my husband certain things, so I would act as a devil's advocate in certain conversations, in an effort to bring out my point—to change him in one way or the other. But I later learned, to act as the devil's advocate is to do the devil's work, and the last thing I wanted to do was to be an instrument in the devil's hand, so I humbled myself and came to realize, my husband was in many ways my tutor. We have since learned to harmonize our best efforts as best as possible even within our individual weaknesses."

We heard a speaker once say, "You can love your country but be a poor citizen. And you can love your spouse yet be a poor

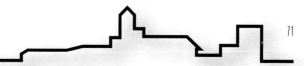

spouse." We don't know how true that quote is, but just in case for the sake of understanding, we feel it's important we define "love."

When we speak of "love" as it applies to a married couple, we speak of that kind of love that places the spouse above all other interests, next to God, of course. It is a covenant relationship that strives to make two people as one, to be growingly endeared to the last breathe and beyond. It is our best effort to think of our spouse's needs above our own.

As it applies to our children, it shifts to a different kind of love. With our kids, our "flesh and blood," we see in them an added degree of legacy being built, of our name being carried on with honor and respect well beyond our lives. We give them our all in time and effort to ensure as best as possible their success in life, particularly in their early years. We adore them and see an extension of ourselves in them. For that reason, our love for them is best exemplified through our willingness to endure through the struggles of child raising, to keep our resolve strong for the sake of our kids, knowing well that our kids, most likely, will be blessed or harmed by our degree of steadfastness to our resolve to teach and nurture them in solid, lasting principles. In a very real sense, we can determine the level of love we have for our children by the amount of dedication we place on getting them prepared for independent living.

Hopefully, you can see why we chose that family as our model to try to follow. We've tried the best we've known how to duplicate what they modeled for us, and it has made for a wonderful life. It has given us direction on how to influence our children to help them be the best they can possibly be.

Our children are now passing these principles on to their children which make us as grandparents very happy.

So then, do you hope to raise your kids up to be the best they can be? Although there are many parenting styles and ways to nurture our children, there's no one and only way. But we're confident in saying that whatever parenting style you use, these

four fundamentals will be included: *respect, obedience* to parents, *industriousness,* and *love.* With these four added to whatever else you do, your kids will be wired for success.

Teaching, Disciplining, and the Moods Parents Set

"Good morning, little sunshine. What made you wake so soon? You scared away the little stars and shined away the moon."

This little children's song was sung by Sandi to our kids every morning to wake them. It was lyrical and light and invited a mood of happiness within our little ones. Parents have within them the gift to make their children's day begin with a smile and laughter or grumpiness, depending on how we approach them first thing in the morning and throughout the day. Certainly, we're all aware children have a tendency to mimic their parents' moods.

When teaching, disciplining, and nurturing children of any age, it is important we make the habit of communicating confidence and optimism. We have a choice. Phrasing our comments to our children in such a way that it shows respect, love, and trust has a tendency to bring the best out in them. So instead of saying, "Billy, pick up your room now!" said in the tone of an army drill sergeant, we might say, "Billy, your room needs some attention. I'm sure it will be clean before lunch time," spoken in respectful tones. To speak to our kids in such a way and with tones of kindness rather than harshness and rudeness will most likely bring the best out in our children, not to mention the parent. When we can speak confidence and trust with an optimistic and accepting tone, they feel accepted and appreciated, yet they know what is expected of them. To do anything less is creating a problem between you and your child, building walls not relationships that separate, not relationships that build.

Sandi and I have felt the frustrations of trying to get action, obedience, and favorable results out of our kids, and we've made many, if not all the common mistakes. We've also applied the softer and more gentle and loving approach, and we can state without any hesitation that the gentle-toned approach, using optimistic language, is more likely to bring out the best in the kids. As a special additive, the optimistic approach invites a loving spirit in the home and the relationship between you and your children; you can't say that about the not so gentle approach.

No doubt, there are times when some kids choose not to favorably respond even to the gentle, loving approach, but by and large, the majority of kids will. For those that don't, persevere with the gentle approach, and you will, over time, see their positive actions come out. There are times they simply need to feel and be assured our kindness approach is heartfelt and not a fluke. Kids are very perceptible and able to determine sincerity versus words to trick them into action. They want to see authenticity and not contrived words to get the action they want.

We should train our minds to think in these terms when striving to get the most out of our children. Always begin with soft, loving, and gentle tones, but be willing and prepared to go to firm if necessary. Soft to firm tones but firm only when absolutely necessary. One great man said, and we paraphrase, the only time we should raise our voice in our homes is when there's a fire. When we have the need to go to the more firm tones, we should learn to apply them with love, as Paul counseled, "Speaking the truth in love" (Ephesians 4:15).

Also, if we lose it, so to speak, we should be willing and ready to apologize to our children. They already know we're human and very capable of error, but with the sincere apology, they can learn the transition to the gentle side of relationships even after a slipup that teaches them how to ask for forgiveness, how to apologize.

If you've not already discovered, there is a spirit (or a mood) in your home and you (the parent) hold the joystick that deter-

mines which direction that spirit will go on any given day—a mild, sweet, loving spirit, or an angry, loud, or sullen, moody, and selfish spirit.

What do we do when we wake up cranky, unsettled, and irritated? How do we adjust to soft, loving, and gentle tones? Everyone has their own methods, and there's probably multiple ways of changing the spirit in your home after you've already begun the day hard. Let us make something very clear: It is we, the parents, who determine the spirit and mood in the home, and *no one can make us have a bad day. It's a choice we make,* just like what we choose to wear each day. We can choose to wear a sincere smile or a frown, speak a hard tone or a soft. It is our choice. It is true; some days we wake up feeling somewhat off our game, but that need not be the cause of a poor spirit in the home.

When we awake feeling irritable, we strive to remember prayer (no kidding). We go to our room, kneel down, and plead for new eyes and a new heart. Sound weird? Sorry if it does, but we're just being honest with you. We have found that that is the finest and fastest way to turn a bad day into a good day. If you've never tried it, we hope you will. Our prayer, though not a written prayer, generally goes something like this: "Father in heaven, please bless me with love, tolerance, and patience in my heart and mind. Help me to be loving, kind and gentle with my children and my spouse."

On one occasion, I awoke to some bad news business-wise, and I allowed that news to spoil my morning with Sandi and the kids, or at least, it tried to. After a few minutes of my bossy and rude language, it occurred to me I had a problem, and with the increased noise in the home from the kids waking one by one, things were going to get worse for me if I didn't try to adjust my mood—my spirit. I realized my attitude could spoil their morning. I went to my bedroom, knelt at the bedside, and said something like this: "Father, I just got some bad news which I allowed to spoil my attitude. Please help me look past that news and see the joy in my kids' eyes. Help me do my part in inviting thy spirit

into our home this morning." With that prayer, I left the bedroom with hope and optimism in my step and my smile. I could have spoiled my morning and said and done things that could have hurt my wife and kids, but instead, I was able to participate in the joy and happiness my wife and children were sharing.

On another occasion, Sandi and I woke one morning, and at the breakfast table, I could tell something was bothering her. She was not herself. I rose from my chair, walked over to her, and wrapped her in my arms. I expressed my love for her as we stood there embracing. Immediately, the mood changed in her and in our home. Gone was the feeling of tension which was replaced with a calm feeling, a closer feeling.

Our youngest son, Joseph, reminded me recently of something Sandi and I made a habit of doing, which seems to have influenced him with his sweet wife, Rachel. He has instituted in his marriage what Sandi and I did and do every morning. Each morning (and a few times each day), she and I embrace. While embracing, I massage her back, top to bottom. It allows our embrace to last a little longer, and I know it makes her tired back feel somewhat better.

It turns out our kids took notice of that morning ritual, at least Joseph did. Joseph, as a young boy in our home, saw his parents embracing and performing the ritual of morning embrace and massage, and that memory created a sense of unity and togetherness in his mind. We can only imagine to a young child, watching this each morning would create happy feelings of parents being together and soothing each other. It starts the day out right.

As our kids grow old enough to understand and communicate clearly, we should teach them these same principles. We should remind them often that within them are the power to create their day. Happiness and contentment are choices and habits we form. Truly, *happiness is a state of mind*, and we are capable of selecting which thoughts we choose to give attention to. The sooner we help our kids understand that principle, the sooner they begin

WIRING KIDS FOR SUCCESS IN LIFE

taking responsibility for their own moods. This learned habit of happiness goes a long way in maturing our children and preparing them for life and the challenges life sends to all.

In a nutshell, let us say that the joy and happiness in raising kids is a daily choice and is a learned habit. To make the habit of joyful, loving communication with our spouse and children is one of the most fundamental and essential principles we as parents should learn. And the sooner we can *show* and *tell* this truth to our kids, the sooner they begin to be wired for success in life.

Let's never forget too that it is not enough for us as parents to teach these principles to our kids. We have the God-given duty to make sure they *understand* them. Hearing something and understanding it are two different matters. We must teach for *understanding*.

The Steel Cable of Conscience

During a family get-together, one of our married daughters, Hilary, and I were sitting in the kitchen talking, while the rest of the large clan was in the living room, visiting with each other. In the kitchen ran Max, one of my seven-year-old grandkids. He went to the candy jar to get himself some more candy when Hilary asked, "Max, did your mother say you could have more candy?"

"Oh yes," he said and proceeded to help himself.

Hilary questioned him by asking, "Max, are you sure?"

I saw an opportunity there, so I said, "Oh, Hilary, you can trust Max. He never tells a lie." He immediately took his hand out of the jar, ran to his mother in the living room, and asked, "Mom, is it okay if I have some more candy?"

At that moment, Max had another strand of strength added to his conscience, which, as it continues to grow, will turn into a steel cable, able to withstand any and all the temptations and trials life throws at him. Honesty, integrity, and character will be his hallmark. For Max, as for most of us, it began as a little child.

Similarly, but from an older child, comes the following story from our son, Joseph.

"I was on the ninth grade basketball team, the A team, coached by Coach Rowe. We were playing a tough rival. I just stole the ball, and it was a one-on-one fast break. Hilary, Dillon, and you [me, Joseph's dad] were in the stands watching. Rather than just go up to the rim and lay the ball in, I tried a spin move to get around the defender. The ball sailed out of my hand and out of bounds. I was so mad at myself I threw my arms down and yelled, 'S——!' The crowd, unfortunately for me, heard it loud and clear.

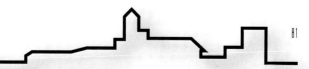

The sound of that word echoed throughout the whole gym for everyone to hear. Most people started to sort of giggle...even the referee. But because of the rules, he had to give me a technical foul. Also, Coach Rowe had his own rule: technical foul, you sit out the rest of the game. As I was heading to the bench of shame I looked into the stands, everyone was smiling or laughing, including Hilary and Dillon. But then I noticed the expression on my dad's face, which was one of disappointment. That little facial expression actually had a big effect on me. Since that time, I have never had issues with cursing, but almost all of my friends got into the habit of cussing during sporting events or just for the fun of it."

Both stories remind us that we, as mere mortals, can change our direction in life. We can feel certain things within that cause our hearts and minds to feel shame, causing us to decide change in our lives. Joseph's story reminds us that building and molding our conscience is not accomplished in a day and not always just in our childhood. Most people spend the majority of their lives forming the kind of conscience that makes them feel surer of themselves, more confident in their inner self, their character, and their integrity.

What are those feelings of shame or jubilation that come to us when we feel we've done poorly or well? It's our conscience. It may be compared to a microscopic computer chip placed in every person at birth that acts like their own personal GPS (Global Positioning System) to guide us to the higher, nobler road and to the achievement of our best, true goals.

The conscience of man comes to all at birth and, ideally, will be well developed before we become a grown man or woman. We are the only creatures (if we can, for this purpose, call ourselves creatures) on earth who can choose to change. Animals and insects cannot. The geese, for instance, when the weather begins to cool for winter, always fly south by nature. Do they have a choice to not fly south? No. For no less than six thousand years,

geese have flown south for the winter. You can say the same about all other creatures on earth.

But for humans, we not only have agency (free will) to choose, but we have feelings within telling us what is right and what is wrong. That's the very purpose of conscience. We can feel that we've done well and revel in it and use it as momentum to improve. Or we can be deceitful and feel inner pain causing us to choose a different direction in our lives and decisions. What's more, as we learn to become more sensitive to that God-given conscience, as a result, our lives become even more directed and happy and peaceful.

In many respects the youth of today have many different choices to make than what we were faced with decades ago, yet their conscience (and ours) has the savvy ability to comprehend it all and place the truth in its proper context, perfectly applicable to the individual and to any era of people.

It should be stated, too, that the conscience of man does not vary according to the individual; after all, murder is murder, lying is lying, and cheating is cheating no matter what the custom or tradition you live in. It has always been so throughout all recorded time. We all have the same influence by the same spirit we call conscience.

Let us define conscience as "the awareness of a moral or ethical aspect to one's conduct together with the urge to prefer right over wrong" (dictionary.reference.com/browse/conscience). That "urge" referred to in the definition is a spirit influence that has been placed in every particle of matter throughout the universe and within every person.

This is a standard definition and one we agree with. The problem is some kids never get the moral/ethical training in home allowing other forces, including society, to have a greater hand in molding the child's conscience. There is much evidence of this today, with our jails and prisons bulging at the seams. Crime seems to be at a record high in much of the world. Had most

of those people had a stronger conscience, nurtured by parents, chances are they would have chosen not to have committed crime.

How then do we, as parents and grandparents, help our children and grandchildren develop the kind of conscience that will guide them to success in life? How do we wire our children with such a moral and ethical *compass* that when they are on their own, they will likely choose the right?

Let us offer a few suggestions that seem to have worked pretty well for us.

First of all, love them, embrace them daily, and tell them sincerely you love and value and even treasure them, and help them feel safe and appreciated. Help your little ones—children and youth and children of all ages—feel connected. One significant purpose of life is to feel connected to family. This connection invites peace and assurance to our children and people of all ages. We are all wired to desire feelings of family connection.

Second, teach them right from wrong, which helps them gain that "*awareness* of a moral or ethical aspect to one's conduct." The moment they are old enough to understand, help them differentiate between right and wrong. Tell them, "This is right. That is wrong." Draw the contrast in their tender minds early in their lives. At our home, we would say, "What you did really made me happy and proud of you, and I'm sure heavenly Father is very happy with you too" or "What you did is wrong. It made me sad that you did it. Please try not to do that anymore, okay?" And then follow it up with a sincere hug. *Be specific* when speaking with them, that they may plainly see what particular behavior that brought about your praise or disappointment.

It's not enough that we teach them not to touch a hot stove or a fire. Teaching them safety guidelines is wise for their own protection, but it's not the same as teaching them "a moral or ethical aspect to one's conduct." We need to help them understand *why* and *how* their "moral and ethical" decisions affect their lives and

the lives of others and how it made us feel as parents when they made those choices.

Children are wired to please their parents. They instinctively feel desire to make us proud of them. Kids will go to great lengths to gain a glance of approval from a parent. Many children who never sense that look of approval or receive that encouraging comment gravitate to levels where they will get some degree of approval but will seldom lead them to a successful life. Gangs come to mind.

Third, we need to "urge [them] to prefer right over wrong." Although we are born (unlike animals and insects) with an inner voice (our conscience) helping us to feel or sense what is right and what is wrong, that gift needs to be nurtured, and fashioned and developed. Children (and youth and adults) can be trained or train themselves to *mask* those feelings and create their own skewed or twisted view of right and wrong. For this reason, we should begin as soon as possible to wire our little ones with a clear sense of what is right versus what is wrong.

We are aware of some parents who feel there are no absolutes in life, who allow their child to believe immorality, for instance, is acceptable, and that it is acceptable behavior to the parents if it's agreeable to the growing child. They teach their children this for the purpose of removing any and all so called restrictions from their child. Their thinking, it appears, is that a restricted child is bound up in a box of moral ethics which, they think, restricts the child's social growth.

We couldn't disagree more with that kind of reasoning. We believe there are absolutes and that history proves such. We believe that premarital sex, for instance, has a tendency to skew the child's moral compass, his God-given compass (conscience), and that if continued in the child's life, will hinder his moral development and place a sort of film over his conscience.

If there are no moral or ethical expectations placed upon that child, he writes his own laws contrary to nature's laws and God's.

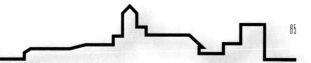

That is dangerous territory for anyone to enter into, let alone a child or teenager. Historically, that child will experience heartache by and by.

Logically then, as parents, we should validate our own moral and ethical standing. Is a little so-called white lie here or there okay with us? How about any degree of lying, cheating, or stealing or any form of immorality? Are we training our children away from their God-given conscience? Parents and grandparents, beware. Our children are watching us closely and most often form their own moral and ethical standards by what they see and hear us do.

Without question, one of the most significant responsibilities of parents is to help develop and form their child's conscience, to make it active, vibrant, and very much alive. Anything less is to shirk our duty as parents. In order to wire kids for success in life, we must train and nurture their God-given conscience by teaching them and living exemplary lives ourselves; their social, emotional, and spiritual welfare depends on it.

> Train up a child in the way he should go: and when he is old, he will not depart from it.
>
> —Proverbs 22:6

Parents as Teachers, Connecting the Dots

Some years ago, when all the kids were home, we were sitting around the large oak dining room table, having supper. I proceeded to ask the kids what they learned in school that day. Cali, our ninth child, said with some enthusiasm, "We began learning about planets out in space." So I asked her some questions to see how much she knew and to determine if she'd like to learn more. It turned out that her grade school teacher that day had entered into that specific aspect of science, so Cali was still quite sketchy as to her knowledge. I asked her if I could show her some things about our Milky Way solar system we live in, and she agreed.

I quickly pulled out an encyclopedia to show her some pictures of the solar system we reside in. She showed interest, so I proceeded with a question or two. I asked her, "How many planets do you think are in our solar system—the Milky Way?"

She responded, "I don't know, but there's a lot."

I explained to her that our solar system is so big that scientists can only guess the number of planets, but that the number is probably bigger than we have a number for. That didn't seem to mean anything to her, so I asked her, "How many people can fit into our local college football stadium?" She had seen the stadium filled with people, so she could relate to that question.

She said she didn't know but thought it was a lot. I told her the stadium fit about fifteen thousand people, and that that was less than half the amount of people in our local community where we lived.

I then pointed out that there are three zeros in fifteen thousand. Trying to connect the dots in her pretty little head, I said, "If scientists do not have a number for the planets in our solar system, which means there could be more than a centillion of planets in it." I used centillion because it was a large number I was somewhat familiar with.

She asked, "What's a centillion?"

I said, "Let's look it up in the encyclopedia," and so we did.

Her eyes lit up when she read that a centillion was a number followed by 303 zeros! Cali responded, "Do you mean that there are that many planets in our solar system?"

I said, "Yes, maybe even more." And then, I followed with this comment, "Cali, are you aware that our solar system—the Milky Way—is considered one of the smaller solar systems scientists have found and that the number of solar systems are more than we have a number for also?"

As I watched her, I could see her mind trying to take all this information in and that she was in absolute awe as to all the creations in the heavens. I then proceeded to explain to her what our religion teaches regarding *who* created all these planets and solar systems and *why*. I also taught her that even though we may seem like little ants in a huge sky, we are God's children, and we are the *primary purpose* he has created all these things.

As I watched the expression on her face and the amazed look in her eyes, I could see that many dots were connecting in her mind regarding this earth and the sun, moon, and stars, and of the purpose of life.

Granted, parents can over teach at times, especially given the short attention span of children. But when the time is right, we will want to get the most from it. Maybe this quote will help, which comes from a great teacher. Hugh Nibley said, "A student is only a student when interest reaches excitement." All parents wish to have their kids get excited for life, learning, and success,

don't they? However, many parents *assume* their child will find his or her path in life and get excited about it on their own. Statistics show that is most often not the case, but rather, kids need more help from parents to find their groove. *Assumption* by a parent is not a good strategy. So in order to *wire our kids for success*, we must learn how to teach our children. We, the parents, are teachers and there's no other way around it.

One mother said to me, "I hate teaching, I'm really bad at it." The truth is, this little mother was wired to teach her children well. She simply hasn't tapped into this grand truth or the gift she has waiting to be found with her. This is true for all of us as it relates to our children. We have our specific children because we're the best ones to teach and nurture them.

The Nibley quote makes sense to all who read it. After all, who among us do not learn more on subjects we're most interested in? Our job as parents is to figure out how to instill interest in our child's mind. *Curiosity* can help develop that interest. We noticed that with our kids when they were beginning to learn to read and when we would ask them before turning each page, "What do you think happened next?" In other words, we invite them to guess what's going to happen next in the story of the book. This little exercise not only exercises their brain, but it also has a tendency to encourage curiosity. We can apply that little exercise with almost anything we do with our kids wherever we may be—in the home, in the car, etc. *Curiosity* develops *interest*, and interest breeds *learning*.

We can, in fact, help our kids become more *curious* minded. Curiosity comes with our child at birth. Virtually, all children have that curious nature from birth from a greater to lessor degree. All children come to an age where they begin to feel their own independence and with less dependency on the parents. However, if we can aid our children early in their lives to be *curious* about most everything (hopefully, it goes without saying, some things regarding their curiosity, we should manage more closely), and do

nothing to squelch their natural tendency to be *curious* but rather help it along, they will more likely need less pulling and tugging from parents to learn. Their natural *curiosities* to learn will grow, not diminish. The psychology of curiosity is a subject all parents should be somewhat familiar with.

Woven into the job of parenting is that of teacher. The remaining questions could be the following: how good a teacher am I and am I willing to sharpen my teaching skills?

The dictionary defines what a teacher does: "giving instruction and guidance with a specific end in mind until rapid and successful execution of assigned duties and tasks is assured" (*www.slide-share.net/.../the-essential-coach-john-wooden*. The John Wooden website is filled with helpful hints for coaches and parents). Wow! That sounds like what parents try to accomplish every day, don't you think? Let's make this clear: a "good" or "great" teacher is a relative term when you are speaking of a parent teaching their child. *Our role as parents is to get our kids ready to tackle the challenges of life and to find and fulfill their life's purpose; we all have one.* If we can do that successfully, we are a great teacher and a great parent.

Thank God for great teachers. Thank God for parents who see their proper role and teach their children. It's a wonderful day for a parent when they (or he or she) realize that to become a great parent, they must become a great teacher—an effective teacher.

Our little ones are watching us so closely that our mark will likely be on them forever, and the words we speak to them will help form the remainder of the lives for good or ill. Should we not take more responsibility in examining how well we're doing as teachers?

We all know learning comes to a child when they *observe* their parents and others (learning by *example*), and we all know that learning by *example* is most often the best way to teach and learn. "Example is the best teacher" is still true today. It was so in earlier centuries when children worked side by side with their parents

on the farm, and when the day's work was done, they often spent time together communicating one with another in the home, unhampered by television, telephones, and the like. *Example* was certainly the best teacher in those days and is still a crucial part of teaching and learning today.

But today, there is less opportunity to work side by side with a parent. Also, we're living in a day that is not as simple for child rearing. More *things* steal our attention and our children's, and more people are vying for our eyes to watch and our ears to hear their messages. Added to those distractions is the fact that a great many of those vying for our kids' attention are sending messages we would prefer our kids not see or hear. Without a doubt, we are living in an ever-growing secular society, a godless society, a threat that has become uniquely skilled at turning our minds and our children's minds from good to the secular. This is ever more reason for us to be more determined parents, more vigilant parents.

Another form of learning is by *precept*, meaning, our children are *taught* by their parents and others in the traditional form of educational learning. When we, as parents, open our mouths and speak in an effort to help them learn, we are teaching them by precept.

So we have less time with our kids than our grandparents had with theirs, and there are more threats to our children's minds and hearts. What's a parent to do?

We offer an initial thought: since we cannot or should not avoid our duty in teaching our children, wouldn't it be better that we embrace the role of teacher rather than try to ignore or avoid it? We are teachers. That's all there is to it, so we might as well choose to embrace that fact, and we might as well choose to sharpen our teaching skills.

How do we sharpen our teaching skills as parents? One suggestion: making the assumption that you read books and hopefully you enjoy reading (as a parent, we absolutely must learn

to love to read and to learn). When you do read, do so *from the perspective of the teacher*, the one who will be taking all or much of what you learn from reading, and passing it on to your kids. When we accept the teacher role as a parent, we can choose to make the habit of self-learning from the teacher perspective, meaning, from this point on, all we read or learn will be potential information to share with our students—our kids. This strengthens us as parents in a few ways:

1. We automatically become more observant of learning opportunities. Also, we always search for principles to pass on to our kids or to implement in helping them become the best they can be.

2. We become more selfless, charitable. Our thoughts and desires are turned to our children, not ourselves. This is a noble thing to do. From this point on, every aspect of our lives will be wrapped up in fulfilling our role as teacher, but not just any teacher—the teacher and coach of our own little ones.

3. Since we've come to realize our role as teacher, we begin to seek the best ways to get our messages accepted by our children. We see each of our children as individuals and each with their own separate needs. Each child has his or her best way to learn; not all kids learn in the same way or at the same speed.

4. When we put our all into our role as teacher of our children, we will see through new eyes. That's right. We begin to see life from a different perspective. We see our role as parent differently, more clearly. Why? Because our whole heart and soul is committed to wiring our kids to be the best they can possibly be. To approach our role as parent in this way turns our role into more of a divine position, one that literally has eternal consequences. And because it is such a selfless approach to parenting, we can call upon

the Lord and trust he will be there for us in times of need in our position as parent—teacher. When we're on the Lord's errand, we can expect the Lord's help.

Hopefully, if you didn't know before, the role of parent-teacher is the most noble and thrilling position on earth. The good thing about parent-teacher is that you never get fired; you never get divorced from the calling as long as you live.

The role of parent-teacher is filled with adventure. We, as humans, do best when we are engaged in *meaningful projects.* Moreover, when our own kids are the "project," we find ourselves getting genuinely excited. At that point, the adrenaline kicks in, which makes it a high adventure filled with a rush. This "adrenaline" and "rush" can carry us through our more challenging and difficult days.

We should be pleased when we observe our kids making even the smallest of progress. Also, when you see their small progress, compliment them with a smile and a hug or kiss, and show enthusiasm for their progress, like a good coach that roots them on to success. Obviously then, *we look for opportunities to praise them, which is a very important principle to implement daily.*

Added to that, we look for opportunities to teach, train, and coach. Again, since we seem to have less time with our kids than our forefathers did, we must take advantage of every opportunity we can, and that requires that we be observant parents. This does not mean we're always hounding our kids with this instruction or that (my kids probably accuse me of that), but it does mean that we stay closely engaged with what's going on in their lives—the best we can—and that we observe situations in their lives that we can use either on the spot or at a later day to teach, train, or coach them to become better and to connect the dots of life in their minds.

Effective teachers and coaches strive to improve their duty to *connect the dots* in the child's mind. When two previously unconnected principles in a child's mind finally become connected, mental lights turn on followed by a more enthused child. When their mental, spiritual, or moral lights begin to turn on, that represents part of the payback for parents. It also represents maturity beginning to take hold in their lives, which is a very good thing.

Anyone who has tried to stay continuously engaged in a learning process knows well how valuable excitement is to learning. For that reason, we shared with you the Hugh Nibley quote. Let us state it again: "a student is only a student when interest reaches excitement." We hope you will reread it often and put it to memory, for we've found it to be a true statement. The Nibley quote applies as much to parents as to our children. We *can* get excited about our parent-teacher role, and we *can* get excited about performing the daily tasks of a parent-teacher. For our children to be *wired for success*, we must find purpose and excitement in our parental duty. Without some level of excitement for the parent-teacher role, we will become bored and tired, which will eventually wear us out. A worn-out parent for lack of excitement is not a place any parent should go, and if we ever find ourselves there, we will want to remind ourselves of our divine duty and calling as parent and return to enthusiasm.

So much of *wiring kids for success* has to do with education. After all, how can we expect our kids to succeed without knowledge—knowledge how to act, how to live, how to learn, how to interact with others, and how to overcome life's challenges? It is more evident: the fact that we parents are also teachers, coaches, counselors, and advisors. For a fact, "the hand that rocks the cradle is the hand that rules the world" (from a poem by William Ross Wallace dedicated to the noble role of motherhood).

Education is so important to our kids' success, and we simply must guide them through to success in their *school work*. Helping them to gain momentum and confidence in learning at an early age is crucial to their success.

What more can we say. Motherhood and parenthood is the noblest work on earth, and of that noble work, the parent as teacher is the highest of parental duties. Our determination to accept that fact and then strive to sharpen those skills should be high on our priority list.

Don't Raise Wimpy Boys

After I'd gathered my four young sons together, I said to them, "Okay, boys, listen up. Smiths are lovers not fighters. You know what I mean by that?

"No, Dad. What do you mean?" the youngest, Joseph asked (age five).

"Well," I said, "I don't want any of you to ever, and I do mean ever, start a fight with anyone. Got it?"

"But, Dad," Dillon, age eight, asked, "what happens if someone keeps pushing us or tries to start a fight?"

"I'm glad you brought that up," I said, "because I also want it made clear that there are no wimpy Smith kids. Do you understand what I mean? Smith kids end fights, but they never start them, understand?"

"Ya, Dad. No wimpy Smith kids. Got it."

I proceeded to teach my sons how I expected them to handle situations when an abuser threatens harm on them and won't leave them alone. I said to them, "Okay, kids, if someone continues to hit or shove you and is acting as though his actions are not going to stop soon, simply tell him 'Stop it.' Tell him you don't want to fight. If he continues again and again, you say the same thing each time, no less than three threats on you, okay? But if he continues after three times and he ignores you each time and continues to come at you to hit or harm you, you then have the moral right to defend yourself, and I will back you up, understand?"

About five years passed with no fighting incidents of any serious nature, at least that was reported to me. Not until Joseph,

who was then age ten, came home with a story to tell his parents. Actually, Sandi and I first heard about the incident from a school aid that saw it firsthand, she called us immediately after the incident occurred.

She told us the school bully was picking on Joseph all recess long, even after he told the boy to stop. She told us that Joseph took three hits to the head and body from that boy. After each hit, Joseph told him to stop and that he didn't want to fight. After the third time, the bully took another swing at Joseph, but this time, Joe blocked his swing and reached back and hit the bully in the face, causing his nose and mouth to bleed. She said, "It knocked the boy down. After the bully realized what had happened, he began to cry like a baby."

Joseph, it turns out, followed instructions perfectly, obediently, and in the end, showed that bully he couldn't get away with that kind of thing with him any longer. It boosted Joseph's confidence in defending himself. He wasn't a bully, nor was he a wimpy kid. Joseph's resolve to do right grew in one, short school recess. In addition, we can only imagine that young bully gained new insight regarding his own behavior, and who knows, it may have ended his bullying.

Raising kids to have the courage and the willingness to stand up for themselves is not always as easy a task as I had with my boys. Some boys are quite timid, and some are very reserved, and some are both. Others are physically weak, who often become easy targets for bullies. In order to get our boys (and girls) to learn the courage it takes to stand tall in the midst of life's battles, we should begin with them when they are quite young. We should begin when they are younger to help them understand that being a bully is not acceptable, yet they can and should stand up for themselves when the need arises.

Helping our kids increase their confidence and assurance to take care of themselves without becoming bullies themselves is a wonderful position we should want for our kids. Several of our

chapters deal with helping kids see their strengths, roles, and purpose in life, which gives our children confidence. A child who is self-assured in honorable strengths and God-given gifts has little purpose in pushing his or her weight around or sabotaging his or her own growth and development.

For the child who struggles with self-image issues, he needs some serious coaching from a parent. Typically, I've found that kids who learn to be bullies or intimidators simply don't see any other alternative way to behave. If we can help our child see more alternatives to his behavior, he will have more data to work with and will likely make better choices. Parents should be quick to address those matters as soon as they are noticed.

Helping our kids see alternatives to self-defeating behavior is one of the parents' major jobs. This kind of parent coaching is helping the child become rewired and is creating avenues for that child's success that previously didn't exist in his mind.

We've learned it is helpful as parents to learn some fundamentals as to how children, including ourselves, make decisions in life. This knowledge provides helpful information for parents who wish to change their child's behavior, or to prevent problems before they begin.

We have learned that kids who are acting out poorly have made the assumption that their *map is the territory*. That may be a new phrase to you. It is a metaphor, meaning the "map" (our child's perspective as it relates to a given situation or even life in general) is not the "territory," meaning the actual truth. The map is how we see life. The territory is the actual truth, often something quite different from how we see it, our map.

Often, we adults buy into certain perspectives and later find what we once believed was not true—was not the territory. You could also say we were looking at the wrong mental map or through the wrong lens.

Imagine being in a large city, say, New York City, and trying to navigate through the streets. Imagine also that you thought you

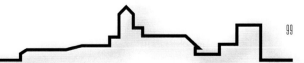

had the NYC map, but in fact, you had a map of, say, Chicago. Your frustrations would hit high levels quite soon. Likewise, when we live life with the wrong map (inaccurate perspectives), everyone but ourselves could say, "He's operating with the wrong map." It's like a blind spot. Everyone else can see it but you. It would be fruitless to say to the map holder in NYC, "Change your attitude and things will improve" or "Try harder and things will work out just fine." None of those approaches would work for a person who has an incorrect map of the territory. No other approach to fixing the frustration would work, only to find the true map. (A must read on this is and other related subjects is Stephen Covey's best seller *7 Habits of Highly Effective People*. All of Covey's books are encouraged for parents).

On the other hand, when we obtain or learn the correct, true map, we can compare it to the territory (the truth), and life goes much smoother with fewer misunderstandings and fewer frustrations. *Therefore, as parents, much of our personal time should be spent on finding and being students of the true maps of life as it applies to every aspect of life—spiritual, physical, emotional, social, and educational, as well as all other aspects of life, including dating, marriage, child raising, etc.*

The time-tested fact is kids pick up much of the unwanted baggage parents have (our incorrect maps) and then carry it on to the next generation. We absolutely must stop the destructive cycle by becoming students of correct behavior, the kind of thinking and actions that history has proven is more likely to bring about happiness and success. When we do that, our own lives will be much more content, and we'll have the information and tools to share that knowledge with our kids and grandkids.

So then, how do we know we've discovered a true map? Please read the chapter in this book entitled "Our Compass, Our Conscience." The key to finding true maps is found within each one of us. Granted, some of the facts we gather are no-brainers. We can learn them by observing other successful people or by

reading biographies of successful people and certainly by being students of God's Word.

Being a student of history is not enough, however. To safely navigate through this life as it pertains to self, marriage, and parenting, we need to learn the language of our *conscience* and then follow it. When we, as parents, learn to become sensitive to that inner voice—the conscience—remarkable things begin to happen in our lives, within our marriage and the way we nurture and train our children.

One set of parents ask, "How do I know when I'm living by my conscience?"

One of my wise mentors stated it this way: "The language of our conscience is mostly felt rather than heard or seen." I asked that couple, "Think about it. When you've had a moral choice to make, for instance, and you made the right choice, didn't it feel right and good, often followed by a feeling of peace?" They agreed. "And in contrast" I said, "when you've chosen wrongly, didn't you feel unsettled inside?" They represent the most common feelings our conscience send to us.

As we become students of the language of our individual conscience, we begin to move on to more and more true paths, paths that will result in better, happier lives for ourselves and our children. Our conscience, because it is God-given to all of us at birth, will always lead us to the territory, the truth.

As we pass this knowledge (learning the language of the conscience) on to our kids as early as they are capable of understanding, we do a work that will positively impact virtually every aspect of their lives—every aspect! They will gain self-confidence because they will be operating with true maps. They will not likely resort to bullying because they will see no need; they will be fulfilled in better ways, higher ways to behave. They will be comfortable in their own skin because they will begin to sense their purpose in life and see a clear path to fulfilling that purpose. Doesn't that sound thrilling? It's even more thrilling when we

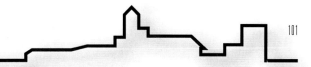

see our children accept these principles, apply them in their lives, receive their own assurance that they are true, and move on to become capable, confident, self-assured teenagers, young adults, and adults.

No one need be a wimp or a bully. The weakest of all kids can still know their way in life and proceed forward each day with dignity and courage, willing and able to stand up to any and all kinds of ridicule or persecution.

The Law of Increased Capacity

Sam, our eldest son at age eight, had had several jobs that helped him begin to learn responsibility and how to stay focused on a job, so Sandi and I thought it time to move him to the next level.

One beautiful autumn day, Sandi, the kids, and I were at the city park, a city population of about ten thousand at that time (late 1970s). While there, I saw the distribution manager of the county newspaper. Always trying to find work projects for the kids, I went over to him, introduced Sandi and myself, and proceeded to sell him on our son, Sam, as his next paper delivery boy in our little town.

He asked me how old Sam was, and I told him eight (he had just turned eight that month). He said, "We have a hard-and-fast guideline that the kids cannot be any younger than nine, and even nine is pushing it."

I followed by explaining how responsible Sam was and that he would do him a great job. I then played on his heart strings by telling him the truth, "Sir, we're just trying to get Sam and all our kids ready for life by teaching them good work ethics." I could tell that had some impact on him, so I proceeded to remind him that Sandi and I would work with Sam until he mastered it well. With that, he said, "Let me think this over, and after I get back to my office on Monday, I'll give you a call."

Monday afternoon, he called as promised and offered Sam the job. Sandi and I were ecstatic. Sam, on the other hand, was a little nervous.

The day came for Sam to begin training with a seasoned delivery boy. Sam was to awake at 5:00 a.m. each morning rain, snow or shine, roll the papers, put them in his bags, and bike off to the other side of town to deliver his papers. Sam learned quickly and was soon on his own.

Sam was a late bloomer height-wise. In fact, he looked younger than eight. So for him to get all those papers on his bike, keep the bike steady, and ride across town were no easy matters.

Sandi and I awoke with him at first and helped him roll and bag, but the day finally came (about a week later) that he was pretty much on his own.

Sandi and I have reminisced of those days, how we were so driven to help our kids learn the principles of work, commitment, discipline, and money management. Now that those days are over, we sort of cringe at some of the lengths we would go to in order to bring about our child-raising goals.

The first morning Sam was loaded and on his bike and it was pitch-dark outside, we watched him through our living room window as he strained to even keep his bike up. We watched as he struggled to get out of our driveway. The load was so heavy for him. We just held each other and cried.

"Are we doing the right thing?" Sandi asked.

"Yes," I said, trying to comfort her, but all along, I was worried about him too in the dark, crossing streets in the early hours each morning.

"But he seems so young, so small. All those papers weigh more than he does," Sandi said. We would go into our bedroom, Sandi and I, kneel down, and plead with the Lord to please watch over our eldest son.

Autumn was replaced by an early winter snow storm that left a foot of snow on the ground. Nothing changed for Sam though. Just as the train must be always on time, Sam knew he had customers waiting for their morning paper. Again, watching

him try to ride through the snow with a load of papers almost too heavy for him to balance tore at our heart strings, but we endured the pain and allowed him to endure the pain, with the earnest hope that what would come out at the end would be a solid, faithful son and human being.

Sam, as with all our kids, would graduate to more challenging jobs, each one designed to teach them the value of work along with all the wonderful extra benefits that come with it. Each job further prepared them—molded them—to become amazing young men and women and, later, as wonderful spouses, parents, and where necessary, providers for their families. With each job our kids performed and completed, we observed their inner confidence grow.

We all have our own unique capacity for growth in every aspect of our lives—spiritual, physical, social, emotional, and educational. In fact, we, as parents, are grownup babies still trying to complete ourselves. But at the same time, we have the awesome and sacred responsibility to help our kids achieve their maximum capacity by preparing them in every aspect of life while they are still in the safety of our home. We call this the law of increased capacity.

Capacity is an interesting word. It speaks of volume, capability, and aptitude. Capacity, as it applies to the human system, is far different than how it applies to a container, like a bottle for instance. If you desire to fill the bottle to its maximum capacity, you will find that it holds only so much and no more.

However, our God-given minds have no maximum capacity; they can hold as much as we wish to fill them with. Moreover, we can continue to fill our minds with knowledge until the day we die. Many people believe after we die, our mental capacity expands beyond our present *capacity* to understand, a wonderful thought. Our minds can be filled with not only knowledge, but it's capacity can grow to include a desire to seek truth, to live truth, to obey laws, to be kind, thoughtful, generous, loving, for-

giving, loyal, trustworthy, etc, etc. Our minds will accept whatever we choose to give it and with no limit to its total capacity and with no questions asked. After all, our mind is literally our servant, as long as we treat it like one, otherwise, it could become the master, to our dismay.

In this life, however, we all have different gifts and talents we were born with, and our duty as parents is to help our little ones find and magnify those gifts to the best of their present ability (capacity), realizing that our child's capacity at his age will expand as he grows up in knowledge and experience. For them to be the best they can be as adults, we always want to help them reach their full capacity for their present stage of life, thus preparing them always to move on to the next level of expansion gracefully (well, not always "gracefully" but successfully nonetheless).

Troubles often occur when a child reaches a certain stage of life unprepared. It often causes undue stress on the child and the parents. It can cause good kids to make foolish choices that can affect the rest of their lives. We parents should not allow any other activity to trump our duty to get our kids ready for that next stage of life.

We grow "line upon line" until we reach "the measure of our creation" or our highest potential development—what we were sent here to become, our fullest capacity. Each one of us is to do the best we can with what we have, and do so with our best effort until our last day on earth. The promise is that those who enter into that great educational developmental process become the most fulfilled; we've found that to be true. The most fulfilled are the most content and happy, knowing they have done their best and reached their fullest potential.

As parents, we should always be cautious to remember that all our kids have different gifts and talents, and all have different capacities at different ages. Therefore, we would be mistaken to compare any of our kids with their siblings or

anyone else for that matter. We are all unique, and we all have unique gifts, talents, and God-given roles and purposes in life. What's more, we all develop at our own rate of speed. We've all heard the term "late bloomer." Well, that might have been you, or it could be one of your kids. We can't rush kids' development any more than we can rush nature. But we can and should nurture and encourage it. Algebra follows basic math, it doesn't precede it. For us to press our kids in the algebra of life before their basic math of life is learned, we can confuse and frustrate our children. Wise parents will learn the capacity of each of their children and help them advance in life's learning as they are ready.

Failing to move our kids to the next level can also create frustration and can create a softy as a child. Mental muscles need to be exercised just as with all body muscles.

A very wise confidant of mine recently said, "We live in a world where the majority of children are not 'raised' they just grow up." We cannot afford that modern trend to rule in our households—with our children. However, if we want to be the exception and not the rule in today's families, we must apply ourselves to the hard part of parenting—planning, close observation, willingness to change methods, and most important, putting the kids' individual development higher on our parent priority list. These things take great foresight and patience, truly the hard part of parenting. We're confident any parent or set of parents can do this successfully with some effort.

To stay on track with your kids' personal development to advance them, you might consider making a chart with each of the kids' names down the left side of the page. Across the top from left to right, you could list all the areas of life you wish to influence your kids' development in—spiritual, physical, emotional/social, and educational. If you can think of others, write them down as well. Then begin with your child on the

top left and record how you feel their *present status* is in each of those categories.

Now that you have a sense of their present status as it applies to each category, do the same thing again, but this time, record *where you think they should be* at this age of their lives. Remember not to compare child to child, but rather, each child to their present capacity to grow. We're always trying to "beat your best" and not keep up with Johnny or Mary.

Now you know where each child is in each category, and you also have a good idea where each child should be. Now you simply need to record *action steps* you are willing to take to help each child get from where they are to where you feel they should be. Prayer is a great help in these matters. The next important step is to *do the action steps!*

Is this worth the effort? Parents, some day you will look back on your efforts to help your kids reach their highest capacity, and you will see them as hard times—challenging times. But you will also see them as some of your most fulfilling times of your life. They will be happy days. You will come to agree if you hadn't before that "no success in life can compensate for failure in the home" (David O. McKay). As it applies to getting our children ready for life, any and all sincere effort is worth the effort, we assure you.

Interestingly but painfully, we remind you, that even with our best efforts, some of our kids may choose wrong paths in life, paths that will cause us heartache. That being the case is ever greater reason to do all in our power to ready our kids for the challenges and trials of life in each of their phases of life.

When we help mold our children to become their best selves and if they choose alternate unhappy routes, the likelihood of them returning to their roots becomes very high. It all turns out to be one big success story in the end. We should teach them and train them so that if they do choose a wrong or even a destruc-

tive path, they will have the correct map to follow back home. As parents, we learn to never give up on our children. The truth is, as we give our hearts to them, they will always return to the family. Sooner or later, they will return.

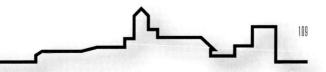

Ready, Aim, Fire

No, only Jesus can walk on water.

Our grandson, Luke, age five, was with his parents at the food mart recently when they came across the man who would be Luke's swimming coach this summer. The coach greeted them warmly, then addressed Luke and asked, "So, Luke, are you the kind of swimmer that can float on water?"

Luke looked at him quizzically and then answered with a serious tone, "No, only Jesus can walk on water." Young children don't understand sarcasm (we should strive to never use joking or sarcasm with children).

Luke's answer tells a whole story to us—that his parents are taking time to wire him for success, meaning, from the inside out. His parents are getting him ready for the next phases of his life. How? By teaching him there is a God in heaven and He can be trusted. Granted, he will eventually learn that the Apostle Peter also walked on water, but that's not the point here. The point is that Luke, a busy, active little boy (the kind that cause his parents to wonder if he's ever listening to anything they teach him), *is* soaking it all in, and it's already beginning to fashion his life around divine principles.

Luke is learning the proper cadence of life. His parents are giving him a solid foundation to his learning and to his life, a spiritual foundation, which should come first in a child's life, at least from our experience. What is the proper cadence of life? We like to think of it like this: "Ready, Aim, Fire." In other words, there is a proper or a preferred learning and preparation model we parents should try to follow as we get our kids ready for life. The seasons of our lives all have significant meaning and purpose. It's not an accident that we begin life as helpless babies, fully dependent upon our mother, our parents, or our caregivers. In that beginning stage of life, the full responsibility lies with the mother—the parents, primarily the mother.

As we've said before, we have made more than our share of child-raising mistakes. As parents of ten kids, you can imagine how crazy it got from time to time. Most of our mistakes fell into one or two categories: Fire, Aim, Ready or Aim, Fire, Ready. What we mean to say is this: we would go through the process of raising our kids just taking one day at a time and letting the daily activities of life lull us into a parental sleep walk. Yet this parental sleep walk was causing us to forget our duty to ready our kids for their next phase of life. Thankfully, we were always awakened to reality before too much time had lapsed. However, notwithstanding our many errors, our kids are all pretty amazing. So take heart—you're probably doing better than you know.

We should strive to prepare them for life's challenges, twists, and turns, before they leave the safety of your home.

With that preparation, they are much more ready prepared to *aim* with a steady and confident resolve toward their chosen path in life. Finally, they can then *fire* or *execute* their plan at life with grace and dignity and intelligent effort.

Parents have a lot on their plates, and we often find it difficult to accomplish all we hope to as it relates to our children. At

times, we may feel like the confused army sergeant who mixed up his sound and said, "Ready. Fire. Aim." We're sure he didn't make that mistake again. Well, maybe he did—we seem to make some of the same mistakes over and over.

It was Benjamin Franklin who was credited with saying: "Experience is an expensive teacher, but fools will learn from no other." As focused and determined parents, we can make our experiences a happy partner and not a foe. As we firmly establish our cadence for teaching, nurturing and training our children, we can be sure to eliminate many of the foolish mistakes parents often make at their kids' expense. And, too, we will be giving our children the wisdom and knowledge they need to avoid many of the most common, youthful mistakes. Ideally we will organize our parental role well enough that we won't need to repeat the same mistakes again and again.

During war time, it's particularly important to get the cadence right, "Ready... Aim... Fire." After all, if solders fail to properly understand the fundamentals of when to pull the trigger, how can they expect to survive the trials of battle? And how can they ever be expected to protect their home land as they are commissioned and committed to do?

You may not feel (yet) that you are preparing your children for the battle and struggles of life, and you may not see any correlation to proper weapon use versus child-raising. We assure you they are very, very much the same, particularly in the times we're living. Our children had better understand the fundamentals of those parts of life that will sustain them during tough, challenging times; otherwise, they will repeat the same youthful mistakes again and again, causing them to spend much of their young adult years wrestling with problems that should have been resolved years before. (When we say "survive," we're not referring to life or death as much as living true to the standards you hope they will be loyal and faithful to.)

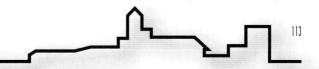

There are very real enemies that threaten us and our children. They have modern weaponry aimed directly at your offspring and they mean business. They don't use conventional ammunition like bullets or bombs, but rather the kind of ammo that will canker the soul and harden the heart as well as other painful wounds. And unless our kids have at least a fundamental idea of how to successfully battle against those threats, they will be easy targets for the enemy. Your sweet, beautiful children have a target bull's-eye on their backs all ready. We must do all we can to help them—particularly for the day when our babies are no longer babies but teenagers and young adults.

Let me interject here that I was born into a very dysfunctional family—loving and kind but dysfunctional. Then my father died at my age seven, which made our home even more dysfunctional. My purpose in sharing this is to express to you that I know somewhat about missing the *Ready* stage of life. My *Ready* stage began as an adult, which made life quite difficult and frustrating for me. So I've been there, and I assure you, you won't want your children to experience that if you can help it. On the other hand, I'm a witness that life can go on after delaying one of our fundamental stages of life.

To help our children, whatever their age, to catch the vision we hope they will embrace, we had better learn for ourselves the importance of the fundamentals—"ready, aim, fire." After all, do we expect them to learn all the vital lessons of life by trial and error? Wouldn't it be better to give to them now the ammunition they will need to navigate through the rough waters of life and successfully weather through the wars and battles life inevitably sends to us all?

Let's take a moment to examine how we can better *ready* our kids. *Ready* is to *prepare* and *equip* our children to better assure their overall success. How do we do that? What do we equip them with? To ready them is to equip them with the fundamentals of a successful, enduring life. Imagine playing on a professional ath-

letic team without having been taught the fundamentals of the sport, it's almost unthinkable that one would even attempt it. If that is true of a professional sport, how much more important should it be to the one and only life we have been given?

The following are a couple of fundamental suggestions and are the points we tried to emphasis with our kids. These are points we learned were best to truly *ready* our kids for life:

- First and foremost, our kids will need a solid *moral* and *ethical* foundation before they leave the nest. Moral and ethical principles provide boundaries they will not cross (not without their conscience harping at them), thus saving them from a multitude of problems. This typically speaks of a religious or spiritual foundation. One must be taught to feel and understand the whisperings of the spirit to be guided by a lively *conscience* that will help them clearly determine the difference between right and wrong, good and evil. The moral and ethical foundation cannot be firmly set without an active, well-working conscience.

You might want to consider teaching your kids that they are too good to make some of the common moral/ethical mistakes many kids make today. "Too good"? Yes. If kids realized their remarkable potential, they would turn and run from the common, foolish mistakes of many. Without a doubt, life is a test, and our time here on earth is no accident (Darwin might have been a nice guy and accomplished many good things, but he missed the mark when he stated our progenitors are from the slime of the earth).

Life is too precious to waste on activities that canker the mind and soil our résumé at such a young age, or ever for that matter. Diametrically opposite to Darwin, your children and ours have a divine mission to perform on earth, so yes, our kids are too good to muddy themselves. All the more reason for us parents to learn and teach the correct cadence of life: To prepare them from the

inside out. Your kids and ours are too good to lower themselves to some of the common behavior many kids today are participating in.

They are sent to earth with a great mission to perform, and to dirty them before they even get into the saddle of life would be to take lightly the high office they hold: to do much good and influence for good many people. Yes, they are too good to contaminate themselves and weaken their perfect moral and ethical résumé.

You see, if the moral and ethical principles are not tightly woven within our children, which is the *ready* stage, they will run the risk of slipping into the kind of behavior we see among many of the troubled children and youth of our day. This need not happen, particularly if our children are lovingly rooted into the *ready* stage of life— their moral and ethical standards.

When Sandi and I would attend parent-teacher conferences to review our children's school progress, the first thing we would ask the teacher was this: "How is my child doing in relations to honesty? And, is he showing respect for you, the teacher, as well as for his fellow students and the school administration? Is he showing you and others respect?"

We made it very clear to our kids those were the first things we asked their teachers during the conferences. From this approach, our kids and their teachers were put on alert to watch the moral and ethical behavior. A high standard was expected, and as a result, a high standard is what resulted. After all, we generally get from our kids what we expect and make clear in their minds.

After receiving that report, we would then move on to questions regarding our children's test scores, etc.

Granted, we should want our children fully prepared for life in every aspect of development including their educational progress, before we give them up to live their own, independent lives. However, we have learned from experience, the most important preparation we can give our children and nurture them in is that

of a solid moral and ethical base. For us, that has tied directly to our faith in God and the church we belong.

Example: Our eldest daughter and her family came to our home to visit. As kids will be kids, her two boys went out of control for a short time and in the process accidentally broke a window in our home. Our daughter and her husband took the matter very serious. Sandi and I were willing to just ignore it and pay for it ourselves, but we kept that thought to ourselves, for we know what our daughter would expect of her boys.

Cari, our daughter, and her husband, Justin, took the boys aside and taught them about responsibility, and that they destroyed someone else's property, therefore they were expected to replace it in full.

Cari had her boys sincerely apologize. She then called a window company and replaced the window, and then set up a series of work projects for her boys to work off the expense of the window, which took them about a week to complete. From this, the boys learned several lessons of life which has stayed with them to this day. Moral and ethical lessons were learned from a very natural consequence.

- For best results, we will want our children to be *goal-driven* (you can learn more on goals from two separate chapters earlier in this book). This is an outstanding quality to have when they're on their own. A moral and ethical person who's driven to succeed with goals and aspirations and with clear, concise *purpose* in mind, is not only likely to have outstanding success in life but will most likely discover the *optimism* needed when setbacks and apparent failures come their way. A goal-oriented child is more likely to be *willing* and *eager* to establish more and shoot toward worthy targets. A goal-directed child will also most likely be or become *industrious*. Being goal-driven, our children will likely find greater purpose in formal education, which will likely bring a finer lifestyle and prepares them to be of greater service to mankind. Imagine, all this from simply being rooted in high morals and becoming goal directed.

We have tried to make a habit of identifying kids we know who have become goal-setters. It's been quite telling to learn which kids are or are not goal-setters. Almost invariably, we can pick out of a crowd the kids who have at least some degree of parental direction with personal goals. Simply by observing the kids for a short time, it becomes quite obvious. Without question, kids introduced and encouraged in goals are more settled in life, and certainly more focused on their own progress. Most generally, kids with even some goal direction can be spotted by their social maturity. We've also noticed kids not directed in goals do not value time and often don't value education either.

You might consider sharing this with your kids: Imagine the NCAA National Championship (USA College) basketball game between Butler and UConn. It is halftime, and with the score tied. Both teams come to the floor to warm up for the second half, only to find there are no goals to shoot at, no rims attached to the glass backboards. "Where are the goals?" the players and coaches yell.

Imagine a basketball game with no goals, no rims to shoot at. Players wouldn't strive and fans would certainly not watch. No one would even want to participate any more in any capacity. Cheerleaders would stop cheering. Coaches would stop coaching and fans would look elsewhere to find entertainment.

And then ask yourself these questions: How long would the players remain excited to play the game without a goal to shoot at? How long would the coaches stay enthused? What about the cheerleaders and fans? Would they encourage you any longer, or would they leave for home? Obviously, we need goals to shoot at to add spice, purpose, and enthusiasm to our lives. You and I are the same, as are our children. When we fail to create meaningful goals we lose enthusiasm for life. Our daily efforts become lackluster, and without purpose in our minds, we become lethargic and weak.

But we should never allow our kids to feel bad when a goal is not reached. After all, repositioning and adjusting are all part of life. It is important we remind our kids that there is no permanent failure when we are striving to improve our lives with goals. Getting back up off the mat of life after being knocked down is a key element of success. If we learn to always get back up after being knocked down by life's experiences, we've already achieved a remarkable degree of success. So let's remind our kids often that when life knocks us to our knees or flat on our backs, it's the getting back up with a solid resolve to continue that constitutes success.

I thought to add an example of one without goals or purpose, but there are so many, I didn't know where to start. Who do you know who's given up on life, stopped working at things which were once important to them, or have basically turned their life over to government handouts and welfare? Our society today has grown to nearly fifty percent who fit into that group. If they only knew how simple it is to determine in their minds what they want, then establish meaningful steps to move them toward their wants and needs, life would magically become exciting again.

- The Ready principle (as well as Aim and Fire) can be applied to all of life or to a single event or project. For instance, your child can learn these helpful hints as they work a school project or assignment, which will guide

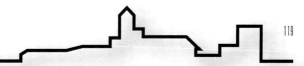

them through to full preparation and completion of the project. They can be applied with assignments given by parents. Boy Scouts use this process when they work their Eagle project and all phases prior. But also, it can be applied to our whole lives and our readiness to achieve our full potential. As parents, we should walk our children through the Ready, Aim, Fire process on small projects. As your child learns to apply each one with small goals and assignments, she will be better prepared to apply each phase with all of life. You, as a parent, can help them see and understand this application to small matters then to life, allowing your child to gain that clear perspective.

When the *Ready* stage is fully developed, our children are quite capable of achieving success in life. They will begin to be *comfortable in their own skin*. With a moral and ethical base, they will likely be respectful to others and willing to give of themselves for worthy purposes. Life will not be overwhelming to that child or youth, but rather a marvelous challenge.

It's also in the *ready* stage that your child's major goals (or many of them) will likely be set and established in their minds.

With the strength of high moral and ethical standards, and with well-defined goals and specific action steps to reach those goals, and with high expectations academically, our children will discover a newfound confidence and wings will be woven from meaningful life experiences of family, work, and faith in God. Anxious yet teachable and itching to get on their own, they will be ready and eager to take their place on the world scene, even in their youth. Not yet fully prepared but eager nonetheless, simply because their parents prepared them well in the *ready* stage of life.

Hopefully by now, you can see that the *Ready* stage is the most important stage to overall success of our children. Interestingly, that is the only stage of their lives they are still within our full care, for after that, they are pretty much on their own. *Aim* and *Fire* are your child's doing, largely—not the parents. Granted,

helping through life experiences such as Scout merit badges leading to the Eagle Scout Award and other such things, will still be in our care. But by and large, once we've locked them and loaded them with morals and a vision with goals, most kids will be pretty much driven from within.

There cannot be enough emphasis placed upon the *Ready* stage. Even though *Aim* and *Fire* are performed by the older, more mature child and youth, we should give them the vision of each stage while they are still at home in our care. Once we've accomplished that, look out world for a prepared and determined young man or women to do his or her portion of good in this world.

Let's now turn our attention to Aim.

Aim speaks of *focus*. Hopefully, this was learned in the *Ready* stage of life. This stage is one where your children are still getting accustomed to their freedoms. In fact, they will likely be on their own and out of the house (but not our hearts and hopes and prayers). Although they may still be working to find their purpose in life, they may well have some clear vision pertaining to their lives.

Focusing speaks of paying attention, being single-minded and steady. It's hard to shoot straight at a target—a goal—if you choose to or fail to concentrate on the target. One cannot expect to move toward the goal if he hasn't got his mind fixed on that goal with sense of purpose. Aimlessness, the antithesis of a focused mind, is one of the most painful conditions of mankind. Aimlessness could be to not know one's purpose in life. It could also be to have no goals. It's foolish to *Fire* when you don't know what you're firing at or to what end. And remember, we should never allow our kids to feel bad when a goal is not reached. After all, repositioning and adjusting are all part of life. It is important we remind our kids that there is no permanent failure when we are striving to improve our lives with goals. A growing number of kids in our day find it hard to focus due to ADHD issues, or other such challenges. Once it's officially diagnosed as ADHD,

you can then address the issue with an assurance your child can become all he wishes to be, it will just take more of his and your time and patience. It surely is not the time to ignore it or sweep it under the carpet. ADHD issues are real, and those who suffer from it need patient, loving help and a gentle hand to assure the child he can and will achieve all his dreams and hopes.

I, Garth, know something about learning disabilities, at least those akin to ADHD. It brings fear and doubt into the mind of the child. They feel stupid, dumb, they also feel deeply humiliated. A loving, understanding parent can turn this lemon into lemonade, but only with much repetitive learning mixed with an outpouring of understanding and love.

As parents we should do all in our power to help our kids learn to focus, mentally—to Aim. A child with even average intelligence, who has good focusing skills, can achieve anything he puts in his mind to achieve.

These points should have been introduced while still in the nest. However, if that's not the case with your child, take heart, for success is still very much within reach. But for success to be within reach, your child will have to learn the *Ready* and *Aim* fundamentals at some point, if he desires to become successful in life. Granted, it will frustrate them and you if they leave home without being Ready and Ready to Aim, but it will still be a wonderful journey of learning and adventure if they leave the nest with a determination to get Ready. What's the old adage, "Don't cry over spilt milk"? If the late or slow bloomers keep their thoughts and emotions on what they did wrong rather than what they now hope to do, they will delay their progress significantly. No matter what, focusing on the chosen goal is significant to their success now and always. Placing emphasis on and becoming single-minded toward a worthy goal are the keys to our children's success. Whether they learn these principles sooner or later, it is essential they do learn them. But learning to Aim—to focus our minds on a chosen target, is what life demands of all who desire success in life.

Once your kids have a solid foundation as listed in the principles above, you begin to teach them how to find their life's purpose. Your kids came to earth already wired to fulfill certain objectives. Our job as parents is to help them find their individual purpose. We take on the role of guide, tutor, and loving parental coach. But for them to find their purpose, they will, sooner or later, have need to focus, to concentrate and stay diligent on their chosen path.

Finding their purpose often does not happen until our children are teenagers at the soonest, well, usually. Often people don't find their purpose in life until they are much older. The sooner we can determine our greatest strengths and how our strengths can benefit ourselves and society, the better, for that is the day we find our primary purpose in life. But, until we learn to focus our minds, at least to some degree, it makes it difficult for us to apply our minds to our goals and aspirations, which lead us toward our mission in life.

Sandi worked with our children to help them learn to focus. Our first three little children all spaced in age about one to one and half years apart, it became more difficult to get all three to hold still and pay attention. This was especially noticeable at church or other functions where quiet was expected. Our three kids were just normal kids, squirming around fidgety and regularly fussing with each other causing some little noise; common for little children

In an effort to help our kids learn to hold still and be more quiet when expected, Sandi began a school at home. One significant purpose of this school was to teach them to pay attention, to focus.

She prepared a corner of our kitchen as a sort of school room, with children's books for pre-school age children, paper and crayons, and other such helps. She worked with them every day, with

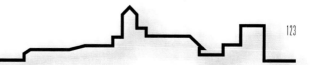

the intent of not just introducing them to numbers and letters and books, but to help them see the difference between holding still and quiet and the opposite.

She wasn't trying to force them to grow up, mind you, but rather, to appreciate, at their young ages, the difference between reverential quiet and disruption that may interrupt others.

It took several weeks before we saw any evidence of change, but when change came, it was very obvious, especially with our two older kids. From this we learned that even little children can reason and make behavioral changes in their lives and still remain happy, fun little children. We often received compliments from others (actually, every week) on how quiet and well behaved our children were. When we added to the three an additional seven kids, it became all the more evident that lots of kids can learn to focus enough to behave and be quiet. That may have been our kids' first lessons on focusing their minds to please their parents. Once they understood what focusing their minds meant, it became a much easier chore for us to teach them other principles important to us. At that point in their lives, they are much more prepared to learn the principle of Fire.

Fire is to pull the trigger of your *energy* and ability to execute your our goals. With your prior planning and developed resources and with your eye fixed upon your chosen goal, you're ready for success. Imagine your child, now an older child or youth, with a fixed determination to remain true to the high family moral and ethical code, and with a strong ability to Aim toward his chosen goals with laser-like focusing ability, he or she will then be much better prepared to execute all his training with maturity and determination. Granted, this level of preparedness may not all come together for each child as quickly as you would like, but as we persevere, all their training will come together for them sooner or later. Some kids begin to show all three facets working in concert in their teenage years, some a little older. But even if it's later, it's much better to have the training than not. Our

children, if they stray away from our teachings for a time, gener-ally return at some point. "Train up a child in the way he should go...". This is a true principle.

Ready, Aim, now Fire, which is for your children to put into execution all their hopes, and dreams and goals, and apply all three parts pretty much on their own shoulders. Granted, they will know we've got their backs.

Your children will now be ready to launch into the dark abyss not with fear, but with faith and hope of a grand result. The bull's-eye will be their target, but to miss the bull's-eye from time to time, will only add additional fuel to the fire of determination.

Watching each of our children execute the Fire principle in their lives was thrilling for us parents to behold. To see each of them as older kids or teenagers, show significant signs of real grownup maturity, helped us to realize all our efforts were worth it. I assure you, we assure you, all your efforts to lovingly teach, train, and instruct your children in ways that will help them see their lives with their full potential, then to give them duties and assignments to work those principles in their lives, will bring remarkable results. And, for them to begin to see the world and their lives from a clear and moral perspective will give them the clarity to live their lives according to their true conscience.

Hopefully, it's been made clear that the Ready stage of life for our little ones is squarely on our (the parents) shoulders and that it is a short window of time. Once that window closes, much (but not all) of the nurturing, teaching, and training ends. It is impossible to put too much emphasis on that period of our children's lives, as well as the duty and responsibility we have as parents to take the most advantage of that we possibly can in that small window of time. So let's get after it! Let's put in the planning, the work, and the prayerful effort to get our kids as ready as possible. Remember, good parenting takes time. This is the hard part of parenting: the planning and executing of the plan. Let's beware not to fall into the common trap of depending on quality time with our kids at the expense of real, day-to-day actual time. Single parents have little choice but to balance their time between kids and work. The rest of us... Well, our kids need our best effort; they need our presence.

Comfortable in Our Own Skin

Freckled faced Max with freckled faced little sister, Sophia.

Things turn out best for those who make the best of how things turn out.

—John Wooden,
UCLA legendary basketball coach

Our daughter, Lyric, gave us one example from her own life and that of two of her three children how to apply the Wooden quote above. Enjoy.

Freckles are a funny thing. It's even a funny word. Say it out loud a few times, and you'll probably chuckle in agreement. I have talked to many people who have no love for their freckles or have bad memories of their younger more prevalent freckle days. As a child, I had the spattering of

freckles. You know, the freckles across the nose and cheeks with the occasional cluster throughout other parts of the face. I loved my freckles. My mom always told me that people with freckles don't get acne. I'm not sure where she got her information, and I really don't know if it's true or not, but I bought into it completely, and I really didn't get much acne, even during puberty.

I also have very fond memories of adults looking down at me and expressing their love for my freckles and my cute little button nose. I really didn't give my freckles too much thought, but when I did, they were adoring thoughts. Now I understand that some people have more than just the spattering of freckles. In fact, my own Maxwell has more than what I would consider a spattering, so to each their own freckle feelings, but I do know that I am completely endeared to Max's freckle face. Don't get me wrong, I think an olive-skinned, spot, and blemish-free child is absolutely beautiful, but seriously, look at that little cropped picture of my cuddle bug, and to me, there is nothing more adorable (including the crazy second grade teeth. I'm admitting my bias!).

I want to make sure he loves his freckles as well, so ever since these little splats of pigment started arriving on his nose (around age three), I started telling him how much I love them. I haven't shared the acne angle yet! I would count them each night, and he loved it. By the age of four, I had lost count, but I still pretended to count and would always stop somewhere around one hundred, and it was around that time that I found my favorite. Meet Mr. Dot! Do you see the almost perfectly round freckle below his right nostril? It's a little bit bigger and a little bit darker than the rest. To me, it is the epitome of the perfect freckle. I no longer count his freckles, but nearly every night, I give Mr. Dot a kiss, and Maxwell loves it. Sophie started to feel left out, so we found Mrs. Dot, who resides at the top of her neck. It is probably even more of a perfect freckle than Mr. Dot, but it's kind of in a ticklish spot, so I'm not really allowed to give it kisses unless I steal them, which means it doesn't get the same attention from me as Mr. Dot and usually falls off my freckle radar!

Max and his Mr. Dot remind us that we all have mountains to climb and challenges to overcome. In fact, it is our belief that this points to the very purpose of life—to endure faithfully through our problems and challenges, to find purpose in life, our own individual life, and to find a way to feel *comfortable in our own skin* that our mountains, our challenges, don't overwhelm us, thus causing us to miss the real joy life has to offer us all.

The idea of feeling comfortable in one's own skin is a weird thing to consider. The thought here is that one such person has such a high level of self-confidence and self-esteem that they are confident within themselves, so much so that most or all of life's issues and trials do not shake them off their solid base; they remain stable and firm in their resolve and commitment to self and others. Kids who have been wired in such a way truly are wired for success and learn to find purpose in their life and therefore become comfortable in their own skin.

The antithesis of being comfortable in your own skin is to focus on your problems (as you perceive them) and not your strengths, to allow your freckles, birth defects, pimples, big nose, the unfairness of life, etc., to take center stage of your mind, so much so that you live much of your life in some sort of fear and an unsettled condition, thus preventing you from being the best you can be. Those in this condition often see themselves as victims, which have a tendency to stifle the growth of that individual. Those who are plagued with the belief they are victims see themselves as mistreated by society or certain groups or individuals. Victims feel they have a ready excuse for their lack of progress and growth. This is not a good place for anyone to be. It is not the way we want our children to begin life, and sadly, millions do.

From a parental perspective, we all should make this a high goal: that as parents we will do all in our power to help our kids

learn to be comfortable in their own skin. Why is this so important? Because as stated, to be so resolved with oneself is the solid foundation of mental health that allows much of the *envy, pride, jealousy*, and other problems of life to simply slide off one's back, thus allowing our children to focus on the real important matters of life, like meaningful and healthy relationships with others (including a future spousal relationship). Being comfortable in one's own skin is to see no need to envy another's position, influence, power, or possessions. They are satisfied with who they are, how they look, and what they have. This is not to say they've stopped striving for more and better, just the opposite. They are likely to be anxiously engaged in many good causes including their own development and standing in society. They simply find pleasure in their present state of being, in every aspect of their lives.

We believe that many, if not most, broken marriages are a result of pride such as selfishness and unwillingness to give all of oneself to their partner and to weave oneself with a spouse in a mutual, loving friendship that grows into a melting together of two people into one.

This kind of united relationship can be had by anyone who is willing to give of him or herself without holding back. *It is a learned behavior*. To achieve it, one must learn to be more self-assured and unselfish. To be comfortable in one's own skin, particularly at such a young age, gives that child a tremendous head start in relationship building, like the kind that results in enduring marriage relationships.

So then, how do we help our children become comfortable in their own skin?

Does your child have freckles that he hates? What about crazy hair or crooked teeth? Does your child have a speech impediment, a birth defect, or anything else that could dominate his or her thoughts with negativism or wishing he or she were someone else? Try doing what Lyric does with Maxwell and Sophie.

Celebrate their so-called blemishes and help them find purpose in them. The truth is many of the problems that dominate our thoughts are only temporary. But if your child has a permanent trial, there is all the more reason to celebrate it. After all, there is purpose in all things in life, even our struggles and heartaches. Let us give you an example.

About a hundred years ago (exaggeration), when I was in grade school, I had a schoolmate who contracted polio when she was very young. This young girl had lost all muscle use in her legs and was unable to walk and run like the rest of the kids. Her parents did her a great favor; they treated her like she had no disability, giving her opportunity to do whatever all her siblings and friends would do as best she could, and with this young girl's adventurous spirit, she was riding horses and doing a great many activities others would do.

But it was her grandmother who spoke to her one day when she was visiting her at her home. She was about seven at the time, not long after she contracted the disease. Her grandmother, whom she adored and trusted said, and I paraphrase, "Sharlene, the Lord loves and trusts you very, very much to give you this mountain to climb. He trusts your ability to reach for high goals and to stay focused in your life. Remember Honey, He will never leave you. Remember, you can make your situation a burden or a gift, you choose. But I'm confident you will make it a gift." Which she did.

Her grandmother's words affected her resolve to be determined and to never let discouragement get the best of her.

Years later, I recall seeing her each day in the halls of our high school as she used her crutches and literally dragged her legs using the strength of her upper body. More noticeable than her crutches and her condition, however, was the smile she always wore whenever I saw her. She was one of the most confident, self-assured young women I knew. She truly was comfortable in her own skin. She knew who she was, what principles of honor

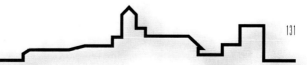

she stood for, and she knew how to overcome obstacles. She paid little attention to obstacles (ones she had no control over). She just plowed forward with confidence and hope. That, you see, is one of the greatest reasons why we should work diligently to help our children become comfortable in their own skin, that they will have the wherewithal to face challenges head-on and unflinching, finding purpose and meaning in all twists and turns of life, as well as the purpose of their own life.

How did her life end up? She never gained the use of her legs, but she persevered with high, lofty goals of education, marriage, and children. She achieved them all, including teaching school for over twenty years. Sharlene and her husband, Jay, are enjoying their forty-second year of marriage and are loving parents and grandparents. A legacy of family has been built because Sharlene saw God-given purpose in her challenge. We all can do the same. (This story of Sharlene and Jay Irvine was graciously given with their permission.)

Sharlene's life with thousands of others reminds me of the words of Victor Frankl: "For what then matters is to bear witness to the uniquely human potential at its best, which is to transform a personal tragedy into a triumph, to turn one's predicament into a human achievement" (Viktor E. Frankl, *Man's Search for Meaning*).

Now, let us speak to you single parents who make up about twenty-five percent of the population and growing.

Your challenges are great, and you may not have the greatest self-confidence yourself, yet you want your kids to be the best they can be. As you can imagine, for them to be their best, they will need to be comfortable in their own skin just like anyone else that endures and succeeds in life. Let us share with you a true story of a single mother who raised her three young children alone after her husband fell ill and died. All three would eventually become parents and professionals in their chosen fields. One son became a high government official as well as an esteemed leader of his

church. How did this mother prepare her three fatherless children for such amazing success? In a nutshell, this is what she did.

1. She helped each child set goals at an early age. Small goals at first, then larger ones. She knew that by teaching her kids to work to complete targets and projects, they would thrill in the process and completion of predetermined goals and thus feel the joy of work, achievement, and completion. Tasks and goals gradually became larger and harder to achieve allowing their confidence to grow.
2. She celebrated those parts of their lives they felt were blemishes. They found purpose and meaning in all things.
3. She expected educational excellence. She patiently helped them gain confidence in learning challenging educational principles. *They learned to love to learn.*
4. She worked diligently to cause them to feel loved and to support them in their own interests.
5. She taught them to feel comfortable in adult conversations even to participate in them, yet to always remain respectful of adults as well as others.
6. She gave them a faith and trust in God and to trust his timing. She taught them there is purpose in life and in death and that death is not the end of living or family connections.

The challenges of being a single parent overwhelm many women and men, and in some cases, they allow those challenges to spoil their joy and then to pass the joyless life on to their kids. It need not be that way; we always have a choice.

To be comfortable in your own skin is, as earlier stated, a *learned habit.* Also, it is not an all or nothing sort of thing. We learn it bit by bit just like all other learned habits until we become proficient in it. So, parents, give your kids the seeds of this principle and then feed it to them daily with some of the above ideas. They will be forever grateful for your efforts.

We've all read the old adage: "Give a man a fish, and you feed him for a day. Teach him to fish, and you feed him for a lifetime." This is certainly true as it applies to helping our kids become comfortable in their own skin. With their growing confidence and feelings of self-assurance, they are equipped to become well-adjusted kids and adults, capable of achieving whatever they're heart desires, feasting on the goodness of life, and advancing from one achieved goal to another until their lives are complete, whole. This constitutes the whole purpose of life—to be the best we can possibly be.

You might be saying, "I'm not comfortable in my own skin. How can I give what I don't have to my kids, for instance?" The answer to that question is really quite simple. If you can recognize something when you see it, like someone who is comfortable in their own skin, then you can begin practicing it—to model it—thus replacing who you are now with who you wish to become. Just like any changes in life, we first recognize what we don't have, but want, and then set a goal to make the change.

At first, it's a sort of "fake it till you make it" sort of thing. Don't worry though, because this sort of faking is a wholesome application of effort—trying to become who we think we can become. Like children practicing to become adults, we are practicing to be self-assured though we've not yet fully achieved it. We become students of what we want, and then we practice it each day until we become proficient at it. As stated, it takes time, but for the sake of our kids, it's worth the effort. And we too should learn to find joy in each progressive, small step.

The phrase "comfortable in your own skin," may lead some to think this is a physical body process only, and they would be wrong but not totally. Most of the work of this Skin process is internal—from the neck up sort of thing. After all, nothing ever really changes in our lives until we first think of it, examine it, become a student of it, and then embrace it in our minds. At first, it's all in our mind.

For many, the Skin process does include the physical body, and it should. If we fail to take our physical body into account as we strive to be comfortable in our own skin, we could likely sabotage our efforts. Our bodies go wherever our minds go, and we have our physical body as long as we're in this mortal world, so we might as well include it in all our goals to improve ourselves—to learn to become comfortable in our own skin. Caring for our physical health and well-being is essential to our success, likewise with our children.

Let's be clear though. We all know people who appear grossly overweight, for instance, yet seem to be very comfortable with whom they are. I applaud those determined individuals. We're all doing the best we know how, so we might as well be sincerely happy with our present stage in life while on the path to improvement.

Now let's turn our attention to the most likely culprit who would *prevent* us from becoming comfortable in our own skin. We've learned how helpful knowledge of the potholes and wrong turns are as we travel the road of life as we strive toward our goals. Of all potholes that work to prevent our progress, this pothole is, without question, one of the most challenging obstacles one could face. History has proven so. We speak of that kind of pride known as *envy*.

One of the biggest problems with our generation of adults and kids today is *envy*. Envy, as defined by Dictionary.com, is "a feeling of *discontent* or *covetousness* with regard to another's advantages, success, possessions, etc."

Envy turns us into judges, criticizers, and conspirators. Moreover, uncontrolled envy is a form of social and emotional cancer; it eats up all that is good within the person by covering over all their good with a film of envy and jealousy. It drains out of one's life what could otherwise be a life of pure joy. It truly is a time waster and a threat to life's joy. The nature of envy is powerfully harmful to those who buy into it, and as C.S. Lewis wrote,

> Envy is insatiable. The more you concede to it, the more it will demand. (*The Quotable Lewis*, p. 186)

Envy has some other close pals—*jealousy, self-centeredness*, and *resentment*. When you put all these together, you come away with *confusion*, and those with a heavy dose of envy find themselves confused. After all, one forgets all the lies and tainted stories they've spread around and to whom they were spread and all to either lift them up or tear down a proposed competitor. So thick becomes the web of small conspiracies, the best the envious can do is conveniently block out of their minds many or most of their prideful deeds.

The spirit of *competition* is woven tightly through every fiber of an envious person. That really is near the root of it. They are deeply invested into protecting their own image as though they are the king at the top of the hill and all others are always trying to steal their crown. They see life like a pie; there are only so many slices, and when those slices are gone, it's all gone, or so they think. So they guard their own pieces of the pie, those allotted to them, and fight to get more, all along trying to maintain their image as peacemaker. The truth is, the slices of pie never end; there is enough and to spare for all, and we'll want to make sure our kids understand that fact.

So nefarious is the sin of envy that when we recognize it in our lives or our children's and desire to remove it, we will find its tentacles fighting to stay attached. Daily, prayerful practice is the only way to totally rid ourselves of it. Hopefully, we can see why it is so important to nip envy and its sidekicks in the bud as quickly as we find any hint of them, whether in our own life or those of our young children. When we sense one of our children demanding or desiring some thing or some influence that is not for them to have or be, at least not now, that is our cue to jump into action to root out the problem as best we can.

We hear our kids say things like the following:

"It's not fair."

"He got more than I did."

"Why can't I have that?"

"I want what she has."

They seem ruffled when something good happens to someone else or when they make excuses for their performance, blaming it on outside forces or influences.

Dozens of examples could be written, but in a nutshell, any time one of our children shows even a hint of jealousy or envy, that event creates an opportunity for the parent to teach and train the dangers of envy and the joys of *goodwill, generosity, satisfaction,* and *appreciation* for what they presently have. Imagine having a few loving sessions with your child on the topic of satisfaction and appreciation and how displeasing it is to parents and God when we are *ungrateful* for what we have.

Your child might say, "But, Mom, I'm happy for what I have, but I want what Billy has too." You can then extend the conversation to include *greediness*. In the end or eventually, the topic with our kids will land on the subject of *charity, love.* When we or our children can truly be happy with life as it is now and when we can be genuinely happy for the success of others, we are on the road to a more joyful and balanced life. That level of happiness is founded in love, love for others, all others. And when we sense that love and see it in the lives of our kids, we know they are becoming comfortable in their own skin. They will no longer be looking to other people's stuff or money or beauty or success. Gone will be the attitude of competition among family or friends. They will find true joy and happiness in their now, their present situation, with their possessions and their status in life. They will come to see God's hand in all things, allowing them to feel satisfaction with what they have, how they look, etc. The election of your teenage child's friend as student body president will be reason to celebrate rather than be envious. Rather than trying to beat or win over someone else can be replaced with a new mind-set to

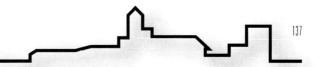

beat our best, simply competing against ourselves. Wow, what a relief that would be. What gladness it would bring.

How many people do you know who are so well-grounded and satisfied with what's been allotted to them? Most would agree it's rare to find such a happy, contented person. This is evidence of how widespread this cancer of envy and jealousy is throughout society, and a good reminder of the importance of insulating our children early in their lives while they are so moldable, so that they will be filled with the desires and habits that will ensure being comfortable in their own skin.

Last but not least is the fact that much of what we learn, positive or negative, we receive our first lessons from our parents, generally by example. As was said earlier in this chapter, envy and jealousy are learned habits. We parents should do some serious inventory of our own behaviors to see if we're the source of our little one's troubles. Placing our kids in holes we've dug is a formula for years of heartache for them and us.

Do we regularly criticize or judge others? Are we often making comparisons with other's in an attempt to raise our worth while depleting theirs? Do we often find fault with others? Do we say and do these things in the presence of our kids? For our kids' sake (as well as our own), the best thing we can do is *stop it*! Yes, stop it, but be patient with self and kids because this is not likely to be resolved in a day.

One of the best things we can do for our kids to help wire them for success is to master early in their lives these principles, never to be troubled by them.

Disciplining Kids Made Easy (Are You Kidding Me?)

I had just walked in the house from a late-night business appointment, tired, irritable, and impatient because my appointment hadn't work out the way I'd wished. Just as I walked in, I heard Sandi say, "Garth, would you settle the boys down? They're keeping every one awake, including the baby."

I walked down the stairs to their bedroom only to see my three oldest boys—ages eight, six, and three—very much awake, teasing each other, laughing, and making sort of a ruckus.

"Listen, boys, I need you to get in your beds and be quiet. You're waking up your baby brother."

Each one jumped into his own bed—Sam in his, Jesse in his, and younger brother, Dillon, in his. I kissed them all, then left the room.

Even before I reached the top of the stairs, loud laughter came from their room. This time I showed some impatience. Raising my voice slightly, I told them to get in their beds, be quiet, and go to sleep.

Back up the stairs I went and again, even before I reached the top stair, more laughter and noise came from their room.

Respect for authority is so important to me as a parent, so I rushed down the stairs, this time in anger. I turned Sam over and gave him a swift slap on the rump then turned to Jesse and did the same. Those two boys quickly replaced their laughing with signs of painful respect. I could tell I finally had their attention. I then turned to the younger one, Dillon, turned him over and swatted him on his rump, but he still held a smile on his face. So I swatted him harder in an effort to see that he knew I meant business but also to see in his face a look of respect for me.

With that last hard swat he still held a smile on his face. So I swatted him even harder but still no look of respect or even pain, only a smile.

I raised him up again to give him an even harder spank when something came over me. I was spanking an angel, a purely wholesome child of God. This little boy, my boy, was just being a boy, and I was inflicting pain on him to bring about some behavior he wasn't even old enough to fully understand.

Who do you think you are? I thought to myself. *This angelic son of mine is taking the pain to impress his older brothers that he's as big as they are and to show them he won't cry because he's thinking "I'm a big boy, too."*

I was the tallest one in that room, but just then I felt like the smallest. I was the father, but I could tell as I looked into Dillon's cute, little smiling face that I was in the presence of a divine soul, three of them, actually, and that my present actions were displeasing the powers of heaven.

I told myself I would never approach discipline in that way again. And with only a few exceptions, I held true to that promise. Did I ever spank again? Yes, but I tried much harder to discipline with love and not with anger. (Spanking was, to Sandi and I, the last option and was used very, very sparingly.)

The root of the word "discipline" is "disciple," meaning "follower," "student," and "learner." It speaks of a loving teacher teaching a willing student. To me, the word "disciple" is all wrapped up in the word "love," more particularly, a loving relationship between a teacher and the disciple or in our case, parent and child.

I was so bent on obedience that night with my three older boys that I clouded my mind and forgot the key point of discipline: to *show* them *how* to act by *showing* them my *love* for them.

And because my mind was overshadowed with impatient anger, I showed them the opposite of what I really intended to show—love, kindness, patience, tenderness, charity, and how to be a parent. For what are we as parents but models to our children, models they can mimic to become loving parents themselves someday.

In fact, one reason this life is organized into families, we believe, is to have parents lovingly prepare the next generation of parents in the right way so they will *see how* to prepare the next generation of parents. It goes on and on and on, each generation of children observing their kind parents on *how* to live their lives and *how* to be good parents to their future children and that when it is their turn to tutor their little ones, they will have a wonderful model to follow.

So we can see that one of the greatest works we as parents can do is to learn of and practice daily the principles of patience, tolerance, kindness, gentleness, understanding, and good, old-fashioned love. We should be students of those subjects and put each one into operational practice as we interact with our children each day. Doing so, we will become more proficient in them as time advances.

Discipline is an action we parents must implement each day to help our children grow and understand. We should put away the stick, the harsh and loud language, and the empty threats of punishment and replace them with loving instruction, the kind that teaches and instructs our kids. After all, what good is teaching and training if they don't understand *what* we teach? *Teaching for understanding* is one of the kindest acts of love we can give our kids.

Is it okay to spank your child with a flat hand or a belt? That is open to discussion. My grandparents on my mother's side had sixteen children (no kidding). Grandpa never spanked his kids, never! He said, "I won't beat my animals. Why would I beat my kids?" All his children turned out well-adjusted and kindly people, and each one absolutely adored their pappa.

How did my grandpa discipline his kids? When they were young, he and Grandma simply loved them, caressed them, and caused them to feel safe and loved. But when they were old enough to understand, he would hold them on his lap or sit them next to him and simply talk to them and help them *understand* in words *what* they did wrong, *why* it was wrong, and *how* it made him feel, and that he *expected* them to try and never behave in that fashion again. Most often, just giving his kids a certain look would cause the kids to modify their behavior to his liking.

Some claim that to never spank is permissive parenting, that the children will be raised without a deep respect for parents and others. Other parents claim that spanking gets good results for them. We spoke with one mother who told us that controlled spanking, although rarely implemented, must always be a tool available when needed.

So the quick answer to the question of spanking yes or no is this: In our opinion, no parent should ever spank their kids with a flat hand or belt *in anger*. A hard spank on the rump or a swat with a belt, if they are done at all, should be reserved for very rare occasions and never with the fist or on the face. Let me give you an example.

At my age seven, my family lived in a gorgeous valley surrounded by the Teton Mountains on the border between Wyoming and Utah in a little town called Alpine (Star Valley). The population at that time was about thirty people. My father, a boilermaker and ironworker, was helping build the Palisades Dam.

Within a few hundred yards of our home ran the Snake River. The Snake River could be swift and turbulent at times, so Mother made it perfectly clear that no Smith kid were to go near the river.

One beautiful afternoon, a neighbor boy coaxed my older brother and me to go down to the water's edge to throw rocks in the river. Forgetting about our mother's rule, we followed the boy (like sheep) to the edge of the river. Little by little, we gained more confidence and began to wade our feet in the water. At that

moment, we heard our mother scream at the top of her voice, "Greg, Garth, get out of that water!" She knew the danger of what we were doing far more than we did, obviously.

My brother and I sheepishly ran up the hill to our mother's side. When we got close enough for her to get her hands on us, she grabbed us both—Greg by his arm and me by mine—and proceeded to kick our behinds with the side of her foot, all the way home. First, Greg, then me, then Greg, then me, all the way home! After we arrived home, Mother lowered her voice and told us how dangerous the Snake River is and how frightened she was for us. She then embraced us both, kissed and held us close with tears in her eyes. We never went to the river again.

What of children ages four to ten or twelve, who are old enough to understand, yet constantly disobedient, how do we discipline them? We bring this up because from our experience, children who regularly are disobedient between these ages as well as older, likely were not taught to be obedient by their parents when they were younger, or the parents' discipline style was harsh or inconsistent.

From our experience, almost all infants and young children, with just a relatively few exceptions, respond well to the loving, kind touch and of a parents' sincere desire to discipline them. They respond positively to love, caring attention, and a gentle hand. They easily sense feelings of affection, adoration, and tenderness. Why? Because they are wired that way at birth—we all were. When we, in our children's first few years of life, fail to give them guidelines, boundaries, and rules and when we fail to expect obedience and respect from them or if we regularly discipline harshly, angrily, and inconsistently, our kids become confused. They often become angry themselves, blaming themselves for the harshness imposed on them. If it continues, they feel unworthy of such high levels of true love later on in life. Many more serious problems often follow.

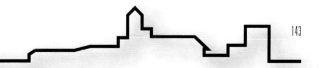

The point is this: We want our kids to be the best they can possibly be and to help them become well-developed, well-adjusted, and safe. We have the duty as parents to teach them the right way to live life to its fullest within the laws of nature and society. We need to do the best we can to nurture them so that they will feel good about themselves and their parents. Teaching, training, and yes, even those times of discipline should be approached with love and tenderness for our offspring. This takes a patient hand, but it's our divine duty to muster up the needed patience and love.

The whole purpose of discipline is to change and improve behavior. In order to improve behavior, teaching and loving must be instituted. Like my grandpa, helping kids to *see* from a broader, clearer perspective is the only real way to change behavior permanently.

Even in the example above with my brother, Greg, and me at the Snake River, our mother, after physically disciplining us (which didn't really hurt us, but made it clear she meant business), set us by her side and tearfully taught us *why* she was so fearful of our lives. Greg and I changed our behavior because we felt our mother's sincere love and interest in us. It turned out to be an excellent learning experience.

We should always remember: Our kids are on loan to us. The day will come when they will be on their own, and when that day comes, we will want them to have tender feelings for their parents, and at the same time have a clear perspective of life. We will want them to have happy memories about their childhood. Even discipline, when done in the true spirit of the word, is love, the kind of love our kids will remember for good.

The ideal to child discipline is this: To have the discipline session end with the child seeing a new, improved direction to go with his behavior and second, for the child to *know* the parent loves and respects him or her.

How then should I have handled the situation with my boys that late night? The answer to that question speaks of the hard part of parenting: Time (the time it takes to patiently follow through, patience) and love. Parenting takes *time*, and often, the call to parent comes at the most inopportune time. There are times we are called upon to parent when other interests or demands seem to be screaming in our ears, and even when we don't feel like taking the time needed, we must. We might feel irritable, frustrated, or simply worn out from our day's activities, yet our highest duty is to put our children's needs above our own, remembering that those tender moments of loving instruction to our child will build strands of loving memory that will stretch throughout their lives and on to future family generations.

Many parents feel conflicted regarding the discipline of their children because they can't seem to balance how they were raised with how their conscience is telling them to raise their kids in the here and now. For instance, some parents are so bent on a near perfectly clean, orderly home so that they place that above the present need of the son or daughter, thus often missing out on teaching, learning, and bonding time with the kids. Other parents struggle in the same way when it comes to a picture-perfect yard. Parents often struggle between the nurture and forming of the child versus the nice yard or spotlessly clean home.

We're reminded of this humorous story:

> A very old man lay dying in his bed. In death's doorway, he suddenly smelled the aroma of his favorite chocolate chip cookie wafting up the stairs. He gathered his remaining strength and lifted himself from the bed. Leaning against the wall, he slowly made his way out of the bedroom, and with even greater effort, forced himself down the stairs, gripping the railing with both hands. With labored breath, he leaned against the door frame, gazing into the kitchen. Were it not for death's agony, he would have thought himself already in heaven. There, spread out on newspapers on the kitchen table, were literally hundreds of his favorite

chocolate chip cookies. Was it heaven? Or was it one final act of heroic love from his devoted wife, seeing to it that he left this world a happy man? Mustering one great final effort, he threw himself toward the table. The aged and withered hand, shaking, made its way to a cookie at the edge of the table, when he was suddenly smacked with a spatula by his wife. "Stay out of those," she said. "They're for the funeral." (http://www.ebaumsworld.com)

When raising kids, a clear perspective of priorities is essential to our success of raising successful children.

My mother loved a nice yard. In fact, she won the Yard of the Month one summer in our small town. But when my brother and I entered into little league sports, our activity and development took precedence over the roses and manicured yard. Don't get me wrong, the yard didn't go to pot, but it would never earn Yard of the Month again, at least as long as we were young.

Wise parents will see a clean, orderly home and a manicured yard as a chore, the kind of chore that will show up on the to-do list again tomorrow and every day. But they know kids don't wait and the teaching and bonding moment is just that, a moment, and that once gone, it cannot be retrieved. Wise, creative parents figure out how to manage both, clean house and nice yard, placing the main emphasis on the kids' needs. With some thought, many creative alternatives can be thought up, but if you have energy for only one, choose the kids.

What should I have done with my boys that night? I should have offered a silent prayer before entering their room, maybe something like this: "Father, I'm tired and frustrated inside. Please help me to patiently give my wonderful boys the love and attention they need to allow them to drift off to sleep and to know how much I love them." If you're not the praying type, maybe you could pause a moment before entering into the stressful situation with your kids and ask yourself, "How do I want my kids to remember this encounter?"

Sandi and I have tried to make a habit of this pattern as it applies to dealing with discipline of our children: First and foremost, love, and then if our human tendencies overcome us with impatience, we always end with love. Over time and with lots of practice, we're generally able to discipline with patience. We should try to make the habit of ending a discipline with a great outpouring of love so that they will know we are not an enemy but rather a loving, caring parent.

The following suggestions are focused on helping us learn to prevent disciplinary action before they even begin.

This first statement is crucial for parents to believe and understand: Our children are wired to please their parents especially, but also grandparents and other significant people in their lives. With this in mind, our language toward them carries great weight in their minds, especially when said in a kindly, respectful way. We can defuse and often prevent would-be problems with our children, thus making it possible to prevent a discipline situation and replace it with just the opposite, peace, harmony, and love. Let us explain with this story:

Just recently our grandson, Krew, age two, was tossing his favorite beach ball back and forth with me while the other adults sat chatting in the same room. But then, another one of our children came to our home with her son, Owen, age three. Owen wanted to get into the play, but Krew felt possessive about his toy and his time with his grandpa. When Sandi and I saw the struggle within Krew and his dissatisfaction and frustration, we began to express loud enough for Krew to hear, "Krew loves to share." We said it several times and even established a little game that included all three of us rather than just he and I.

I could see in his eyes the new social law he just discovered, that sharing is fun. In fact you could see he enjoyed it more than when just he and I were playing. Our efforts defused and even prevented a blow up of emotions. Later in life, Krew will learn that sharing is not only fun, but also invites a wonderful spirit of

peace into one's life. This new knowledge will help him help himself someday, thus preventing selfishness from overtaking him.

The above story applied to two boys ages two and three. Notwithstanding their young age, they were still able to understand what we expected of them which changed their behavior. This can work just as easily with kids at almost any age, even adults. Of course the language with adults would be adjusted some, "Bill, I'm surprised, I know you like to share." When we desire a change of behavior in our kids, spouse, or anyone for that matter, we should use positive language; for best results, positive, upbeat language.

As parents or grandparents, we can learn to act quickly with our kids and grandkids, to apply a natural law that is woven within the child to help them and you change a would be disciplinary situation filled with anger and frustration, into one of calmness.

When we see behavior in our children that troubles us, we can express honest, sincere comments that can and most often will, change their behavior allowing them to better understand the advantages of better choices and behavior.

Education is so important in our household, that whenever possible we try to inch our kids and grandkids closer to a decision to learn and progress on their own. So, we often find ourselves saying to our grandkids, "Wow, you are smart, you love to read, don't you." Or, "(Calling the child by name), we love books, let's read together." And while we're reading, we often comment, "Oh, how I love to read, don't you? Reading and learning is fun", and, "Wow, you are a good reader for your age, good job."

We can literally direct an otherwise stubborn child to become a participant. Other times we can be heard to say to our grandkids, "We love to work; I know you do, too. Let's clean up the toys together." It's not uncommon to see kids dealt with in this way to later be found picking up their own toys as well as other messes they make. After all, they know what makes us happy, and as stated before, they are wired to make us happy. (If you are

finding your child is not picking up on your verbal cues of verbal optimism, examine your own common ways and means with dealing with your child, you'll probably find his unwillingness to follow your wishes are because you've wired him otherwise. Be patient with yourself in your efforts to change, but it's change *you* will want to do, for sure).

As parents and grandparents, we should begin this positive language soon in the child's life, and continue it for the rest of their lives. We all enjoy hearing optimistic words about us from those we love; that never seems to grow old.

We all need to be reminded often, the human mind and heart will most often move in the direction of what we expect of the individual; they rise to our positive expectations. And, just in case there's ever a question in any one's mind about the antithesis of positive verbal expectations, parents or grandparents should never (and we do mean never) verbally degrade their children or grandchildren, not even in a sarcastic way. If we ever think we can get our children to permanently change their behavior by verbally assaulting them or degrading them, we're sadly mistaken. The human mind and spirit responds best to positive, uplifting language, the kind that enriches their perspective of themselves, not reduces, takes away from.

"You're so stupid." "You dummie." "I'm raising a bunch a lazy kids." "You will never amount to anything." These kinds of verbal assaults and dozens of others like them do more harm to the human spirit than most adults realize. Words mean things, and when those words come from the person we adore, those words cause pain that can last throughout a lifetime. Our children are worthy of much more from us, so let's give it to them in positive, uplifting, and encouraging language, the kind that lifts the spirit and encourage better behavior. (You can read more on this theme in the chapter "Educating Desire.")

Now, back to those times when discipline is necessary.

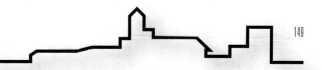

The following story is from a dear friend. From this heartfelt story, we can see there are many ways to discipline (teach and love) our children, but some penetrate the heart and the inner soul of our children more than others. And really, it's our children's hearts we want to win.

> I was about age thirteen, too young for a driver's license. One summer afternoon, after I'd finished all my chores, I, in my usual adventurous spirit, decided I wanted to drive my dad's motor bike. It was something Mom and Dad had made clear to me that I was not to attempt. I knew it was wrong, but the thrill of it all got the best of me. So I hopped on the bike and drove off. I drove through much of the city and thoroughly enjoyed it. But when I got home, I sensed I was in trouble, that I had been found out. I took the bike to the back yard where I saw my mother on her knees working in the garden. She had a belt in her hand, so I assumed I was in for a lickin'.
>
> Mom got up off her knees and walked out of the garden, but instead of lashing me with the belt, she instead tossed the belt to me. I was curious what was going on. She looked me straight in the eye, her look pierced right through me. Then she said something that had more impact on my behavior than anything before or since. She said, "Lance, I need you to whip me with that belt for not teaching you better."
>
> She walked near me so I could whip her, but of course, I couldn't. I loved her too much. And besides, it was I who had erred, not her. I wished she would have whipped me with the belt, the pain would have been much less than what I'd actually received.
>
> Mom's method of disciplining me that morning changed my life, my behavior, and the way I saw family rules and my duty to live them. Most of all, it endeared me all the more to my precious mother. (Story shared orally by our dear friend, Lance Thueson)

I (Garth) once had a mother who came to me, asking my advice, admitting she had wasted most of her kids' young lives by placing her selfish desires above her children's needs. She told me she fed and clothed them well, but that she was often rude and sharp in her language toward them and was very impatient with them and how irritable she became when things didn't go her way or when the kids' needs got in the way of her schedule. She admitted she even tried to find reasons to not be with them, especially her oldest, her daughter, because of the frustration she felt between them. She was penitent now and desired to become a more loving, kind mother, the kind that took advantage of daily opportunities to discipline with love and to begin melting their hearts to hers. She was fearful it was too late, that her kids were ruined, and that her problem was irreparable. It was really quite impressive to sense her honesty and humility in wanting to now become the parent she felt she should have always been to her kids, now ages twelve, nine, and seven.

I asked her a few questions, and then, I reminded her that it is never too late to make changes in our lives. She is an intelligent woman, so she realized she could not change history, and that some habits in her kids have already been established, habits that reflect the way she worked with them. She was mostly worried that her lack of patience in discipline of the kids could seriously impair them later in their lives as they faced struggles of their own.

I reminded her too, that her kids are young enough to form new habits easily and that as she changes her thoughts about her role as mother and the kids, the kids' behavior will likely begin to change as well. I reminded her how important it is to stay focused on her new goal and that the best way to do that is to identify those times, those moments, that previously turned her otherwise smile into impatience with her kids. Once she could identify those moments, she could plan for a strategy to replace

the impatience with her new desired behavior. I reminded her that there was a force in this world that works to stop her progress, so I encouraged her to be very prayerful and to be specific in her prayers regarding her desired result.

You see, what she really wanted was a new mind and a new heart. She wanted to be changed to a different person, the kind of person that would bring the best out in her and in her children. This kind of change requires more than a pep talk and the reading of a few self-help books. This kind of permanent change she desired is the kind of change that we all should want and can have if we're willing to take the simple steps that lead to it. It is, after all, a process and not a singular event. (There are some reports of a singular event changing the whole person permanently. But by and large, it is a process that takes some very real, focused effort on our part.)

I also encouraged her to sit down with each child and apologize for her behavior and to explain to them the kind of inner change she desires to make and to ask them to be patient with her desired progress and that she would strive to be more patient and loving with them.

I encouraged her to work to put in proper perspective her priorities. First, as a religious woman, I encouraged her to make the daily habit of drawing near to God and to daily make and renew her promises to him.

Next was to her *children's welfare* and development and a *tender, loving feeling* within their relationship with each other.

Lastly, all other matters important to her.

The last I heard, she had made those changes and the impact of her changes were showing remarkable fruit.

The time we have with our children in the home goes by so quickly; we will want to do all we can to foster loving, tender feelings and memories for both our children and ourselves. The housework and yard work will still remain long after the kids are married and gone from the home.

Additional thoughts regarding discipline:

1. Choose your battles. If we feel we must correct every error we see our kids do, we will be worn out, and we will wear our kids out, too.
2. Be consistent. Once we choose a point of emphasis with our kids and expect them to follow it, we should remain vigilant until they make it a habit in their lives. God is "the same yesterday, today, and forever," and we should *strive* to be the same as parents. Inconsistency will confuse kids and cause them to think we're really not serious.
3. Remember, no two kids are the same—the same temperament, personality, or need. We discipline the child according to his or her specific need—no more, no less. Since they all learn in different ways and speed of learning, our discipline tactics should be molded to fit the child.
4. Stated again, love, love, love them. Let them know they are cherished by you. *Empathize* with them. Make sure they know that you know how they feel and what they are experiencing. Help them *see* and *feel* you are disciplining them not out of spite or anger or to show you can (power), but because you love them so much, you want them to learn the lessons of life before they leave the family nest.
5. Find them doing something right, and then compliment them. Daily sincere compliments can bolster their desire to do well (something kids are wired to do). Honest, specific compliments will help kids know we are watching them, we care about their progress, and we can help them stay on track with growth and progress to be the best they can be. On the other hand, insincere compliments can have the opposite effect we desire. Kids are quite adept at reading parents, so we should make our compliments honest and sincere. We should be watchful to place our compliments where they will do the best good. Another point: be specific with your compliments.

"Honey, I like the way you made your bed. When you tucked the sheets in tight, you did it exactly the way I showed you, thank you." The advantage of being specific is the knowledge they have of *what* they did right (or wrong). This knowledge provides them with enough information to know exactly *what* pleased you and *why*.

6. Before we discipline, we should make the habit of getting into their heads that we might know the facts behind their behavior. How can we expect to help them grow from where they are now to where we want them to be if we don't know what their thoughts were that brought about their misbehavior?

   You might ask: "Honey, why did you do that? What were you thinking?" Wait for their response. When thinking changes, behavior changes (this is true for our kids but also for us, the parents). Our tone of voice in this line of questioning should be loving, considerate, and nonjudgmental.

7. Wiring kids for success in life cannot be forced or coerced. It must come by daily acts of love and patient kindness. When danger lurks, we may take away their agency and coerce them, but those times are rare. All other acts of discipline should be experiences of heartfelt parental correction, always remembering our children are literally children of God on loan to us. Lastly and maybe most important, the answers we parents and spouses seek in parenting and marriage are already within us. We need only learn to tap into our own loving, gentle, kind, and soft center within. We all have that soft center; although for some it may be buried deep within, it is there. The truth is, there are as many parenting and marriage styles as there are adults and parents. As we seek the divine within each of us, our own unique style comes out, custom made for each child and each parent and each separate situation.

So, we don't need lots of how-to books on parenting and marriage relationships, we need simply to learn how to tap into our true selves. From there, the best answers and solutions will come out.

Just Say "No"

There are few things as frustrating as dealing with a spoiled individual, whether a child, teenager, or adult. It's not natural for a child or teenage to expect unearned gifts from parents or grandparents on a regular basis. These expectations are *learned habits*. And where do they learn them? Generally from the parents.

This represents one of the hardest parts of parenting: to see the difference between giving to their child in the spirit of parental love versus giving to the child and creating a spoiled "gimme, gimme, gimme" attitude, "I want what I want and I want it now" mentality. We've come to believe that by giving in to the child's begging and whining does far more harm to the child than most parents realize.

Sandi and I witnessed a grandchild mugging of her grandfather; we don't think he saw what hit him. We were at a high school basketball game to watch one of our grandsons. While sitting in the bleachers waiting for the game to begin, this cute little high school girl sat down next to her grandfather and said, "Oh, Grandpa, did you notice that famous singer and his band are performing a concert next Saturday?"

"No, honey, I never noticed," he responded.

She followed with, "I would love to go to it, but I don't have tickets." Her comment was followed by a look of disappointment on her face only a drama queen or Hollywood star could manufacture.

He continued by saying, "Oh, honey, don't worry. Grandma and I will get you a ticket."

"Thanks, Grandpa. I love you so much," she said, and after which, she left his side to sit with her friends.

I know this girl because I've taught her in a classroom setting on multiple occasions. We don't claim to know the whole story, but we know enough to say, Grandpa either strengthened his granddaughter or weakened her, one or the other. Maybe he felt he needed to buy her love. It was quite obvious she was well trained in getting her own way, and the confidence she showed on her face told us she was certain she would get what she wanted. In broad daylight and in the presence of dozens of people, this young lady pulled off a well-crafted, perfectly designed mugging. Oscar nomination for her.

When we were raising our ten kids, we didn't have the money to shell out to our kids whenever they so desired. And, with our predetermined strategy Sandi and I had formed in our minds regarding child-raising, the kids learned in a hurry they weren't going to get whatever they wanted, whenever they wanted it, no matter how hard they tried or cried, moaned, or strategized. Oh, don't get me wrong, we may have fallen to a few capers, but not many. There were times too where we saw legitimate needs and requests. Those were the needs we tried to fill, free gratis.

Even the smallest of circumstances can test our parental resolve. It wasn't uncommon, while at a sporting event for instance, for one of our younger children to beg for popcorn or candy. My most common response was, "Mom's popcorn is much better than theirs. Let's wait till we get home, okay?" If begging persisted, I would ignore it. After a while, they got the message— Dad's not giving in.

There are many problems with giving a child nearly everything the child asks for. We can be sure that to give them all or most of what they want does not build strong kids nor does it buy love, not really.

I recall one father who *trained* his kids to beg and beg for what they wanted only to give in to their requests. He did this repeatedly. His common response to them was, "If you ask me one more time, you're going to be disciplined." Never did we see discipline, but we always saw begging and giving in. The father was *training* his kids to beg, manipulate, and to persist in both. They learned

from experience that if they continue, they'll get what they want with no discipline attached. Is that what we want to teach our children, manipulation? There are ways to have them feel love and to be attended to, without always giving in to all their desires.

When kids come to us with a request of a gift—candy, ice cream, money, car, clothes, etc.—we can use that exchange as an opportunity to teach them and to form their character. To begin with, we can help them see that most all *things* in life come with a price tag—either they pay for it or you do ("things," not to be confused with love, which has no price tag). If, by chance, it's something they're willing to sacrifice for, you can work out a deal with them. The deal could include extra work on their part. If they shy away from that, you will know it was never a high priority to them in the first place. If they are willing to work for it, you've created an opportunity for that child to see life and reality more clearly. And the by-products for the child are remarkable— learning to accept a responsibility, learning to complete a job, as well as the patience to wait until the money is earned. Patience truly is a virtue.

Too many kids today have been wired by their parents and grandparents for personal, immediate satisfaction. Anything we parents can do to teach our children to plan and wait patiently for something they really want will build within them wonderful character traits. Better yet, if we can have them wait patiently until they themselves complete a task to earn it and pay for it with their own hard-earned money, more character and moral muscles will be built within the child. At that point, it's not a gift any more, they earned it, and to earn it creates even more personal satisfaction for the child.

One of the most difficult parts of parenting is learning to say no. Imagine saying yes to everything our kids ask for, and then imagine what the end result would be: a very spoiled, demanding child. A spoiled and imbalanced child will find real life much harder to deal with once they're on their own.

Parents must learn how to say no more often, to do otherwise will be detrimental to your child's overall well-being. The perfect parent said, "Ask and ye shall receive." Parents want to say yes as often as possible, but even the perfect parent says no sometimes, and at other times, he says, "Yes, but not now." There are times God says yes, but then he gives it to us on his timetable, not ours, and in his ways, not ours. He says, in effect, "What I give you will be more suited for your needs than what you're now asking for, as well as perfectly timed." Teaching our children the benefits of delayed gratification is a lesson that never stops giving.

For parents to be successful in saying no, they need to have a good imagination. They need to at least try to imagine how their child will end up with the kind of parenting style they are presently using. Do you see trouble on the horizon for your kids? If so, then change your parenting style. The power is in us to make the changes as well as the divine duty to do so. Learning to say no with a smile could be a good first step.

We have millions of selfish, "gimmie, gimmie, gimmie" kind of people; people willing to receive without effort on their part. Let's not be the parent or grandparent who adds one more to that kind of society. Do you want independent, hardworking kids? If so, you're more likely to have them if they hear no from time to time. As you can imagine, there are many ways to say no. It can be said in anger or disgust, or you can look your child in the eyes and say, "Honey, I'd love to give it to you, but I love you too much to give you all you want," followed by a smile. Some parents have learned how to humor their kids into a no answer. The kids have learned, however, that even though Mom or Dad said no in humor and a smile, they really mean it. And how would they know that? Because Mom and Dad stick to their decisions—they don't waffle, they don't weaken, nor do they tolerate continual whining and begging. Other parents I know have so trained their kids that when they say no, they are to never ask for it again; for if they do, that is a sign of disrespect, and respect for parents in

their household is rule number one, and to violate it means trouble for the kids, the kind of trouble the kids have learned they won't want to repeat.

Some parents give in to their whining children just to shut them up—to get some peace and quiet. The parents that slip into that pattern are doing far more harm than they realize. Often our own selfish desires forms the way we interact with our children. Parents, in order to get the most growth from our children, must ask themselves why they do what they do in relation to their children. Our motives often form the effectiveness of our teaching and training. We absolutely must realize we have our little ones for a relatively short time. The truth is, most of their habits will be formed by their age ten. Can we really afford to slacken our resolve at such a crucial time of their lives?

I played a lot of basketball in my youth, and as I'd mentioned in a previous chapter, I was quite a troubled kid, one with a sort of chip on my shoulder. So it was not uncommon for me to see my opponent as an enemy and not just an opponent. That must sound weird to you, but the truth was, I had bottled up inside me much anger. I also would see the referee or umpire as an enemy as well.

While playing high school ball, I remember this one particular referee that I learned to respect and even enjoy. When he would call a foul, he would blow the whistle, point at you, and then put on the biggest smile as though to say, "Silly you, I caught you. You can't pull the wool over my eyes." His smile took all the anger out of me. In fact, when he would call the foul and then smile, it always brought a smile on my face. As much as I wanted to, I couldn't get angry at such a playful yet sincere smile, even if I felt he missed the call.

Parents can do the same when they say no. They can put a smile on their face and maybe even a little giggle, look the child in the eyes, and say, "Silly you, you know Mom and Dad are not going to allow that."

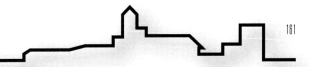

What we give our children, *how often* we give it, and for what *purpose* will affect our children for good or ill. Let's do our part to build the next generation of kids who are respectful to all and who expect to work for what they get. This builds children wired for success.

The Brick Wall

Sandi and I wanted a large family. In fact, when she was in third grade in Arizona, she read the book, *Cheaper by the Dozen* and fell in love with it. She told herself, "Hey, I can do that. But instead of a dozen kids, I want thirteen." She carried that desire with her always.

As for me, I was in fourth grade when it occurred to me that I wanted to be the father of lots of kids someday but put no number on the size of family. So you can see that Sandi and I were wired for a large family.

Decades ago, large families were the norm, but not in these more modern times. It's really quite amazing that the two of us would meet and marry, both having the same desire since our childhood years, to have a large family.

When Sandi was expecting our sixth child (our oldest was eight), her uterus began to tear causing severe pain. I took her to the doctor, and he sent us to a specialist. The specialist told her she would have to live with the pain, that there was nothing he could do while she was pregnant, and that any repair work would have to take place after she stopped bearing children.

Keep in mind, we both wanted as many kids as the Lord would send us, and our hope was nearly double the amount we presently had. Sandi was very concerned because, she thought, "If I have to go through these tearing pains with the rest of my pregnancies, I don't think I can do it." She was quite discouraged to hear he couldn't do anything for her at that time and that it would be an issue with any future pregnancies.

Sandi, saddened at the possibility that we might stop at six, asked the doctor if this is all the kids she should have.

"Should this be our last baby?" she asked.

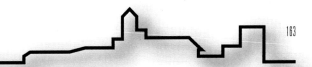

He answered, "The female body is very strong and resilient and capable of having numerous pregnancies over their childbearing years—fifteen or more." He went on to say, "I can't answer that question, but you will know when you're there. It will be like you've hit a brick wall, physically, emotionally, and mentally."

Neither of his comments was very comforting to Sandi while in the latter months of her sixth pregnancy.

When he said that, she thought to herself, "I'm in lots of pain, but I don't feel like I've hit that brick wall yet."

A few months later, when Sandi was in the hospital, preparing to give birth to our sixth child (Hilary). Her contractions began to be so severe she knew the baby was about ready (Sandi had all but one of her children without any pain relief. Sandi told me, "If I have another contraction like that last one, I will die—my heart will burst." She asked me to call for the nurse to check her again. The nurse checked her and said, "No, honey, it won't be for a while. The baby is posterior. Be patient." The nurse's comment frightened Sandi thinking that she couldn't bear any more contractions similar to the last one she felt.

The nurse left the room, and Sandi said to me, "This baby must come now. I literally cannot take any more contractions like that—I will die." Just as she said that, she felt the urge to push, and as she did, she said, "The baby's here. Go get the nurse!"

You must understand, with all Sandi's deliveries, they have all come nearly a month early, and when they do come, they come very quickly.

Knowing that as I did, I felt I hardly had time to get the nurse and doctor in the room. Nonetheless, I did leave Sandi's side, ran to the nurse, and informed her, "The baby is here. Come quick!" The nurse appeared a little put out because she just told us moments ago it would be somewhat longer. Nevertheless, she did check Sandi, and to her great surprise, the baby's head had crowned. I will never forget the look of surprise and concern on that nurse's face as she screamed for the other nurses to inform

the doctor (the doctor had been informed by the nurse that there was no rush, so he was not washed up and ready).

To read of Hilary's grand entrance into this life, read the next chapter, "Hilary's Grand Entrance."

Did Sandi ever run into that brick wall? No. She had her thirteen pregnancies and ten deliveries, the last one at age forty. No more children came, so we assumed it was simply a matter of having all the children the Lord allotted to us.

However, Sandi informs me that many women do run into that brick wall and that when they do, they know it. You see, because "multiplying and replenishing the earth" is a divine decree and because it is the means whereby God brings his spirit children to earth, the numbers are predetermined and set.

All of you sweet mothers should fully understand that you are literally wired for the number of children you *can* bear. Obviously, you are not all prewired to have ten kids as we did. You may choose to have less than is allotted to you, but it's not likely you'll get more than your allotment. Some will hit the brick wall after one child, others after more. But whatever your number is, it is our hope you will be perfectly satisfied with what you receive and not envy those with more. We all know, don't we, that God knows all things, and something as crucial as divine birth, he keeps a close eye on.

In closing, we should also beware not to judge those who have many kids, few kids, or no kids at all. We're all trying the best we can under our present circumstances. Judging one another hurts not only the judged but those who judge.

Hilary's Grand Entrance

From the last chapter, you got a glimpse of one of the tense but wonderful experiences we had in our desire to fulfill our purpose as parents. Although we had special (even spiritual) experiences with the birth of each of our ten kids, Hilary's grand entrance added a special flair.

To begin, we have to go back before Hilary was even thought of. Sandi had given birth to our fifth child, Dillon. We loved Dillon, of course, but with four other little ones under foot (ages seven, five, four, and two along with Dillon who was nine months), Dillon's inquisitive nature almost took Sandi to the brink, emotionally speaking. He never had a mischievous bone in his body, but he was overactive and more inquisitive than most little ones. Dillon couldn't be left for a minute because of his active nature. He created one mess after another, more than most kids his age. It was not uncommon for Sandi to tie him to her chest; otherwise, she couldn't get anything done.

So here is the setting: Dillon is now crawling about and somewhat out of control, and we're at church—the whole family. Sandi, feeling worn out, was sitting in a Sunday school class with Dillon in her arms, listening to a lesson, when the overwhelming thought came to her mind: "It's time for you to start another baby."

She said to herself, "No way, not now! I'm too overwhelmed and tired." But the voice inside her persisted. She became so emotional that she had to leave church and go home. She became quite beleaguered at the thought and decided it best to simply go home.

She took Dillon and proceeded home in the car, leaving the rest of the family at the church building. While at home, she put Dillon down for a nap and then fell to her knees in prayer.

"Heavenly Father, I can only assume these feelings are from you, but I'm telling you, I can't do this again so quick. I feel drained of energy and strength. I can't do it!" She screamed the last sentence. (Yeah, she really did scream it.)

Still on her knees, she opened the scriptures that were next to her and let it simply fall open and began to read. The verse she read spoke of faith and trust in the Father's will. Her tears by now were gushing out and her emotions at their peak. She called out audibly, "Okay, okay, I will have another one now but only if you can send me a gentle and quiet little one, one that will not require so much of my energy. I need the best one you've got up there." With that plea, she began to feel some comfort and assurance that all would be well.

About eight months later (literally all of our kids came nearly a month early), Sandi was on the hospital bed, feeling the severe contractions for the delivery of baby Hilary as mentioned in the previous chapter. Let us continue the story from there.

The frantic nurses wheeled Sandi into the delivery room. All the nurses were much unprepared for this event. And then the doctor came in, unwashed and with a look on his face that did not engender confidence to me.

Our doctor, Dr. Foote, was a very kindly, gentle man and godly too. He took a look at the situation, calmed himself down, and proceeded to take control of the special event.

Within seconds, Hilary was born, but there was a problem. She was not breathing on her own. Dr. Foote did the normal things a doctor would do to arouse a response from our newborn, but still there was no breathing. All went quiet in that delivery room. Not a person, nurses or I, dared move or say a word. It was all in the hands of our good doctor, or was it?

Seconds passed and the tension grew within the hearts of all present, except our doctor. After trying all his normal approaches and with no success, he held our little Hilary in his big hands and

said, "Okay, little Smith girl," then turned toward the wall where none of us could see his face, and then he bowed his head.

Tears were streaming down my face, first out of fear, but then out of faith in my good doctor and the promise the Lord had made to Sandi that she would have this little one.

The doctor's back was still to the nurses and me, time seemed to stand still, and the tension grew except for the new feelings of faith I was feeling. We still heard no sound from Hilary—no cry or gasp for oxygen. Seconds passed and the anxiety grew, and still there was silence in the delivery room. With the doctors head bowed as in prayer, holding little Hilary, she finally put out a little cry much to the joy of all in the room.

I later realized why he had turned facing away from all of us and bowed his head. He was offering a prayer or a blessing on little Hilary. He was pleading with the powers of heaven to give her life, and life is what resulted. The Spirit of God was in that room to aid in helping to fulfill a promised blessing given to a sweet mother who was willing to go the extra mile beyond her own strength—to do "not my will, but thine."

The Lord was true to his word. Hilary was a healthy, beautiful baby, the kind of baby that needed little care or attention. Oh yes, she received plenty of attention but not because she demanded it. She would lay and watch and smile but never (and I mean *never*) fussed—well, except for food or if she was tired. She was the most contented newborn we had.

Where are they now? Dillon is happily married to a sweet wife, a father of three, and is an architect. With the poor economy, he returned to school to become a physician's assistant. Hilary is a happy wife to a kindly man, an attorney by trade. She is a homemaker and mother of two. She is a trained dental hygienist.

The Little Red Wagon

Sam age 4, Cari 2 1/2, Jesse 1 and Sandi
6 months pregnant with Lyric

One thing is certain in this life: change. And as parents who desire to give their little ones the best of ourselves, our individual change should be upward improvement of our lives, regularly and often, that our kids may see the best in us and hopefully embrace that good.

Yet as parents, sometimes we're slow to see the need for our improvement and added to that, for those who are only somewhat introspective, they are daily reminded of their faults and weaknesses. As we all well know, family life can bring stress in our lives, which brings out both the good and bad in us, either to enhance our progress or stifle it. With our effort to train up our children in the way they should go, such things come to the forefront regularly—our impatience, intolerance, envy, judging others, anger, bitterness, and sometimes even hate, as well as the rare fault of seeing oneself as perfect. We are duty bound to seek and destroy each of these weaknesses and all others like them from our natures as quickly as possible.

It is our duty as parents to show by example good character traits with the hope our children will latch hold of those rather than our weaknesses. Hopefully our lives will not end before each of us learn and apply the good character traits so our children may have that example from us as they search for models to form their own lives. We've found that those kinds of changes are all centered in charity, the highest form of love.

In our effort to make progress as individuals and parents, it is well for us to remember that we all learn life's lessons at our own pace. Some learn the life lessons quickly and effectively while others are late bloomers, and still others spread between those two extremes. The bottom line of life, though, is that we finally do learn them and hopefully before we leave this frail existence for our kids' sake as well as our own.

The following family story reminds us that it's never too late to make the needed changes as long as we are *willing* to try.

Because one of the key figures in this story is my mother, I should explain that my mother never appreciated Sandi—well, not at first. In fact, when we were dating, my mother was rude and bitter toward her. This was not my mother's typical way of behaving. She was generally kind, generous, and sweet to people. So why would she act this way toward my girlfriend and future wife? Some of you mothers may relate to this: "No one's good enough for my boy." And in this case, it was her baby boy, Garth. She really believed that. Oh, she never said it nor would any parent, but it was perfectly clear to those who knew the situation. I never showed interest in a girl that she approved of.

While Sandi was expecting Lyric, our fourth child (Sam was four, Cari was two and a half, and Jesse was sixteen months), an

amazing change took place in the family, a miracle actually. It came at a time when I was working in a city 150 miles north of our home town. I was able to come home only on weekends.

Whenever Sandi came around my mother, Mom became cold and angry, and resorted to rude comments. These comments caused tremendous hurt to Sandi and me. Anyone who knows Sandi finds this very hard to believe, that someone would be so hateful towards her, but that's how it was. When my mother would talk with any of her friends about me or my family, the way she would bring Sandi's name into the conversation was "Garth's wife." Never was it Sandi or Sandra. It caused tremendous stress within the family relationships.

As for me, I adored my mother and always desired to please her; but on the other hand, I had found the love of my life, the woman who I would share forever with and who would be the mother of our children. It caused serious emotional pain at all levels of our family. That broken relationship continued for years.

We had just moved from Arizona back to the town of my birth and lived in a home only a few blocks from my mother's home. I had accepted a job as manager with an up-and-coming company. The only problem was my territory was 150 miles from our home, too far to commute each day. I worked at my territory office all week, and then on the weekends, I would come home. It was winter time in that area of the country that saw lots of snow, slick roads, and freezing temperatures.

We only had one car, so whenever Sandi would have need to go anywhere (shopping, visiting family or friends, etc.), she would bundle the three little kids up, place them in a little red wagon, and pull them through the snow to her destination.

The miracle began when my mother became ill, was operated on, and sent home to recover. She was about sixty years old at that time. She couldn't care for herself and often couldn't even get out of bed by herself (her husband, my father, had died many years prior).

Sandi saw her needs, and in her own wonderful way set up a daily practice of helping her mother-in-law both morning and night. In the middle of a cold and snowy winter, Sandi would dress the kids warm, arrange them in the little red wagon, and then pull them through the fresh fallen snow to mother's home. This was done twice each day, morning, and night, all through the cold winter months of snow and slush. If mother needed additional attention, Sandi would make a third trip with the kids in the little red wagon.

With the old canyon wind blowing in her face, her thoughts were racing, wondering how this would all turn out. After all, it had only been a few days prior to Mom's operation that she lashed out again at Sandi, causing Sandi to leave the room in embarrassment and hurt.

Sandi would stop on her trek periodically to check on the kids' welfare. The cold wind could be a threat to any one, especially children. The distance she was going was only three city blocks, but pulling the kids through the new-fallen snow made it seem like a mile. Pulling up the hill, then down another made the trip seem extra long.

When Sandi would arrive at my mother's home, she would begin by making her breakfast and then bathe her, followed by cleaning and redressing the incision. She would then clean the house and then get her settled back in bed, all along caring for the three kids. Following a short uncomfortable visit, Sandi would bundle the kids back up, load them in the red wagon, and return to our home. This routine repeated itself at least twice daily through the whole winter season. At first, Mom was cold toward Sandi though obviously appreciative for her help. I can only imagine Mom's thoughts: "Okay, what's her motive? What does she want from me?"

But as the service went on and on, something began to change within my mother. She became so affected by Sandi's selfless service it warmed her heart toward Sandi, or rather, it melted her

heart. No more was Sandi "Garth's wife." Now she was Sandi or Sandra. From that time forward, she had a loving respect and appreciation for her. My mother's countenance changed from bitterness to one of kindness and acceptance. That new loving relationship grew brighter and brighter until my mother's passing a few years later.

I see many life lessons from this true story, lessons we can each learn as well as principles we can pass on to our children:

1. My mother's need for change
2. My mother's willingness to change
3. Sandi's willingness to unconditionally serve an appeared enemy
4. The power of tolerance, patience, and love to change one's heart

I suppose there are other points that could be addressed as well, but let's focus upon each of these for a moment.

My Mother's Need for Change

As stated before, who among us is without faults and weaknesses? No one. And the truth is, and as my mother's story reminds us, we're much happier people when we identify our frailties and begin a process to turn those weaknesses into strengths. We are all in the same boat when it comes to that. I think we can all agree, changing our heart--our character--is a painful, humiliating and sometimes embarrassing process which causes many of us to ignore the need to change or to run from it when we see it coming.

Granted, we shouldn't be in the business of trying to change others, especially when there's so much work to do on ourselves. But it's a sad day when one chooses to stay the same when they have (as we all do) great untapped potential in so many aspects of their life. This attitude is particularly painful when that person is a spouse, one of our children, or loved one.

We should begin early in our child-raising responsibilities to wire our children to realize that life is largely about change and that we should welcome and even seek regular improvement and progress in our lives. The day we stop changing is the day we stop growing and developing. Remember, it is our job, each one of us, but especially us parents, to strive to become the best we can possibly be. That also means change and growth, as well as disappointments and joy. Disappointment when we seek progress and progress appears nonexistent or slow coming. And joy when we see growth in our lives or that of our children.

This quote may be helpful to those who get frustrated when their progress seems slow coming: "There is no such thing as failure, only feedback." This quote reminds us that as long as we are *willing* to improve our lives, that willingness brings forth some action allowing us feedback information to determine some degree of progress. Even an appeared failure should be welcomed as long as we are sincerely willing to try. Regular, consistent personal improvement is essential to our happiness.

My Mother's Willingness to Change

As we all well know, discovering flaws in our personality, character, or viewpoints is not the same as a sincere *willingness* to change those flaws. My mother's *willingness* to address her flaw and her *humility* to change, allowed me to see a whole new dimension of my mother. I can only hope I can prove to be so willing, so mature about my life.

The best part of my mother's willingness and victory over her discovered flaw was the peace and love it brought into her life, our whole clan, actually, as well as the new mother-daughter relationship that was allowed to take root and begin to blossom between my sweet wife and my dear mother.

My mother, before her passing, would express to her friends her love and appreciation for Sandi and that she considered her one of the best mothers and homemakers she'd ever known. She also regularly praised her industriousness. A newfound unity had taken hold. I've found unity in relationships to be one of the most significant powers for good we can attain.

Bitterness between people is not much different than a growing cancer. A new found unity between the two, not only expels the cancer, but it invites the most sublime feelings of love and togetherness this life has to offer.

The importance of our own self-examination regarding our opinions and viewpoints, as well as our personalities and character, cannot be overstated. And that we wire our kids to likewise make regular internal soul-searching, with a willingness to address the issues they find within. Such a practice ensures regular growth and progress.

Sandi's Willingness to Serve an Appeared Enemy

Sandi longed for acceptance from her mother-in-law, something she never experienced for the first five years of our marriage. It brought great emotional pain and hurt, especially to Sandi, but also to me and all other members of the family.

So for Sandi to decide to serve her mother-in-law, she had to make some assumptions. The first assumption was that her mother-in-law would accept her service and not turn her away, making matters even worse. The greatest assumption she made though was that my mother was acting contrary to her real nature, that she was instead, a very good and kind person who had, unfortunately, accepted a bad viewpoint, an incorrect mental map.

She ran the risk that her selfless service could have no meaningful impact on my mother. For this reason, her service could

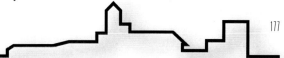

not be based on the hope of Mom's change or some other ulterior motive. No, she had to enter into this service with pure motives, which she did. Most people can read underlying motives, and when they do, it generally makes matters worse than before.

Seeking the best in people is always the best way to go, even toward those who ridicule or disdain us. This is something we should want our kids to embrace. Wiring them early in their lives with this trait will position them to be loved by almost all people. We may want to encourage our kids, when they are still quite young, to look for the good in people, even the porcupine type, you know, those who are hard to love, or even snarl as if to say, "I dare you to like me." For the truth is, and you'll want your kids to know this, every single soul desires acceptance and friendship. We are all wired that way. Knowing that fact makes it easier to assume even the porcupine type can, with patience and tolerance, be loved and give love in return.

The power of tolerance, patience, and love to change one's heart

Honest, sincere love changes hearts. This kind of enduring love, mixed with tolerance, breeds patience and is the kind of medicine needed for those individuals who have allowed their hearts to harden. Thank God for my angel wife, who applied the combination of virtues to work on my precious mother's heart.

How do we place within our children these enduring virtues? Complete books have been written on that subject. In a nutshell, however, we can say with confidence that as we are kind, gentle, patient, and tolerant with each other as parents, the kids will see it first hand and will likely model it in their lives.

Added to that, if we teach our children these principles using the technique of spaced repetition, the kids will begin to understand. It's lots of fun to observe our children both model their

parents' loving actions and implement their parents' teachings, too.

Many years have passed since that cold and snowy winter, and many things have changed. For one thing, all our ten kids are raised with children of their own. Since those days, we've had many additional challenges including relationship challenges. But one thing has not changed over the years: relationships are precious and need regular nurturing. Also, for relationships to grow to become healthy and to endure requires that we seek and destroy the pride in our own hearts and replace that pride with tender feelings for all, which cannot come to us without a sincere willingness to change where change is necessary.

A Great Awakening

Earlier in the book I described my father's passing when I was seven and the impact it had upon me, my mother, and my siblings. I also described how I was raised in a nonreligious home or, rather, not active in our church, nor did we practice religion in our family, and that matters of church and religion came to me later in my life.

I remember the day my dad died like it was yesterday. It was an early October morning. I would arise early with Dad so I could sit at the kitchen table and have breakfast with him. I also remember clearly my dad and mom standing out on the back porch prior to Dad leaving for work. He would pick her up in a big bear hug and kiss her so sweetly. It's a great blessing for a child to see his or her mom and dad love each other so tenderly.

Dad drove out of our driveway off to work and I returned to bed. But we would all be aroused by a phone call that would come less than one hour later. The phone rang and my elder brother, Greg, answered it. Greg sensed instinctively, the voice on the other end was filled with emotion. He handed the phone over to our mother.

Our mother tried to hold her emotions, telling us Dad had a small accident at the steel mill and she had been asked to come over to be with him. My eight-and-a-half-year-old brother knew instinctively that Dad had died; he burst into tears and became inconsolable, screaming, "Dad is dead, Dad is dead." What actually had happened, however, was our father, an iron worker/boiler maker, had been gassed with poisonous fumes, which caused him and his partner to lose consciousness just as they were trying to climb out of the risk-filled area of a huge, enclosed pipe, causing both of them to fall about seventy feet.

Dad's partner on the job was hurt but lived. My dad, on the other hand, fell directly on his head without his helmet to protect him. He would die about an hour later on the steps of the hospital. He was in his thirty-eighth year.

When we kids finally got the news of his passing, we were at a movie theatre (Mom had put us in the hands of some relatives, and to take our minds off the situation they had taken us and some of our cousins to a movie theatre).

Our fourteen-year-old sister, Sandy, come to the theatre, ran down the dark aisle until she found us, whereupon she burst out in tears, "Greg, Garth, come home, Dad is dead."

How does a seven-year-old manage that kind of news in his mind? I had never experienced death before, with the exception of our family dog, Toy. I ran home and into the house, it being filled with family. I immediately ran to Mother's side. She was weeping and being consoled by her brothers, sisters, and parents. When she saw me she held me close. I felt her tears as I kissed her cheek and felt her hands and arms quiver as she held me.

I could not comprehend the death of my father, but I could see and feel the pain of my dear mother. I hurt so much for her; I could hardly take seeing her suffer so much. I said to her, "Momma, don't cry, we'll just bring Daddy back to life." Her response changed my life, she said, "Oh, honey, we can't bring him back, he's gone."

I went to my room and cried more tears than I knew I could. That event would begin a struggle in my life that seemed to never end—a constant struggle to find myself and learn who I really was. I struggled for years to overcome severe feelings of inadequacy. I was a little boy who needed a loving, caring father, but it was not to be. My mother was unprepared to handle the load placed upon her, at least the part of teaching and training children. I would have to learn the lessons of life for myself, without the encouraging voice of a father. For a number of reasons, my struggles would continue for many years, well into adulthood.

Many years would pass. I was married to an amazing woman, Sandi, and we had begun growing our family. I still struggled with feelings of inadequacy and doubt. I still found myself longing for a father figure, my father, whom I could call on the phone and talk to for advice, for counsel. I needed good counsel and advice, and even though many of the memories of my father were not particularly positive, I knew him to be a kindly man within, and I almost begged for a relationship with him even though he'd been gone for many years. I had many joys in my life, but with many of the struggles I still labored over, I felt I needed the sound, loving advice from my own father, along with a kindly relationship with him. Oh, how I longed for a closeness with my father.

So there I was years later, the husband of an amazing woman and the father of a large, wonderful brood. Life was good—lots of joys in my life. And even though I had lived to age thirty or so and had had many wonderful answers to prayers and spiritual experiences, I still found myself longing to call my father to ask for advice.

I often found myself feeling envious hearing other men speak of their relationship with their dads and doing this or that with them—staying close to him.

While still in Kansas, I had a tough decision to make, and I found myself, again, feeling quite alone. I recall thinking to myself how wonderful and helpful it would be to pick up the phone and call my dad for advice or to just get his opinion. I just sat there pondering the matter with feelings of melancholy and worry over my present struggle before me.

When at that moment at my lowest point, the thought entered my mind like a flash of light, "I'm your father. Call on me."

Of course, I thought. *Why hadn't I connected that spiritual dot years ago?*

It seemed so simple, yet that exact thought had not entered my mind previously. The thought brought such feelings of peace to my soul, feelings of assurance and confidence. I had learned to

be a praying man, but for some reason I'd never made that solid connection that God was my father. Sometimes the obvious is not very obvious, at least for me.

With tears rolling down my cheeks, I immediately fell to my knees, thanked the Lord for reminding me of that fact, and proceeded to pour out to him my worries and concerns, asking for direction, and help regarding them. The feelings of peace continued long after that.

That simple mind-set adjustment changed the nature of my relationship with my God in my mind. For many years, I had made the habit of prayer, but now my prayers became more personal. After all, I saw more clearly than before that my prayers are to a personal God, the Father of my spirit, and that he is literally my father, and that just as Howard Barber Smith is the father of my body, Heavenly Father is the father of my spirit, literally! I was never the same again. I found him to be more than ever before, "Wonderful, Counsellor… (my) Everlasting Father" (Isaiah 9:6).

Preparation: Our Children's Launching Pad

Sandi and I raised ten wonderful children, who all survived into adulthood (notwithstanding our many weaknesses as parents), and our kids did just fine—well, more than fine. We weren't financially rich nor well educated ourselves. But we chose early in our marriage that we would give our kids the best start to life we could possibly offer them. The following is a concept that helped us; maybe it can help you too.

Wiring kids for success in life requires some serious planning and strategy. What do we strategize and what do we plan? The approach Sandi and I took was to try to see every aspect of our children's lives and then work plans around each one. We were not so naive as to believe we should pigeon-hole our children into who we wanted them to be. No, we simply wanted as any parent does, to prepare the foundation for them to help them be the best they can possibly be. That is why as parents, we don't force our children (with a few exceptions: "Johnny, get out of the road, now!"). We *guide* them, *teach* them, *lead* them, *show* them, and *embrace* them. What do we show them? We guide, lead, and show *how* to get the most out of life by following certain tested and tried principles. These principles had been tried and tested from the beginning of recorded time; we simply trusted the principles and tried our best to wire our kids with them.

Our children's lives (which is true of all of us) can be looked at in the following categories:

- spiritual
- physical
- social/emotional
- educational

You might sit down with your spouse, or if you're a single parent, take the time to focus on these categories regarding your children. We would go on a date, sit down for dinner at a restaurant, and dedicate that time to filling the needs of our children, on paper at least. With paper and pencil in hand, we would brainstorm ideas as they applied to each child individually. You can do the same.

Examine each child individually from the perspective of each category, to see if her or she is making progress in that area, how much progress, and if no or little progress, what can be done to correct it.

The following are some general questions we asked ourselves as it applied to each category.

Spiritual:

1. Is my child showing interest in spiritual matters?
2. Am I doing anything to prevent his spiritual growth?
3. What can I do to correct my errors?

Physical:

1. Is my child getting enough physical exercise?
2. Am I feeding him nutritional foods?
3. If not, what can I do to correct it?

Social/Emotional:

1. Is my child getting enough social interaction with others?
2. Is he interacting well with his siblings and others?
3. Is he learning to share with others, to be kind, and to think of other's needs?
4. If not, what can I do to help him learn these lessons?

5. Am I doing anything to prevent his social and emotional development?
6. If so, what changes can I make?

Education:

1. Is my child progressing at or above grade level in school? If not, what action steps can we do to help him?
2. Is my child showing interest in learning—reading? If not, what action steps can we do to advance his interest?
3. Am I doing anything to prevent his growth and interest?
4. If so, how can I correct it?

You will come up with more of your own thought-provoking questions to help gauge the progress of your child. As you develop your own series of questions, you will want to ask yourself along the way, "What is the end result I desire for my child? Who do I want her to become?" Some may think we cannot mold our children into what we want, and we agree. But *we can help them to be the best they can possibly be.* In fact, we must do our strategic part to help them be successful. That is the very essence of child strategy/planning meetings—to do our part in helping them be their very best. We're certain we can all agree that a child with a firm foundation of the above principles will be considerably more likely to succeed in life. We should want our children to have that kind of foundation.

We are certain you will also agree the last thing we want to do is become a barrier to our child's development. That is why questions are designed to account for our methods to determine if we are stifling our child's progress in any way as it applies to each category. Because this process is so crucial for our kids' sake, you might consider beginning your strategy session with prayer.

Years ago when our children were young, my employment took me from one end of the state to the other over any given month. My favorite thing to do was daydream; daydream of my kids and

how they would turn out as adults. In my mind's eye, I couldn't see what employment they would choose, but I could see they would be at the top of their field whatever that field would be. I could see them as honorable, faithful, and courageous against life's challenges. I saw them as wonderful spouses, outstanding parents, and noble members of their church and community.

Parents and those who hope to be parents should daydream of their children's futures. Daydreaming of your children's progress and future is a form of parental goal-setting. It helps us stay engaged and on track with their progress. Daydreaming can be a form of pondering which is a form of prayer. See them in your mind's eye as noble, faithful, and strong in every way. See them making a difference in the world for good. Many children of our time will be great. Why not yours? They will be great, but we as parents *must* give them a solid foundation to stand on, to grow from. When I say "great," we need not suppose they will discover a new vaccine to cure the ills of the world. But if they are honest and noble in their lives as well as true companions to their spouses and loving, caring parents to their children, they will be great. The solid foundation you set for them will be like a *launching pad* to propel them into the future with confidence, resilience, courage, and determination. We live in troubled times. We all can agree we want our children to face the challenges of life with confidence and determination. A certain scripture we like says, "If ye are prepared ye shall not fear." It is our divine duty to see to it that our children are prepared in every aspect of life so they might stand with confidence and withstand whatever life's storms come their way.

Parenting is an interesting thing. Here we are, nothing more than grownup babies ourselves, and we have the divine call to ready and prepare our little ones to become the best they can be. As parents, we're always under construction just as our kids are. We should strive to be students of our parental role, for our kids' sake, and much of our strategy is to encourage our kids to be stu-

dents too. It seems we're all in the same trade, parent and child, them and us striving to do our best, yet we have the leadership role simply because we have much more experience, not to mention we were elected to take this sacred calling. Obviously, we all need much patience with ourselves, our children and with others.

The single most important thing we can do as parents is to love each other, husband and wife, for our kids to see and feel. At first, it may feel like we're faking the immense love we have for our spouse, but if we persevere in our sincere effort, the "fake it till you make it" will turn into real love, enduring love, the kind of love that will create a family legacy.

When we first marry, we feel as though we deeply love our spouse, and maybe we do. But over time, that love will expand to a near reverential tone. In other words, as we endure faithfully with each other in the marriage covenant, our love for each other begins to tie to something beyond ourselves. Enduring, caring marriages know what we mean, because they likely feel the reverent, sacred feeling within their marriage. We all should strive for those connecting feelings. These sacred feelings within marriage come sooner or later to all those who selflessly serve their spouse, placing spouse above self.

It is this kind of love felt between spouses and felt and seen by our children does more to prepare our kids for their success than anything else we could do; it prepares them for life in marvelous ways.

You see, as we continually work on the love part of marriage, the rest of the pieces of the successful family puzzle will likely fall in place almost like magic. That is so because sincere love between husband and wife is the key that opens up advanced knowledge and know-how regarding parenting. It's a revelatory sort of thing.

So as we strive to launch our children onto success in life, we must show them and teach them about the true concepts of enduring love and let them know you've always got their back.

GARTH & SANDI SMITH

They will know they can always count on their parents for encouragement and to be in their corner helping them along the way—the rocky path of life. As we show this kind of support, love, and back up for our spouse, the kids will feel it for themselves as well.

And because none of us know what tomorrow will bring or how long we will be in our children's life (death comes to all), we should desire and strive to prepare them effectively, affectionately, quickly, lovingly, and to aid them in becoming parents of their own family legacy, some day.

Change the Cycle

I spoke with a father not long ago. Our discussion was on parenting. He made the comment, "I can't expect my kids to do something I'm not doing or have not done in my life."

"Let's see if I understand," I answered. "So even though you know something that would be a great help and benefit to your kids, if you've not learned to implement it so well in your own life, you think it's not right to teach it to your kids and expect them to live by it. Is that what you mean?" He said yes.

I've thought back on that conversation many times, comparing it to real-life examples I've either lived myself or observed, and in each case, I've come away with the thought that my friend's view is well intentioned but slightly skewed.

From our perspective, our children must be pointed in the right direction by their parents, even if the parents are not so well directed themselves. If parents feel guilty they've not done as well as they could have, that means they can see a better way, or could with some sincere pondering.

Why, we've wondered, would we wish to transfer to the next generation the habits and problems that have plagued us for so long? Of course parents would not intentionally pass on bad habits to their children, at least we hope not, but if we don't see it as our duty to advance our kids to a higher standard, they will not likely expect it from themselves.

Obviously, our children learn best by a sterling example, and example is the best course for us to train our children. If, however, we can't seem to muster up the discipline to overcome our most serious weaknesses that should not excuse us from being open with our children and making it clear they know our expectations of them. I've seen parents retain habits yet through full disclo-

sure, telling and teaching their kids to seek higher moral ground with some degree of success.

Our greatest assets should be our spouse and our children, and assuming we mean well by our children, few mistakes we make will permanently damage them (some obvious exceptions we can all think of should be avoided like we would the plague—child molestation, etc.).

Raising kids brings the best out in us and sometimes the worst. For us, though, to avoid expecting change and progress from our kids simply because we've not learned to master a habit or principle, to us, is a serious mistake. When we see ourselves as flawed individuals and parents, with bad habits and character flaws that trouble us almost daily, it makes life much easier to advance forward with high expectations for our kids, notwithstanding our weaknesses. You see, for failure to be permanent in our role as spouse and parent, we would have to walk away from our marriage and our kids, and *never come back!* That would be permanent failure. Everything short of that, there is still hope for us in this life as it applies to our family.

Real failure is falling down and failing to get back up. Using this definition of parental success then, as long as we're still trying with ourselves, our marriage, and our kids, there is still a degree of success, even or notwithstanding our obvious and many weaknesses.

Are you still breathing? Are you still in the home with your spouse and kids? If not, do you still have any degree of influence with them? If you can answer yes to these questions, there is still time to change the cycle and begin a new family legacy of your own. And even if you cannot answer affirmatively to those questions and if you're reading this, there is still hope for you to build a family legacy. But you must choose to begin the task, and the sooner, the better. It all begins with connection, connection with spouse and kids.

There is a wonderful quote we like that for many offers hope: "There's no such thing as failure, only feedback" (John David Hoag). This quote relates to the person who, sooner or later, desires more for his children than what he was taught but also more from himself. It speaks of being *introspective* for the purpose of positive change in our lives. But the change doesn't occur unless and until we look for feedback in our decisions and behavior. Using our missteps as feedback provides us with valuable data to help bring forth better choices in the future.

But if we've given up on ourselves regarding personal growth and moral development, we're reading off a bad mental map. We all can change; we can all find areas of our life where we can make even small advances, don't you agree? The exciting news is this: when we focus with diligence and patience to make a small improvement in our character or behavior, when we begin to recognize even small improvement in our lives, adrenaline kicks in followed by feelings of hope to make even bigger changes. Hope is a powerful friend. But remember, "Hope" is not the strategy; it's the benefit of making new, better choices in our lives; setting higher or more realistic goals and stretching to reach them.

Even better, however, is this: when we decide to engage in personal and family improvement, an unseen power comes into play. The moment one positively commits oneself, Providence then, moves too. For a fact, "when the student is ready, the teacher appears." History proves this out.

Personal change is hard for most, but for our wife and kids' sake, we should begin now to make a strategy for improvement in our own lives. We may want to begin with small improvements, and over time, if necessary, we can work on the larger issues. Some have found the benefits of hiring a life coach to help them get focused and to stay on track until new habits are solidly in place.

Our little children still see us as Superman and Spiderman wrapped up into one, but as they get older, they see us without

our Superman and Spiderman suits and magic powers, and at that point, we become human to them. Not only human but pretty flawed humans. The truth is we're all quite flawed. And when a spark of desire comes to us to change the generational cycle, we begin to feel like hypocrites or at least the fear of appearing as hypocrites. For many, that spark of desire is quickly snuffed out because of doubt and fear.

That fear of being seen as a hypocrite is powerful. The thought of being the parents who say to their kids, in effect, "Do as we say, not as we do," is based on an incorrect map, causing many parents to shy away from expecting greater improvement from their kids beyond the parent's current level. That mind-set also creates fear in the parent as it applies to personal change. Failing to expect character and educational growth from our children for fear of failure or the appearance of looking hypocritical creates serious damage to child and self. In the end, it affects the whole family—the whole generation.

What parent can't relate to that? Who wants to be seen as a hypocrite especially by their own children? That mind-set, how-ever, reveals a problem and a trap many parents have stepped into from generation to generation, family to family throughout time. With that incorrect mind-set, no changes occur and personal and family culture remains the same. The kids embrace their parents' flaws thus they grow up and leave the family nest not any bet-ter off than their parents, often worse, having adopted the same habits and problems. This creates another generation of exact or similar problems. In the end, the kids always come out the loser. There is a better way.

Before we address the better way, let's expose a common trap, the kind of trap that has prevented millions of people from mak-ing the needed changes in their lives. It is bound up in the word "hypocrite." Hypocrite or hypocrisy speaks of one who tries to act like someone he is not. It typically refers to one who wears a mask to deceive or trick someone.

Of all the people we've known over our lifetime, a very, very small number fit into that definition. The trap we fall into is that we will be *perceived* as hypocrites. Yet it is absolutely impossible to change behavior and character without running that risk of being so labeled. For us to change our lives, we go through a phase where we are *practicing* to do better when inside, we still may feel very weak and vulnerable, thus causing us to feel like hypocrites, yet we are not. The definition of "hypocrite" is based on one's *motives*.

The best thing we can do as we begin to desire change in our lives is to check our motives—our reasons for wanting change. If motive is unselfish, you can allow your critics to say what they will because you will know that the true reason (the "why") for your desired change is for your kids and families sake. You can go on to the remarkable business of positive improvement and change knowing that your cause is just and honorable. Let the naysayers say what they will. The naysayers of life have always been there. We should refuse to let their words or opinions prevent us from doing what we know is best.

One fellow said to me, "But what if I fail at my effort to change?"

"Remember," I told him, "failure is only permanent when we refuse to get up after we fall. After all, we all fall sometimes. "Your job," I told him, "is to be so firmly committed that if you stumble in your efforts and fall off the wagon, so to speak, you will get right back on track as soon as possible."

The better way is found in the parent(s) desiring more for their kids than what they had. We're not talking about money or gifts, but rather, principles, knowledge, and habits. It requires parents asking themselves some tough questions and a willingness to seek for true, correct answers as it applies to us all, parents and children.

The bottom line is this: we can change, we can improve, and we must if we're to change the generational, vicious cycle. You can say to yourself, and we encourage it. "The problems of my life and of my parents and ancestors will end with me! I refuse to pass on to another generation the issues that have been so painful to me. I love my kids too much to let that happen."

That's a bold statement and an even bolder decision. We can promise you with an assurance, that to strive to hold to that resolve will prove to be the most significant decision of your life.

As we face that new commitment but are daily reminded of our bad habits, poor decisions, vulnerability, and feelings of weakness, we ask ourselves, how do we begin and when? As stated above, we *begin now* and we begin with what will be easiest to change, followed by more challenging issues.

One father I know had multiple problems, problems he was determined not to pass on to his kids. He determined the easiest vice to tackle first was swearing. He made a deep and sincere commitment to himself and his wife that he was resolved to eliminate that vice from his life. In his case, he chose to find acceptable words to replace his crude and offensive words and simply began injecting those words into his vocabulary. Over a matter of weeks, he mastered the problem. A weakness became a strength!

With that victory his confidence rose so he dove into another vice, smoking. That took a little longer, but with the help of a nicotine patch, he mastered that vice (after a great struggle, I might add). With those two vices out of the way, he was feeling like a new man, which gave him even greater confidence to tackle the next one, drinking.

He was a heavy drinker, so he began studying Alcoholics Anonymous Twelve Steps. Over a period of one year, he was well on his way to being alcohol free. Granted, these changes required major adjustments in his life, like changing friends, as well as major work on his thought processes. It was a tough battle but

well worth it. Why? Because he was striving for a cause greater than himself: his wife and children, as well as a deep desire to change the cycle and create a family legacy. He determined that with a solid "why" in his mind, he could fulfill any "what." His "why" was his strong desire to build a family legacy, one his wife and children would be proud to be a part of. His "what" was eliminating damaging vices from his life, vices that had been part of his family for decades.

I knew a single mother of three; she had her hands full to say the least. She shared with me her story which I will paraphrase:

> When it finally occurred to her that she wanted more for and from her kids than what she was raised with, she settled on the idea of getting her kids involved in religion (an unusual decision for her since she was not raised to be religious). She called upon a church leader at the nudging of a friend. She told him of her plan, whereupon he arranged to help her reach her goal. Each Sunday she would dress and prepare her kids and then drop them off at church into the hands of a member of the church. When the meetings were over, she would pick them up.
>
> The kids were gaining new, good friends as well as learning so they looked forward to Sundays, and she was pleased that they seemed more content. As time went on, he asked to speak with her. In their meeting, he asked her a simple question: "I'm pleased you are bringing your kids to church, but please tell me why you are doing this? What is your motive?"
>
> She said she wanted a better life for her kids. He proceeded to help her see her goal from a broader perspective. He said, "I'm thrilled you want better for your kids and that you had the *courage* to take that big step. But if you really want to build a great family and give your kids more than you were raised with, I suggest you begin to come with them. You'll be amazed how much more it will positively affect the future of your three children as well as the culture in your home."

197

She said, "Sir, I can plainly see the value of my kids getting involved in religion, but truthfully, I would feel like a hypocrite going to church when, for me, my heart is not in it—I don't feel like a religious person and don't want to be a hypocrite."

He responded, "You've got it all wrong. Religion is not for the whole—the perfect—for there are none. We're all sinners and will be until the day we die. The church is not a *country club* for the socially and morally well-to-do, but rather, it's more like a *hospital* for the *sick*, and we're all *sick*!"

He went on to ask, "With the exception of the 'hypocrite' concern, is there anything else that prevents you from joining your children each week?"

She said, "Well, I'm simply not a believer in God, or I don't think I am."

He followed by saying, "So you don't think you're a believer, but you're not sure?"

"Right," she said.

Calling her by name, he said, "Remembering your goal, to help your kids to receive more from life than you were given, can you see that being united with your children in their growth and development would do so much more for them than sending them? Can you see that?"

She agreed but was still hesitant to commit.

He went on, "It appears to me that you're putting all hope in your kids and making the assumption that you're lost and beyond hope yourself. Is that how you feel deep down?"

She said, "Yes. Honestly, I can't see myself changing much, but I want my kids raised with it."

He continued, "Your answer tells me that your faith and belief is much, much deeper than you realize. Wouldn't you agree?"

She agreed. "But I'm afraid," she said. "I'm afraid that if I commit to attendance and then fail to change, I could make matters worse for my kids rather than better. That's why I thought it better to just drop them off."

He said, "Fear then is your biggest concern, right? Fear of failure in the eyes of your kids?"

She said, "Yes, I guess so."

"Don't you realize," he said, "that we all face that, every last one of us, me included?"

"You do?" she asked.

"Yes, most definitely, and that's why active members of our church continue each day by fortifying themselves by learning, praying, serving others, etc. In this way, they're more likely to stay active and engaged in their progress and to be examples to their children. Remember, just because we become committed churchgoers doesn't necessarily mean we're any stronger people. It simply means we're *willing* to give it our best effort, and in your case, it's also for your kids." He went on, "I would encourage you to try seeing that point, which by trying to *change yourself* from within is the best and most effective way to ensure a straight course for your children to follow. The most important thing we want our children to learn is to keep going, never give up, right? And if we slip up, we get back up, brush ourselves off, and get back at it again, and that the best thing you could do for your kids is to try to do the hard things, the right things. And one of the worst things you could show your kids is how not to commit. By committing you're not saying how good you think you are, but rather, how *willing* you are to go to great lengths for your kids and yourself. It's an act of *courage*," he said. She felt somewhat satisfied by what he said. She followed his counsel, took the bold step, and raised her kids in a religious family. She changed the cycle that had not been broken in her family for generations.

The bottom line of parenting is the same as the bottom line of life: when we practice daily to be the best we can be, good things happen notwithstanding struggles of every sort. As humans we're all *wired* to change and progress, and when we stop expecting advancement and growth in our lives, inertia (apathy, inaction, and sluggishness) becomes our life, followed by unhappiness and lack of personal perspective, which is followed by loss of hope for our future. When hope is gone in our lives for long periods of time, disaster is often to follow, a place we should never want for ourselves or our children. Hope is a powerful tool.

Both of the above stories exemplify courage. The root of the word "courage" is "cor," which is the Latin word for "heart." In one of its earliest forms, the word "courage" spoke of one speaking his mind and telling all of one's heart or allowing others to see their vulnerabilities.

The mother of three above and the earlier story of the man with many vices, shows how they showed their heart for all to see. They did it by stepping into territory they had never been before thus running the risk of allowing all to see their weaknesses, their vulnerabilities. Courage is essential for all of us to muster up in order to make the kind of progress that would constitute being the best we can be, and showing our children how to do the same.

It is progress and hope we want to pass on to our children, and that's best done through example. Therefore, to change a vicious generational cycle for the sake of our spouse and kids we can begin with our kids; but sooner or later personal, internal changes will be required of each one of us.

So back to my friend from the beginning of this chapter, the one who said, "I can't expect my kids to do something I've not done so well at myself."

We must—we must—place our children's best interest above all else. But along the way, sooner or later, and for best results with the kids, we will want to begin the change within ourselves—that is, if we really desire to wire our kids for success and build a family legacy. Courage to become better must become a big part of our priority.

Educating Desires

Because the following method of child behavioral modification worked so effectively for us, let us restate what we mentioned in an earlier chapter.

When our children were young we noticed we could often change their behavior by *what* we would say to them and *how*. By offering *sincere compliments* we would see immediate behavior improvement. After some success in that area, we decided to take it to another level. This is what we did: if a particular child was having issues with honesty, for instance, we would find a time when that child was within earshot of our words. Sandi and I would speak to each other as though our child was not able to hear us, yet we knew he could.

"Garth, our son —— is one that can be counted upon. He's honest and trustworthy, which makes me very proud of him."

"Sandi, I agree. You can always count on him to tell the truth."

Using this approach we would see changes in his behavior very soon before the day was out. From this example, deeply held desires were either formed or firmed up.

This chapter could be, in our opinion, the most important chapter in the book. Why? Because it addresses what drives the thoughts and actions of both parents and child and the very root of what creates a happy, fulfilled life.

Educating desires is possibly the most significant subject we should be students of, yet it is seldom addressed—seldom even thought of. Educating our desires speaks of things we absolutely believe, principles we're willing to fight for to the end. It speaks of our most powerful hopes, our longings and deepest anticipations and passions. They are the things we spend most of our thoughts on.

Few parents realize the influence they have over their children's futures. If they did, they would likely change the way they parent their children. As we work with our little children, we're working as co-creators of their desires in concert with the child. We become managers, as it were, to help oversee the formation of their earliest, most heartfelt desires. As we strive to change our own desires, as adults and parents, it's quite a different process. Let's begin with the adult process for shaping and educating our desires.

Speaking of adults: There is an inner core to every human that is a sovereign territory we each possess. It is that spot in our most inner core that is ours individually, and we alone create and control it. Even though the influence of family, friends, and culture affect us greatly, that inner core is solely ours to create and form. Moreover, this inner core is being strengthened or weakened daily by our thoughts and actions, both of which have their beginnings with our deepest and most heartfelt desires. Desires become choices and choices turn to actions. It's as simple as that. Honorable thoughts will create honorable desires, and honorable desires will bring about honorable choices and decisions we make. Poor decisions are the reflection of poor desires brought to life. We're speaking here of moral choices primarily, those that show our inner most feelings about honesty, integrity, morality, obedience to law, and respect for others. As adults, we can change or reeducate our desires thus changing our outcomes and our lives as we know it, which we will address later in this chapter.

Speaking now of our little children: Their minds and desires are not yet fully formed, so their ability to form and create their own desires is largely in the hands of their parents. Need we point out how big this responsibility is on our shoulders as parents? Our *example* and *teachings* as parents largely determine the nature of their inner core—their desires. We literally have the greatest impact upon their desires, interests, hopes, and dreams for their future. Granted, as they grow older, they can adjust those desires

as they please. But initially, we create for them the path they will follow. If it's a path they become passionate about, it will become their path, self-chosen, but initially guided by their parents.

So as we go about nurturing our little ones, day in and day out, we're helping to form and educate their desires. In a subtle way, the things we *say* and *how* we say them and the things we *do* and *why* we do them are seen and felt by our children. Each of those images they see and feel help to form their initial desires, which as we said earlier, will likely form their actions and behavior for good or bad, evil or righteousness. A person's inner most will (desires)creates the environment that eventually determine their choices and decisions.

The impact we parents have on our children's future is probably greater than we prefer, but it is what it is. For that reason, we have great need to examine our own deepest desires and passions and how they form our behavior, actions, words, and attitudes. We're being watched closely.

Of course parents can, and many do, relinquish their leadership role to television, music, other adults, electronic gadgets, or the like but at great risk. I think it obvious why we should hold tight to our role as parent and co-creator of our child's most precious inner core.

We have choices to make and those choices will affect our children. Do we desire our children to grow up with some of the same problems and issues we've had, issues that have been painful to us, or would we prefer our children to go in a different, better direction with their lives? If we would choose the latter, inner changes are required of us. In as much as permanent changes do not happen overnight, we might want to begin as soon as possible.

Do we want our children to be honest? Then teach and show honesty in all you do. What about morality? Do we want our children to live by a high, moral standard devoid of teenage pregnancies or sexually transmitted diseases and all the emotional problems that follow? Do we want our children to live by situ-

ational ethics, where their ethics and morals change depending on the situation? Or do we want our children to live by fixed, time-tested values, ethics, and morals? If so, let's begin to show it and teach it, now.

What about fair play? Do we want our kids to embrace it? Then we'd better show them how it all works. From parents, kids learn their earliest lessons on how to be a grateful receiver or a demanding child. From us they learn to be materialistic, vain, greedy, and covetous. From parents they learn humility or to be prideful, to be giving or selfish. From us they learn impulsiveness or the wonderful advantages of delayed gratification and the virtues of patience and thoughtfulness that flow from it. We subtly teach them to be industrious or lazy, a taker or giver, independent or dependent. From the parent they learn to place the most emphasis on their body shape or their spiritual and moral development. One can turn them to arrogance the other to be genuine and unpretentious. All these and more we teach and show our kids as they observe our daily walk and talk. We can show and teach our children the positive or the negative of every aspect of life. We can provide for them a sort of insulation from future would-be struggles of life. From us they get their first lessons on the benefits of a disciplined mind, the kind that will create in them confidence and hope. Or we can lead them toward an unruly mind, the kind that makes progress a struggle. It all comes from the learned habits formed in their young, tender minds while they are still on their mother's knee and the relatively few years that follow.

The infant and child's life is one of struggle—struggle to eat, crawl, walk, talk, and learn. In their tender, beginning years and shortly thereafter, we can teach them and show them the good path of life, the path that leads to a greater likelihood of success in their choices. Or we can extend their struggles to span years or a lifetime. It all hinges on their inner most desires which we help form.

Our intentions to show our love to them can turn to hurt. "Oh, you're so beautiful" will not cause any harm to the infant, but to continue it to the young girl can create in her mind that her natural beauty is the real her, causing her to miss her greatest gifts of mind and character.

As we strive to educate our children's desires in directions that will help them to be the best they can possibly be, we need double vision. We can look into our kids' future, so to speak, and at the same time, see the details of the here and now of their lives. We need a microscope in one eye and a telescope in the other. The microscope observes the details of their lives and the telescope looks into their future to envision how we see their full potential being realized.

The microscope, when used effectively, examines every aspect of their lives. This allows us as parents to make necessary adjustments for their best good. It is this part of our vision for our kids that keeps them on the straight and narrow path, the path that will likely lead to their greatest potential for success. To stay on course for their potential, details are very helpful to parents. Granted, it requires we be more observant and studious of their budding lives. But that is our job—our duty if we want them to be wired for success.

The telescope looks long-term in their lives. This allows us to have a target to shoot for as we point and direct our children in their lives and as we strive daily to form and educate their desires.

Hopefully, it's obvious that we parents hold claim to our little one's hearts, at least for now. Doesn't it make sense that we make sure we're going in a good and right direction as parents? We're all climbing the ladder of life. Let's just be sure our ladder is leaning against a true, good wall, for our kids' sake as well as our own. Equally important is that our children discover and desire that "true and good wall." This requires self-examination and lots of introspection in our lives as well as our children. As it applies to our children's welfare, we don't want to get that one wrong.

Much of what we teach our little ones that influence their desires have to do with two points particularly: *relationships* and *discipline* (meaning, teaching them to not only be *obedient to parents*, but to learn how to *discipline* their own lives). We parents can strategically focus our efforts on those two points of interest (relationship building and discipline), which would significantly help us strategically focus our efforts on our kids' progress and development.

Something as simple as showing love, tenderness, and respect to our spouse, shows and teaches our kids how to do the same, thus helping them educate their own desires regarding relationship building. How? By seeing and feeling the benefits of such acts of kindness and patience, they will likely desire the same. They will feel the wonderful mood in the home as loving, kind, and respectful and will likely work to feel those things in their own lives. Without a doubt, the greatest blessing we can pass on to our children is how we treat our spouse; a feeling and assurance dad cherishes mom, and mom dad.

The key here is that we guide our kids to *want* those desires of kindness, love, and respect for others, as well as the desire to gain other's respect for them. Over time, that desire to "want" those same traits in their lives will grow to a *love* and *passion* for those things. History shows that people will overcome great odds and any obstacle for things they deeply desire and are genuinely passionate about.

Our desires can be an *ally* or an *enemy*. If our desires are directed toward things that help us, improve us, unite us with our spouse and family and with others and create a healthy life in every respect, that desire is an ally and friend. On the other hand, if our deepest passionate desires are likely to create chaos and frustration in our lives or in the lives of others, frustration and pain is what will result. Our desires are either friend or foe.

Years ago, I developed a friendly relationship with a fellow who shared with me his story. He was a very talented kid in almost

every way—intelligent, athletic, and socially well-adjusted. His father had a hobby of race car driving, his greatest passion. So as expected, his son picked up the same passion. The problem was that the environment of the race car events, at least at that time, was not the kind of environment a young boy should be in—that is, if a parent's desire is to train up a child to avoid excesses and poor habits such as drinking alcoholic beverages, smoking, and drugs, not to mention the kind of language that was often heard in that type of setting.

Unbeknown to the father, his son would have a tendency toward excesses in all the wrong areas of life. Later in life, my friend became an alcoholic and a drug abuser. It cost him multiple marriages and placed his children at risk. Who knows how many generations it effected?

Parents have influence over their little ones. Their likes and dislikes often become the likes and dislikes of the kids, for good or ill. We have the divine duty to examine what we expose our children to and how. Using the example of my friend and his race car father, had the father been more sensitive to what he wanted his son to grow up to become, maybe he would have realized that type of environment was not healthy for his son. We can only suppose the father did the best he knew how, but with 20/20 hindsight I'm sure the father would have encouraged his son in different directions.

After my friend grew up, married, and had a family, he could have chosen to change his life and habits by changing and reeducating his desires. However, he would be climbing out of a very deep hole. We parents would prefer (if we're introspective and observant) to place our kids on a trajectory of progress and growth rather than place them in a deep hole they will likely spend the rest of their lives digging out of.

We parents can and do help form our children's deepest desires and passions whether we know it or not. We can best form those desires as we teach them by *example* as well as *explanation*. They

see our desires acted out each day. If we want them to embrace a certain desire and to make it a passion, we *explain* to them *why* we desire it and *why* we hope they will too. So, *explanation* (teach and clarify) and *exemplification* (illustrate and demonstrate by example) are our parental tools to form their desires.

My friend, now an adult, may wish to change his desires—to turn his life around. How would he go about that major change? How would he reeducate his desires that his behavior would change? And how do parents who desire improved lives for their children's sake make those inner core changes?

As we search for answers to these questions, we begin to enter into one of the greatest adventures life has to offer—changing self, changing our inner core. Not simply change for the sake of change but the kind of change that will make our lives better and happier. The kind of change we will want our children to model and embrace. That kind of change requires far more than words—it requires our greatest commitment.

It seems that when we desire to improve and educate our desires in a new and better direction, unseen powers seem to hedge up against us. However, we can be sure there are also unseen powers working for us. *When we begin to feel divine discontent within us regarding our misguided lives, we know it's not only time to change but also, and more importantly, we can be assured we're receiving divine help in our newfound desire.*

With this new budding desire to change, we'll want to take seriously the next few steps that will be required of us. Think of it, we won't want to waste that new and fresh desire to change, nor do we want to miscalculate what will be required of us. A miscalculation here could cause us to fail in our all-important desire to improve our lives. *Discouragement* is what we want to avoid, often caused by thoughts of "It's too hard," or "What's the use?" *Bridging* our new untested desire onto a successful inner change should not be done nonchalantly.

When we desire to make major changes in our lives we enter into a process that will require of us to build a solid connection from where we are now to where we want to be. Sometimes total and complete changes are required of us. In those cases, we don't want to build a bridge to our new self; we'll want to create a whole new self, a complete transformation. In a very real way, we're working on a rebuild from the inside out. I assure you, it's all worth the effort. For a person to have a sincere desire to improve their lives, that willingness is enough to carry him through to the end if he keeps that purpose for change clearly in his mind. It is that purpose that acts as fuel to propel us to endure to success.

Let me use my own history to illustrate. Note, I'm not suggesting I'm the best example, but rather, I know my history better than anyone else's. As an adult I found the need to make many major changes in my life, so my life may be similar to many of you readers.

Sandi and I had predetermined that we would have as many children as possible, and with that new decision, I felt greater weight on my shoulders to be a better example for my children.

Having been raised by kindly parents but who were challenged with many severe problems, problems they had adopted from their parents, and problems I'd learned to embrace, I found the need to make a break. I chose to stop the generational cycle that had afflicted my family for many years. These changes were major and radical; they had to be because the new direction in life I desired was far different than the one I had been on.

These are the steps I took to change my desires and to find, at least for me, success in life. I learned that habits were not easy to change, so I learned to *be patient* with myself. Often my progress was not as rapid as I'd hoped, but I came to realize that even small incremental steps upward was still progress. Daily and weekly progress is what I needed no matter how seemingly small the changes were. I was determined to make the kind of inner changes that would literally change the course of my life. I knew

it would require many years, maybe a lifetime. I learned that one can be more patient if they have a clear, concise *purpose*. My purpose was to create a *family legacy* which inspired me to stay on task to the end.

Another important step had to do with education. Previously, having not been a daily reader of books (that's an understatement), I saw the need to *reeducate my mind*. I learned that educating my mind was a key ingredient to successful change of inner desires. I handpicked books that spoke to the kind of changes I hoped to make. Many were self-help books at first, books on optimism and encouragement, all pointed to make daily progress toward the honorable and good of this life. Those books reminded me that I could learn to control my thoughts, and that to do so was my duty. I learned to appreciate biographies of great men and women. Their examples often gave me courage to remain diligent in my quest.

Daily reading from the scriptures provided additional, well-needed knowledge but also gave me regular doses of peace of mind. I came to realize that dramatic changes in one's life are not likely to be permanent without knowledge of truth. The word "truth" scares some people.

Truth seekers in our society are often mocked. Many in this world believe truth is whatever they want to do or whatever they believe is true and that if it feels good, do it. I learned, however, that there are absolutes (unchanging principles) in this life, thousands upon thousands of them. These absolutes provide anchors for those who choose to embrace them for change. Some argue, "how can you know what is true?" I learned one simple test to determine what truth is. I learned that if the principle has endured throughout time, I felt to trust it. I learned that eternal truth is stable, solid, and can always be counted on, always. So for me, the way to determine what is and what is not truth, I followed this pattern.

These principles of truth fall into virtually every aspect of our lives: physical, social/emotional, moral, and spiritual. There are natural truths (gravity for instance), moral truths, and spiritual truths. Physical laws are more clearly seen and felt. We all know natural law like gravity never fails, it always holds true. We're able to have confidence in it and count on it 100% of the time. Likewise, laws that apply to social/emotional, moral, and spiritual, any time we try to skirt past any of those laws, heartache is what results. On the other hand, as we learn to understand and live true to these laws, joy, happiness, and success is what results, automatically.

I learned that truth has no agenda. Truth is not for or against anyone or anything, it just is. Truth is a constant reminder that there are powers in this life that are constant, we can be sure they will hold true in every situation or condition.

Once I found there to be absolutes in life, laws I could count on—principles and laws that have endured throughout recorded time, I became an enthusiastic student of them and to search for them daily. It became a thrilling adventure for me as I pored through books searching for even one nugget of truth. I found that the scriptures, if interpreted correctly, are packed with truth. After I found a truth and confirmed it to be so, I began trying to implement it in my life.

Next, I began *sharing* it with my family and others. The sharing process solidified my new knowledge in my mind but also satisfied an inner urge to hand down truth to my family which was part of my *purpose* in reeducating my desires. I learned that *teaching* is a central responsibility in parenting. So I worked to improve my teaching skills, for my kids' sake.

My new habit of daily learning became a deep love, a fresh and powerful passion. I learned that *leaders are readers* and to create a family legacy I must learn to be a leader of which knowledge of truth was a prerequisite. Gaining new knowledge of truth provided much evidence by way of new and improved desires. I could feel and see the improvements my new desires were giving me. I felt my time was too valuable to waste on simple information only. I didn't want to waste my time on books that did not further my progress. I became convinced that only time-tested truth would give me the needed fuel and motivation to get where I hoped to go.

When it occurred to me that truth was what I needed, my daily reading always began with prayer. My prayer went something like this: "Father, I'm reading now in the scriptures [or this biography, etc], and I'm searching for understanding and truth. Please enlighten my mind that I might understand the truths from this book You would have me learn."

I've never known anyone who has changed their lives significantly who did not exercise a *prayerful* heart and a *humble* attitude. When it came clear to my mind that there were absolutes in this life, I began desiring to find these truths. From the scriptures we read, "Then said Jesus to those Jews which believed on him, If ye continue in my word, then are ye my disciples indeed; *and ye shall know the truth and the truth shall make you free*" (John 8: 31-32).

I've pondered these verses many times, and have come to the conclusion they (truths) are far more practical than most would want to believe, choosing rather to apply some mysterious application to Christ's words in this verse.

I've also concluded that Christ was speaking of "truth" as it applies to all laws. How happy and "free" we are when we learn to live the laws of health. Happy are we when we learn to apply the laws that apply to all things, including spiritual truth. Imagine how unhappy we are when we fail to learn and apply the physical laws, including Sir Isaac Newton's laws of motion. Understanding something about Newton's laws of motion, gives us the freedom to live by those laws. We know to go contrary to physical laws could cost us our lives. Living by them brings joy, freedom, and happiness. Likewise with all physical, social/emotional, and spir-

itual laws. Live true to them and we're free to enjoy them. Fail to live them and we live at risk.

It also holds true with God's laws. Just as Cecil B. Demille stated regarding God's laws:

> "We cannot break the Ten Commandments. We can only break ourselves against them- or else, by keeping them, rise through them to the fulness of freedom under God. God means us to be free. With divine daring, He gave us the power of choice." (*Commencement Address*, Brigham Young University Speeches of the Year, Provo, 31 May 1956).

The most beneficial course correction I made, turned out to be a gift. I can take no credit for this myself, but in some miraculous way, I was given an inner motivation to grow myself not for my sake only but also for my wife and children's sake, as well as for others I may come in contact with over my lifetime. Stated differently, every truth I learned, I learned for the purpose of sharing that truth with my wife, my children, and others. That new desire to share increased the size and strength of my motivation to learn. My new desire was bigger and greater than me; it was for the overall welfare of my wife, my kids, and others. I learned from this experience—that when our desires are unselfish and turned primarily outward rather than inward, greater motivation to continue the process ensues.

Well, here I am, much older now, and I'm still working on the education of my desires. I was right in my initial perspective. It could take a lifetime and probably will. I've learned, though, had I not entered into the quest of educating my desires, my goal for a family legacy would never have been reached. As it now is, I still have much more work to do on self, but I'm far advanced from where I began the process. It seems I'm always under construction. I feel my greatest achievement has been my willingness, desire, and endurance to create a family legacy. Some say the journey is the best part; I have to agree.

I can take but little credit for the family legacy that's been built. Along with my dear wife, there have also been powerful influences on both sides of the veil that have made it all possible. But it all began with a single decision to change desires, attitudes, and behavior.

The desires we give place for in our hearts and minds creates our behavior, which determine our state of happiness or sadness, joy or sorrow; it's our choice. Things do not change in our lives unless and until we do. As parents, we are in charge of forming our children's fundamental desires, and if we must change our own desires first, we should. Please remember, the task of changing ourselves is very doable.

I hope I've made this point very clear: Nothing is any more important in this life as the attention we give to the deepest passions and desires of our minds and hearts.

Pride, the Personal and Family Cancer

Our years of experience in marriage and raising kids tell us that our marriage has been pretty much like that of many others— "mostly sunny and clear." However, like most others, we've had our times of "partly cloudy with a chance of rain." Less frequent have we had "cloudy with rain and gusty winds."

As a married couple, one committed to making it endure, we've seen our job as making the sunny days last longer and recognizing when dark clouds come that we might prevent them from becoming a ferocious storm. Our biggest obstacle in reaching that goal has been the attitude that has caused the downfall of nations, the cause of nearly every war ever fought, and the breakup of millions of marriages and families. Probably the cause of every painful division known to mankind. We speak of *pride*.

This pride we speak of is not the kind of pleasure we feel from a job well done, nor is it the feelings attended to a well-kept home and neatly dressed children. No, this kind of pride is that devilish attitude that gets in the way of clear thinking and true communication. It is the pride that darkens our minds and rearranges our thoughts so that the "we" is replaced with "me." It is a selfish attitude that blocks unity and demands personal rights. It is the thing that single handedly tears hearts apart and turns an otherwise family legacy into ruin. And unfortunately, the pride in the parents' hearts is most often the cause of the children's emotions to be filled with fear and their hope of the future to appear bleak. Sadly, those with heavy doses of pride are so blinded by that fact they don't have a clue they've got a pride problem.

We think it's safe to say nearly every living soul has some pride issues, small or large. So to be totally devoid of pride makes that person a true saint. We're familiar with only one person that was totally and completely pride free. For the rest of us, our goal should be to *strive* every day to be devoid of pride, to work on it day in and day out. Not an easy task but one worth the effort, for our sake as well as the kids.

The effort to detect and eliminate pride from our lives (to the best of our ability) is not simply an individual and personal matter. If our pride issues get passed on to our children, the cycle not only continues, but it has a tendency to fester all the more. Whatever we can do to eliminate our pride problems from reaching our children is worth all the focused effort we can muster up.

C. S. Lewis described best the fundamental cause of pride and how to eliminate it from our lives, he wrote,

> Pride gets no pleasure out of having something, only out of having more of it than the next man…It is the comparison that makes you proud: the pleasure of being above the rest. Once the element of competition has gone, pride has gone. (*Mere Christanity*, pp. 109–10)

Lewis's definition speaks of the kind of "comparison" we feel to have "more of it than the next man"—more or better homes, cars, better-dressed children, better or more education, and in our day, more money. Any of these can be either actual or just the appearance of.

We know we have pride issues when we come to the realization that we are in competition ("comparison") with our spouse or anyone else. This is not the kind of competition we feel in the field of athletics. It is the kind of comparison and competition that brings out the selfish in us, as well as the self-conceit, self-gratification, self-seeking, and even self-pity .

Sooner or later, contention shows up in the life of a prideful person—arguments, fights, disturbances, hostility, confessing

other people's sins, spousal abuse—all of which most often end in broken hearts, confused and pained children, and divorce.

Pride is easily seen in others but seldom admitted in ourselves. The prideful person is usually easily offended and holds grudges. They find it hard to forgive because of their desire to hold another in their debt. They don't take counsel or correction well. After all, how does one correct near perfection?

The territory of the prideful is fault-finding, backbiting, gossiping, coveting, and envying. Because of their fear of another being raised above them in the minds of the crowd, they withhold gratitude and praise. They are generally jealous and unforgiving.

C. S. Lewis had it right when he wrote, "Once the element of competition has gone, pride has gone." Our job as spouses and parents is twofold:

1. Make our spouse a partner not a competitor.
2. Teach our children how to see all other people as their equals and not competitors.

To make our spouse a true partner and not a competitor requires that we learn to see his or her true value. For this reason, we should look into the heart and mind of our spouse and see the good qualities; everyone has some. We all saw them when we were dating prior to marriage, now we must refocus on those wonderful qualities. Our job is to elevate those qualities and think on them often. To continue in the prideful way toward our spouse is to continually elevate in our minds their weaknesses, ignoring our own.

I (Garth) had the chance to speak to a US Marine who had served three tours to the Middle East. He told me marines, especially in times of war, have a sort of buddy system and that each marine has a fellow marine he can count on to "watch his back." Each marine learns to trust that brother even with his life and is willing to reciprocate the same at any time.

When a married couple learns to unite in the same way, to always "watch his/her back," the most wonderful kind of enduring love is the result.

When we come to see our own weaknesses and imagine them going unchecked and how our weaknesses can cause the ruin of the family legacy, we can become humbled very quickly. We need to apply that thought more often just to remain more humble, more submissive, and more teachable. Humility is the opposite of pride. However, we shouldn't focus too long and hard on our weaknesses, or we'll get depressed. But to keep our pride in check, an honest self-examination of our strengths and faults is not a bad thing to do from time to time.

Recognizing our weaknesses and our spouse's strengths helps us see our need for our spouse. This is possibly the only time comparison is a worthy effort. It's a wonderful time when we come to see how, as a married couple, we balance each other out. Her strengths seem to minimize our weaknesses and vice versa. That's how partnerships are and why they're created. It makes one think of how all of our frailties are overshadowed by our Redeemer. The truth is, marriage is a type or example of the relationship we have (or should have) with our Redeemer.

Teaching and training our children to avoid prideful behavior blends with the chapter in this book entitled "Educating Desires." Ideally, we will show and tell our kids how things will eventually grow old or break, but relationships last forever. When we can do that effectively with our children, we're showing our kids what's most important to us; they will generally follow our lead.

Small things make the biggest difference when it comes to training children away from pride. When they hear us speak down to a race of people, an area of the country, or an individual, they see pride in action. But when they hear us speak lovingly and kindly of all people, they see the model for tolerance, patience, and loving kindness for all people.

We can teach our kids, "We [our family] love everyone, from every country, from every religion, every color of skin, and every walk of life, and *why*? Because we know the Lord loves them just as he loves us. And for us to dislike anyone is to dislike one whom the Lord loves. We never want to displease our Father, right, kids?"

With little children, you could next *show* examples of *how* to include all children into their circle of friends. After all, we all want to learn to include others into our circle of friends, not exclude. The Lord is all about widening his circle of influence and not narrowing it, and we should strive to do the same.

Again we state that pride is that great cancer that destroys nations, causes wars, family fights, lasting bitterness, and family ruin. We parents have a divine duty to seek and destroy that attitude in ourselves and our family whenever it its detected. A "wired" child, young adult, or adult is one who includes and not excludes others. He is one who fosters acceptance and love by removing the feelings of competition that separates.

Kids and Honest Labor

The following was written by our daughter, Lyric (child number 4), written for her monthly church newsletter. She refers to Relief Society, which is the woman's organization within our church. Our purpose in sharing this kind letter is to remind us all the importance of being diligent in our efforts to teach our children the benefits of honest labor. A warm thank you, to our daughter, Lyric, for sharing this with us.

This last Sunday we heard a beautiful lesson in Relief Society by Sister Bennett about moral discipline and how we can help our children develop this quality. For most of the lesson, I was focusing on my role as a parent and how I can improve; but as the hour winded down, I had an overwhelming feeling of gratitude for my parents. I find them to be near parenting experts in many areas (not that how I turned out is any indication of this!), and as different ideas were discussed in Relief Society, like learning that choices have consequences, understanding the difference between rights and privileges, learning to recognize the Spirit, and learning the value of work, I was reminded that all of these things were a part of the home I was raised in.

For this message, I want to focus on the importance of teaching our children to work. I was the typical youngster and teenager who grumbled when chores were assigned, and sometimes, my parents were the enemy. My parents even bought a milk cow when I was in high school, and we have since learned that they had brought Toto the Jersey cow (we had previously lived in Kansas, hence the name!) to our two-acre lot to teach us kids responsibility. Not only have their teaching efforts been effective because my siblings and I learned how to work hard and become reasonably productive adults, but I have been remembering the many times when their work (it is work to teach a child to work!) was effective instantly.

I remember one Saturday of my precious teenage years that I was not allowed to go out with my friends until I had a section of the very large garden weeded. I whined and procrastinated and whined some more, and then I realized my mom was not budging on this one, so out to the garden, I moped. I worked hard. I weeded that garden beautifully. I discovered that much gratification comes from pulling a weed at the root. I still find it kind of fun, minus the achy knees that result! After several hours, I looked out at the weed-free garden and marveled at its beauty and the part I played in it, and I'm not even exaggerating here! I remember many mornings waking up at the crack of dawn to milk Toto with one of my siblings, again with a mope to my step, and as I would walk out to the pasture, I would experience the beautiful sunrise and crisp morning air, and my mope would be uprighted, and my scowl would turn to a smile. And then there was the sibling bonding that occurred while seated across the cow from a brother or sister. We would have milking races, we would squirt the cat, and the most memorable, we had some of our best vocal performances on both sides of Toto. You've probably never heard a Wilson Phillips duet like ours! I share these stories in honor of the efforts of my parents and also as a reminder to all of us mothers and grandmothers and youth leaders that our efforts to teach our children the value of work are important. It is important to them as youth and as adults. Even during those times when our children act as though we are the enemy, and those times will most likely be the norm, it is vital that we press on. L. Tom Perry said, "I believe that second only to ensuring that every child receives an understanding of the gospel of our Lord and Savior is teaching them the joy of honest labor. Teaching children the joy of honest labor is one of the greatest of all gifts you can bestow upon them.

Again, our thanks to our sweet daughter Lyric, for sharing her memories. She's right, teaching kids the benefits and advantages of honest labor is pretty much a full-time job for parents. It is a parental duty we can't afford to leave out. Learning the principles of honest labor is so essential to our children's overall success, we parents should put in place daily systems and programs that keep our children not only busy, but busy learning how to begin and complete a job, that they might regularly feel the satisfaction of being finishers. Imagine your child growing up with the inner confidence that whatever he starts, he can and will finish.

With this kind of assurance, they will confidently approach life's challenges without the fear of failure. Does that mean they will never fail? Naturally, they will have failures as we all do. They, being wired for success, will not see failure as permanent, which means they will likely not get easily discouraged at failure. They will see it as a process, yet with the experience to know that what-ever roadblocks come their way, they will figure out a way to beat them rather than be beaten. This kind of determination and con-fidence came to them not by accident but because their parents walked them through the process of achievement almost every day of their early life, through work projects and the expectation of completion of each project or assignment.

This subject of raising finishers is simply a by-product of teaching your little ones how to work—how to become industri-ous. Truth is, there are lots of by-products that come from teach-ing this great virtue to your kids. So many that when you begin to examine them you'll likely be awestruck at how amazing it is that so many side benefits attach themselves to it automatically. Here's a short list, just a few to consider:

- responsibility
- teamwork
- obedience
- respect
- endurance

- efficiency
- self-confidence
- joy and satisfaction of being a finisher
- joy of blood, sweat, and tears for a good cause
- appreciation of nature and God
- leadership

As mentioned earlier, this is the short list, but we're sure you would agree with us that when kids learn these traits, they will become remarkable teenagers and adults, and simply from teaching them and showing and expecting your kids to work.

Mother Earth offers so much support for us parents when it comes to this. To engage our kids in a garden provides additional by-products that can be learned in few other places. "But I'm a good gardener," you say. That's okay. Remember, you're not raising produce as much as you're raising kids. The main focus is teaching kids the benefits of industriousness first and foremost, followed by wonderful produce to eat. Do your homework on raising productive gardens, teach it to your kids; you can all learn together.

Imagine having a small plot in your backyard and a whole row dedicated to your son or daughter (depending on their age and ability). If you don't have the garden space, consider a community garden. A growing number of communities are implementing gardens; take advantage of it, for the sake of the kids.

Showing them how to prepare the ground, plant, water, weed, and harvest teaches them the basic building blocks of life using nature as your teacher/helper. Lest we forget, nature follows exact laws in every aspect of our lives. So to involve our little ones early in their lives in the process of nature's lessons, reminds them there is a process to success, and that staying dutifully engaged in the effort (planning and work) is to learn all the lessons earlier listed and more.

Teach your kids to work and to learn to love it, for some of the greatest joys of life come from being a finisher.

We've heard all the excuses, most of them coming from parents themselves. They whine and complain how hard it is to keep the kids engaged in work projects. They complain and argue how frustrating it becomes in dividing up assignments between kids and in trying to keep it fair. Often we hear parents say they've run out of work for their kids to do, as they stare at their walls that have not been washed down for months, or the other deep cleaning projects that happen only once or twice a year, sometime never.

We're familiar with all the excuses; we've been tempted with them ourselves. The hard part of parenting says, "Stick with it, stay focused on the final outcome."

When we parents commit ourselves with a determined mind to instill in our kids solid work habits, creativity enters our minds, and we begin to see dozens of work projects for our kids to do. Whether you are in the country or in the city, there is always plenty of work to do; jobs kids are very capable of doing.

When we're determined and see the amazing benefits of our kids learning industriousness and follow through, it makes it much easier to stay engaged as parents. However, when we take our eye off the benefits of industriousness, kid's whining and complaints win out. On the flip side, imagine how exhilarating it can be to learn to get into a routine with the kids, and to keep your parental eyes fixed on the purpose for the work projects.

Again, we all face severe life challenges; our kids certainly will as they grow older. Wouldn't they face those struggles better had they been taught to work through tough assignments as a child? We know they would and logic proves it so.

Excuses and whining, whine and complaint.

Those parents who complain and whine are not seeing the big picture. They forget it's a process and not a single event. Trial and error is part of the learning, and it's also one of the hard parts of parenting. Something we learned to do was organize a *system* and a *work chart*. Once the system is organized on paper, blackboard, or bulletin board, all that remains is filling in the names, your kids' names, and the specific duties. Even then, you should follow a set pattern so no one can argue. After all, what job your son does today or this week, his sibling will do tomorrow or next week. It all rotates. If someone doesn't like it, blame the system. And too, when the system is built and the kids' names are entered into the job slots, all that's left to do is follow the system. *The system becomes the boss.*

But parents, be sure your system allows for enough jobs to keep each child busy enough for an hour or two of work, depending on the day and whether school is out or if it's summer time and balanced according to the children's ages. "Where much is given, much is required," meaning the older the child more is required and expected. Older children, about age ten or so, much more work time can be expected.

As we start them young, we can mold our kids to love to work and to see advantages to it. And best of all, they will not be fearful of work, of sweat, and of working their muscles. Thrilling is the only way to describe your feelings as you begin to see your kids become self-motivated in assigned duties and work projects.

A child who has been given a good moral compass, but who has also learned to endure through a tough project to the end, is more likely to face life challenges without faltering midway through the decision making process, thus allowing him to make better decisions in life.

From this perspective, it's not enough to give our kids duties that simply passes time. Jobs that are easy for our kids to do are not necessarily character building. In other words, find a job or jobs that are difficult for them to do on a regular basis, jobs that often cause them to sweat and feel achy muscles. When they learn to endure faithfully through those tough challenges, and learn to find satisfaction in their efforts, they will learn not to fear life's tough challenges. These types of work projects offer benefits learning to play a musical instrument cannot match. While we

agree with stretching their minds with learning music or other like disciplines, learning to sweat and work physically hard is a life experience like no other for our children.

As parents, we can make a mistake thinking our child is sweating and working hard on the ball field, but unless their being forced to play sports, which we don't recommend, the child is sweating and working at something that is play to him or her. The experience we want them to learn is to do what they don't necessarily want to do but is expected of them, a job that will teach them how to endure through some hard times. Learning these lessons will bless their lives forever.

We do our kids such an amazing favor when we diligently organize and plan for their lessons in life regarding honest labor and industriousness. Few lessons we give them carry with them such remarkable benefits, benefits that carry throughout their whole life.

We think Ann Landers gets credit for this quote:

"It is not what you do for your children, but what you have taught them to do for themselves, that will make them successful human beings."

Industriousness and a "finisher" mentality are gifts that never stop giving, and are necessary ingredients that help wire kids for success in life.

Attitude Matters

The attitude we choose to adopt each day determines our day. As it is in athletics, music, or any other discipline, so it is in life; attitude really does matter when it comes to our daily performance.

Athletics has been a significant part of our family—basketball, baseball, football, track, cross country, and volleyball. As parents, we've seen how participation in sports has helped form our kids in wonderful ways. They've learned how to be good team players, work toward goal achievement, and of course, they've learned social skills through working with coaches and teammates. There's much to learn in individual and team sports; assuming the sport does not dominate their lives and infringe on significant family time, academics as well as other higher ranking goals.

Our kids took their participation in sports quite serious, always striving to improve their skill to be the best they could be. Our job as parents was to help them feel supported and help them keep the sport in proper perspective and to at least try to never allow it to squeeze out more important things. As one who loves sports, it was a fun but challenging job. For me as a parent, balancing something good with many things that were, in my mind, labeled great, required a strategic balance, and I'm not sure I (we) always got the balance right.

One of our children, Dillon, loved basketball and had developed pretty good proficiency for his age (about age fifteen at that time). He tried out for the junior varsity team and made it. As the season developed he found himself on the bench far more than he preferred. He felt he could play as well or better than most of his teammates who were getting more playing time than him. Having been a competitive basketball player in my younger years, I knew when I saw good talent and I saw it in Dillon. I worked hard to gain a clear perspective devoid of partiality. Every father thinks his kid is as good as or better than all the others and should be getting more playing time. But for me, I wanted to see the situation more from the coach's perspective and not one of an eager father.

I counseled Dillon that there was much that could be learned sitting on the bench, such things as patience, perseverance, humility, and placing the good of the team above his own desires. We had many talks and all for the purpose of making sure Dillon's head was on straight—his attitude right.

I watched his performances and noticed he was playing with great hesitancy, which prevented him from playing his best, yet I knew if Dillon were to prepare himself mentally, when the opportunity presented itself, the coach would see how much raw talent he had and would play him more. So I set a personal goal to help Dillon help himself through optimistic thinking, realizing that when Dillon would get on the court with a well-prepared mindset filled with positive action, he would shine for the coach and all to see.

I shared with him the idea of two creations, found in Stephen Covey's bestselling book, *7 Habits of Highly Effective People.* The first creation is in our mind, our imagination, as well as goal-setting, and the second is the actual creation or performance. I invited Dillon to daydream about playing his best. I told him to see in his mind all his shots going in. I invited him to daydream of his very best effort without any mistakes, missed shots, or the like—a perfect game.

I encouraged him to hear the crowd cheering at his great performance on the basketball court and the look of approval from the coach. I encouraged him to see his play as a vital part of the team's overall success, thus allowing him to feel significant as a member of the team. All this was intended to help Dillon mentally look past his bench-warming experience so that when his time would come to perform, he would be at his very best and

not hesitant or fearful he wasn't pleasing the coach or helping the team.

I want to make it clear: Dillon did most of the work. As his father, I simply pointed him in the right direction, showing him how powerful perfect mental rehearsal can be, and how an optimistic mind can be like writing his journal in advance. I explained to him that when well-prepared skill meets opportunity, great performances happen. And that's exactly what happened.

After days and days of father-son discussions about positive thinking and optimism and talk like, "You can do this, Dillon, because you've got the skill. No one's holding you back but you, and that's going to change real quick," the opportunity presented itself. Dillon came to the next official game filled with positive, optimistic thoughts and prepared for the moment he would be called upon by the coach.

The coach finally put Dillon in to play. He played remarkably well, to say the least. He was unstoppable offensively and scored more points in a few minutes of play than he'd scored in all other games combined. He was literally so adrenaline-infused nothing could have prevented a great performance. I recall him telling me, "Dad, the basketball rim looked as large as a hoola-hoop. It was so big."

That game offered more evidence to Dillon that positive thoughts and optimistic action makes a significant difference in performance. And truth be known, that night would be a microcosm of Dillon's life (as well as all the Smith kids). That game was like life proving that our thoughts do matter and that a positive approach to life's events, small or large, can propel us toward our best effort. We can create in our minds rough roads ahead or smooth, gentle roads. Our thoughts, our attitude set the stage or rather create the way we will accept whatever comes our way in life. Tough times can be made not only tolerable but even joyful.

Dillon played well because he replaced his hesitant, fearful play with confidence and assurance. After all, he had played that game in his mind hundreds of times before the real game actually began. His game, in his mind, was simply a preview of what was to come, and he proved that that principle really works when it is done correctly. We all can apply that principle in any aspect of life.

Victor Frankl said it well, "The last of human freedoms—the ability to choose one's attitude in a given set of circumstances." (http://www.brainyquote.com).

I'm reminded of the marvelous author and speaker, Byron Katy, the author of multiple books including my favorite, *Loving What Is*. In this outstanding book, we get a glimpse into Katie's life and mind. From her (yes, Byron Katy is a sweet, beautiful woman) experience, we learn that whatever befalls us, we can successfully navigate through it by changing the way we see challenges and so-called obstacles. She reminds us that we have a choice to see *purpose* and *meaning* in our troubles and struggles, or we can give in to all the horror the circumstance can pour out upon us. It's our choice. She reminds us that attitude does, in fact, make a considerable difference as we make our way through this life filled with challenges but also with much joy.

As Charles Swindoll has said on numerous occasions, "I am convinced that life is 10 percent what happens to me and 90 percent how I react to it. And so it is with you…we are in charge of our attitudes."

I can say for my own life, most, if not all, of what I have considered severe challenges were really a matter of me not seeing through the true, correct lenses of life. No doubt most of us have a tendency to create in our minds greater, more ominous mountains to climb than is real or true. Katy helps the reader come to that truth, thus relieving much heartache and stress.

Our so-called troubles are really opportunities for growth. Life is designed for those kinds of experiences; otherwise most of us would never learn perseverance or endurance. Our lives are supposed to have much joy in them, yet if we continue to look for

troubles and obstacles, troubles and obstacles is generally what we'll get.

This motto, I've found helpful in my life: "The riddle of life is this: It doesn't matter what happens to us in life, it's just the way we take it" (*You Can't Afford the Luxury of a Negative Thought* by Peter McWilliams and John-Roger). I've found solace in this statement. It reminds me that I always have a choice how I will act or react to life's events. And the interesting thing is, when I'm feeling down followed by a remembrance of the above quote, I immediately begin to feel a rush of enthusiasm and confidence that the new, optimistic thought is true and correct. History, my history, has proven to me, that when I take that more optimistic thought and approach to any given circumstance of life, I begin to receive a nudge of encouragement from the unseen world.

The McWilliams quote above reminds us of the responsibility that rests on every human shoulder, that of choice and account-ability. Whatever happens to us in life, we still have a choice of how we will act or perform during and after that event, either positively, optimistically and with a desire to see purpose in the event, or the opposite, negatively and with bitterness or other negative reactions. We always have a choice.

From the same book we read, "Start looking at bad situations in life as raw material for your 'opening monologue.' Ever notice how much humor is based on misfortune? What's the difference between laughing about something and crying about it? Attitude. Which would you rather do?" (Ibid, p. 297)

Even the death of a loved one, as painful as that is, can be seen through a broader view which can help put in proper perspec-tive for us in our time of mourning and thus help us through the trial. Norman Cousins said, "Death is not the greatest loss in life. The greatest loss is what dies inside us while we live" (Norman Cousins's quotes, *Saturday Review*). While in the midst of a trial, like the death of a loved one for instance, we should be mindful of our attitude and perspective of the trial so that we're careful not to allow the trial to cause us to weaken or die within ourselves, as Cousins stated. Attitude and a desire for a clear perspective of the trial can help us keep our feet solidly on the sod of real life and things as they really are and not as we suppose them to be.

If we can make the habit of proper, optimistic thinking, especially in times of severe trials, we can more easily navigate through life successfully. Learning for ourselves and teaching the following principle to our children, that as Earl Nightingale reminded us, "We always move in the direction of our most current, dominant thought," can give us the reminder that we can control how we advance in life and how well we adjust to life's twists and turns, and that it is our "current, most dominant thoughts" that prove it so.

As we choose to make our most current dominant thoughts optimistic, happy, cheerful, and positive, we can be sure we move in a good direction that moment, that day. Let's learn to care for the moment, the day, and then the weeks, months, and years will be joyful.

Nightingale's statement is so profound! I've proven this a true statement, at least to my own satisfaction. The events and experiences which are about to unfold or explode into our lives are most generally tied directly to our most current, dominate thoughts prior to those events. Amazing and very true.

So as parents, we should look for opportunities to teach our children that no matter what happens in life, joy and silver linings can be found and that there is nothing that can occur in our lives that can permanently knock us down and out *without our permission*. We hold the joystick to our happiness, no one else, just ourselves. As we fill our young children with these truths, we begin to see our children taking more personal responsibility, which is exactly what we want them to do and as soon as possible.

Sandi shared this story:

> I recall one of our little children coming home from school
> with a scowl on her face. I asked her, "why the sad face?"

She responded, "My friend makes me so mad. She's so selfish and never shares."

"Well," I said, "your friend makes you mad. Is that really possible?"

"Yes, she makes me mad every day at recess." So I took that opportunity to walk my daughter through the truth regarding happiness and joy and how she always has a choice to either be happy or sad.

"It's up to you," I said.

I could see her mind working on that thought. After a couple of moments, I asked her if she understood what I meant, which opened up a wonderful dialogue between the two of us, on the power of thoughts, choice, and accountability. I shared with her many other examples in her life and mine, where holding tight to our own joy and happiness is truly up to us and not some other outside influence. I walked her through how one can have bad things happen to them and still maintain happy feelings. I even spoke of the death of a loved one and how good things can happen when we first choose to be joyful and happy even (and especially) when such challenging times come—to always strive to see purpose in life's events. When the conversation was over, I could see she had bought into her newfound truth and was willing to put it into action in her own life.

When we teach and show our children the remarkable benefits of owning their own thoughts and of choosing happiness over sadness and optimism over negativism, we insulate them largely from the many thorny impacts of life's experiences. We should *show* them and *tell* them that no matter what happens to them in life, they always have a choice to wear a smile or a frown and that it's our hope as their parents they will choose happiness and a smile.

Our best efforts cannot come when we give away the responsibility of our own thought processes or when we harbor in our minds anger, grudges, and hard feelings toward others, nor can we see our best effort when we play the blame-game. That kind of behavior takes away our options for happiness and joy, placing them on others rather than our own shoulders. Our best effort happens when we place our full and complete happiness and joy with ourselves and not another. Taking responsibility for our own behavior is possibly the greatest evidence of maturity. Maturity of mind and emotions is what we want for our children.

The sooner we can help our children gain that clear perspective of happiness, joy, and contentment, the better. As we all know, life has a habit of giving all of us plenty of chances to practice these principles. And if we want our children to be wired for success, they will need to see through the true lenses of life, which begins with an internal decision to have a happy attitude. We, the parents, can guide them to this joyful result. Just as our son Dillon learned for himself, that inner confidence rises when we choose our thoughts and begin to see in our mind's eye our successes in advance.

We really can write our journals in advance. We script our lives and our actions when we see through our lens of joy, happiness, optimism, confidence, and faith. Knowing this doesn't happen by accident, we should begin the process with each of our children as soon as possible.

The Problem with Communication

Sandi and I like this quote by George Bernard Shaw: "The problem with communication is the allusion that it has occurred." This quote convicts me, reminding me how deficient I am at effective communication.

Failure to clearly communicate has caused at least one world war. It has been the primary cause of many if not most divorces, thus splitting families apart and wounding little children's hearts. All this pain simply because two adults fail to understand and appreciate each other through effective communication.

Often when we communicate with another, particularly our spouse, we make the assumption (as Shaw stated) that communication (understanding) really occurred when, in fact, it did not. And because of poor communication, false assumption ensues which creates frustration and disappointment followed often by betrayal, or at least the appearance of betrayal. All of this between two people who may have had at least some degree of honesty in their effort to communicate but failed to make a true connection. The problem with communication is that we often don't actually communicate, but we think we do.

One little lady (I don't recall her name) was famous for her wise quips. Long after her death, her immediate and extended family still laugh at her witticisms. One statement she regularly spouted to her kids, nephews, and nieces:

You seem to put the wrong emphasis on the wrong syllable.

This was her way of causing them to think and ponder what she was saying, which worked. Decoded she said, "You seem to

put the wrong emphasis on the wrong syllable," meaning say what you mean and mean what you say and don't mix words be straight to the point.

But instead, we often allow ourselves to get so wrapped up in our own ego (self-importance) that our communication is peppered with much sarcasm, put-downs, cryptic messages or ridicule, and other forms of communication that tend to hide what we really mean, what we really feel.

Even the action of rolling our eyes at a comment is clear evidence of disrespect to the other party and reveals our own faltering, weak ego. Any trace of condescension in our voice or actions is likely to prevent real communication. In fact, none of those types of actions listed above are conducive to true communication and relationship building. On the other hand, true communication is almost automatic when we feel accepted and included. We are all capable of improvement in the area of communication.

Years ago, I was privileged to observe a true genius at work. He was a young man in his late twenties and married with a child or two. He was what I call a "boys' man." That means he understood boys and the boys loved him.

He accepted the responsibility in the church he and I attended, to be the leader over a dozen young men. This young leader had a special gift, a gift of acceptance. He seemed to be blind to the many issues that would be a source of irritation to most adults working with teenagers. One of the youth was extremely immature which triggered much sarcasm and other social gestures that typically disrupted meetings. The leader simply overlooked the issues as best he could and treated the boy like all the others, taking special care to befriend the boy. Another boy had very poor hygiene, but this young leader didn't seem to care. He simply invited the boy into his circle of friends and did so with open arms. And last, there was one young boy who had many bad habits, habits that went contrary to our religion. This young leader ignored the habits as though they never existed and treated the

boy like all the others which caused the boy to feel perfectly welcome and included.

Because this leader accepted the boys as they were, they opened their hearts to him, sharing with him their passions, fears, and concerns. This leader was a modern Pied Piper to these boys; they would have followed him anywhere. When he spoke, they respectively listened because he first listened intently to them. He always acted the part of the adult leader, yet he never acted as though he were condescending to a lower level to be with them. They could sense his honesty and they reciprocated the same to him. He and other male leaders would take the boys out on a scout outing, wear the boys out with hiking and other activities. Then in the evening, sit around a cozy campfire with plenty of goodies to munch and just be with the boys. It was often in those settings the boys would really open up and share their true feelings and concerns, as well as listen more intently to their leader's instructions and counsel.

Thankfully, this man was a solid leader with high morals and pure motives to fulfill his responsibility to guide and teach these young men to greater preparation in life. Best of all, were the changes in the lives of the youth. It became obvious to all, the youth were striving to mold their lives after their adult leader. This was a good thing since the leader was such an amazing example in every way. As you can imagine, the parents of these boys loved him.

This youth leader reminds us of how much true communication is transmitted when we adults truly listen. His example teaches us the importance of not judging another and how much kindly interaction can take place with kids when they can see that our intent is only real friendship, real love. All of us can take a lesson from him.

Granted, parents are not called upon to be friends to their kids, but rather, parents, and teachers. Yet all the ingredients found in a trusting friendship can also be found in a healthy par-

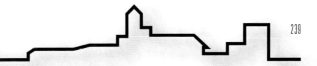

ent/child relationship. We are parents but we hope to also have a friend-like rapport with our kids.

The fundamental issues that create real two-way communication are really quite simple and easy for all to understand. The problem lies in our poor communication *habits*. Habits formed over decades of time, are not easy to break. Habits can be changed, but we should be patient because for most, progress is gradual but well worth the effort.

According to Carmine Gallo of Business Week, four major means are used to communicate with others: body posture, facial expression, voice tone, and words. We know that approximately fifty-five percent of a message is conveyed in body posture and facial expression, thirty-eight percent in voice tone, and a merely seven percent in the words spoken. (Body Language: A Key to Success in the Workplace BusinessWeekBy Carmine Gallo | BusinessWeek – Wed, Feb 14, 2007). From these numbers, we can learn how important our actions are when we communicate with our *children*, our spouse, and particularly our little children and babies. Their vocabulary is so small and understanding so limited; they depend on the expression on our face and the tone in our voice as well as a gentle touch.

Our children will likely model their parents in most ways including communication patterns. Coming to a clear understanding of the components that make up real communication between two people should be of primary importance to married couples and parents. We should ask ourselves what makes meaningful communication, and what barriers prevent effective communication? Let's begin with the barriers.

The most common villain to real communication was spoken of by C. S. Lewis, "Pride is competitive by nature. Pride gets no pleasure out of having something; only out of having more of it than the next man...it is the comparison that makes you proud: the pleasure of being above the rest. Once the element of competition has gone, pride has gone" (*Mere Christianity*, p. 109–10

This is C.S Lewis' quote used earlier in this book but in support of another subject; evidence of the substantial nature of this remarkable quote).

The competitive nature to be right (meaning, the other person must be wrong) is at the root of much of our failure to communicate.

According to Lewis, this is a widespread problem among humans. We might want to examine our own natures and habits to see if we're one of the culprits to that problem in our marriage and with our children. If you have blood flowing through your veins, there's a good chance you are guilty just like the rest of us. We need not feel hopelessly flawed, there is hope and promise for improvement, but like any other significant changes in our lives, it will require effort on our part.

Lewis uncovered the main issue to communication failure: pride, which happens to be the root of most all our inner weaknesses. As long as we think we've got the key to knowledge and that ours is higher and greater than all others, communication between two people breaks down. That attitude of "greater than thou," "smarter than thou" is a cancer to communication. It seeps into our words and actions for the other party to see and feel, and it doesn't taste good to us when we're the one on the receiving end. We feel condescended to, left with a feeling that whatever we add to the conversation is considered unworthy. This places great responsibility upon the heads of those who have acquired truth and/or higher education (Einstein, C.S. Lewis, and Stephen R. Covey for instance) that they teach us in humility and meekness.

Another bad habit many have, is that of engaging our minds in a response while the other party is still voicing his or her thoughts. One need not be prideful or egotistical to practice this flaw. It's simply a bad habit, and it gets in the way to true communication. As skilled as we may be in multitasking, no one is capable of hearing the words and intent of the other person at the same time creating their own response in their own mind. Imagine speaking and listening at the same time. It doesn't work well. Something always falls through the cracks and miscommunication results.

Often the pride Lewis spoke of gets in the way. For instance, for those who feel inferior to the other party they're communicating with (poor self-image), they may compensate by trying too hard. The communicator may feel they have to impress the listening party by replacing their real self with flowery language, not part of their common vocabulary. Their motive is not to truly communicate but rather, to impress another. How refreshing it is when we free ourselves from acting out a part rather than revealing our true self. Our true self is always more interesting.

As one might imagine, there are many reasons why true communication fails to happen. We've mentioned a couple of the most common, but we're confident that by learning how to overcome our pride issues (ego and competition) many or most other communication problems will evaporate. Let's address how we can overcome that key barrier of pride that we may more fully emjoy our relationships.

It's probably safe to say that we all know someone who is a true communicator—the person who is a good listener, patient, respectful in communication, and who seldom uses ridicule, sarcasm, put-downs, or intimidation. How do they do it? How is it they are so secure in their own skin that they put away any ego issues and false pride, are willing and able to share their perspective without any hint of condenscension, are thoroughly interested and respectful of the other person's perspective on any and all subjects? As we interact with them, we sense no competitive spirit; in fact, they seem to be sincerely interested in making us feel comfortable in the social exchange. How do they pull that off day in and day out?

True communication comes from the heart, not the mind. It's all centered in motive. If our motive is one of sincere caring for the other party, it becomes far easier to be patient and desire to clearly understand what they are trying to express. And, if our motive is grounded in genuine love for others, tolerance and patience becomes our habit. Compassionate listening is rare to find and refreshing when we do. The compassionate listener not only listens well but also speaks from the heart with respect for your feelings. He doesn't flower his language to sound impressive, only to express what's really on his mind.

With that level of true caring, respect, and even love for others, our own selfish interests (ego and pride) take a back seat to our desire to satisfy and fulfill the other party. Stephen Covey's "Think First to Understand before Being Understood" (the fifth habit from his best-seller book, 7 *Habits of Highly Effective People*) becomes part and parcel of our very souls, woven into all we do and say.

Replacing our false pride and ego with a sincere interest in the welfare of the other party is the key to improved communication. That kind of internal change is the kind of change that will inevitably impact every aspect of our lives and not just our communication with others. When we can *listen* with sincere interest, we are on the road to true communication.

Again, the problem most of us have is years of practicing poor communication. The answer to our problem is to begin practicing the correct way! Today. We can all begin that practice by implementing one single thing: *listening*. To enhance our practice of listening, we can become better conversationalists by asking more sincere, honest *questions*, then practice listening, listening intently by asking for further clarification from the other party with the intent of full understanding. Ask questions then listen, followed by more appropriate questions in an effort to better understand the initial comments made. As we strive to forget about ourselves and simply focus on what their interest and passion is, wonderful things begin to happen. You will find yourself enjoying the other parties eyes light up with enthusiasm for their subject, and the fact that they've found someone willing to listen to them fully express their thoughts. That doesn't happen often for most people—so rare is true listening—true communication. We will find ourselves really learning from the sender. For some, this can be high drama and for others a new and refreshing experience. With this kind of exercise, both parties win.

As we implement this practice with our spouse, we begin to see them feel validated and supported. We walk away from that experience asking ourselves why we don't do that more often. The answer is that we return so quickly to our own feelings and concerns and forget to place our spouse's interests above our own. True communication with our spouse leads to greater understanding which grows the relationship to one of trust. A trusting relationship with our spouse is a key element in becoming united.

In marriage, we should always be moving in the direction of a *trusting relationship*, where we learn to trust that we are being upheld by our spouse and that we are committed to honor their good name. Each one knows only kindness and respect will be spoken of the other. Imagine the feelings of love and appreciation that each spouse would feel in that kind of relationship. And when we slip up or shift back to our old ways of communication, we quickly apologize and begin anew. This is the model we should be striving for. Learning to truly communicate with loving care is a significant first step toward a lasting relationship.

It's common for our efforts to truly communicate to be sabotaged by the feelings we carry in our mind about ourselves. This is very common with teenagers, but can be found in people at any age. The following poem by Charles C. Finn helps us better understand some of these inner struggles many have; struggles that make true communication all the more difficult.

Please Hear What I'm Not Saying

Don't be fooled by me.
Don't be fooled by the face I wear
for I wear a mask, a thousand masks,
masks that I'm afraid to take off,
and none of them is me.
Pretending is an art that's second nature with me,
but don't be fooled,
for God's sake don't be fooled.
I give you the impression that I'm secure,
that all is sunny and unruffled with me, within as well
as without,
that confidence is my name and coolness my game,
that the water's calm and I'm in command
and that I need no one,
but don't believe me.
My surface may seem smooth but my surface is my mask,
ever-varying and ever-concealing.
Beneath lies no complacence.
Beneath lies confusion, and fear, and aloneness.
But I hide this. I don't want anybody to know it.
I panic at the thought of my weakness exposed.
That's why I frantically create a mask to hide behind,
a nonchalant sophisticated facade,
to help me pretend,
to shield me from the glance that knows.
But such a glance is precisely my salvation, my only hope,
and I know it.
That is, if it's followed by acceptance,
if it's followed by love.
It's the only thing that can liberate me from myself,
from my own self-built prison walls,
from the barriers I so painstakingly erect.
It's the only thing that will assure me
of what I can't assure myself,
that I'm really worth something.
But I don't tell you this. I don't dare to, I'm afraid to.
I'm afraid your glance will not be followed by acceptance,

will not be followed by love.
I'm afraid you'll think less of me,
that you'll laugh, and your laugh would kill me.
I'm afraid that deep-down I'm nothing
and that you will see this and reject me.
So I play my game, my desperate pretending game,
with a facade of assurance without
and a trembling child within.
So begins the glittering but empty parade of masks,
and my life becomes a front.

I idly chatter to you in the suave tones of surface talk.
I tell you everything that's really nothing,
and nothing of what's everything,
of what's crying within me.
So when I'm going through my routine
do not be fooled by what I'm saying.
Please listen carefully and try to hear what I'm not saying,
what I'd like to be able to say,
what for survival I need to say,
but what I can't say.
I don't like hiding.
I don't like playing superficial phony games.
I want to stop playing them.
I want to be genuine and spontaneous and me
but you've got to help me.
You've got to hold out your hand
even when that's the last thing I seem to want.
Only you can wipe away from my eyes
the blank stare of the breathing dead.
Only you can call me into aliveness.
Each time you're kind, and gentle, and encouraging,
each time you try to understand because you really care,
my heart begins to grow wings—
very small wings,
very feeble wings,
but wings!

WIRING KIDS FOR SUCCESS IN LIFE

With your power to touch me into feeling
you can breathe life into me.
I want you to know that.
I want you to know how important you are to me,
how you can be a creator—an honest-to-God creator—
of the person that is me
if you choose to.
You alone can break down the wall behind which I tremble,
you alone can remove my mask,
you alone can release me from my shadow-world of panic,
from my lonely prison,
if you choose to.
Please choose to.
Do not pass me by.
It will not be easy for you.
A long conviction of worthlessness builds strong walls.
The nearer you approach to me
the blinder I may strike back.
It's irrational, but despite what the books say about man
often I am irrational.
I fight against the very thing I cry out for.
But I am told that love is stronger than strong walls
and in this lies my hope.
Please try to beat down those walls
with firm hands but with gentle hands
for a child is very sensitive.
Who am I, you may wonder?
I am someone you know very well.
For I am every man you meet
and I am every woman you meet.

(www.poetrybycharlesfinn.com)

As it applies to our most important relationships, we, as parents, must learn to listen, truly listen, not just with our ears but also with our hearts and our eyes. Our ultimate goal should be to help our spouse and children feel loved, secure, and safe around us, that they may feel perfectly safe in opening up to us their hearts, fears, doubts, and greatest concerns. Only a safe haven can produce such openness.

While serving as a leader in the church I belong to, a sweet middle-aged woman requested to speak with me. During our discussion she said, "I'm always concerned that when I die, my husband will speak ill of me to our children and others. I'm afraid he will emphasize all my faults to them. This is one of my greatest fears."

I tried to calm her fears as best I could. After the interview, I spent much time thinking about how much trust is required between husband and wife and that each one carries the duty to always (in life or death) protect the honor of the other in all they say and do, even if there is evidence they don't deserve it!

Building and nurturing that kind of trusting relationship is a life-long goal we should all strive for. For that kind of relationship to be hatched requires the most honest, sincere and patient communication. It's certainly worth the effort to get there. If we really want to become our best selves, how about we extend that nonjudgmental nature toward all and not just our spouse and children?

This is our new regular assignment—to place our spouse's emotions and needs above our own, which should trigger our memory to ask our spouse a sincere, honest question then listen with all our heart and mind. Ask a question, then listen, question, and then listen. As we apply this selfless practice with our spouse (and our children), we will begin to feel the relationship expand and our own emotional maturity grow. How impactful it could be on their lives if our kids are raised and tutored with that kind of selfless communication.

In our daily struggle of life we often become casual in our communication with our spouse and children. Impatience and ego may get in the way and we feel ourselves falling back into old communication habits. When those times come, we can quickly

get back on track by reminding ourselves who we're talking to: a son or daughter of God. Again, from C. S. Lewis: "There are no ordinary people, there are no mere mortals" *(Mere Christianity)*. This thought can humble us quickly, allowing us to get back on track.

There are also times when crucial issues must be discussed between spouses or children. Emotions and tensions can run high causing civility to slip some. The key is order, and from order, unity is more likely to result. *Unity is our goal* and when we think of unity and the benefits of unity in marriage and family, we're reminded of the saying we heard years ago from an unknown author, but it goes like this: "It is better to be united than to be right." (Of course there are exceptions to this principle. For instance, we wouldn't apply this principle to Marxism or terrorists for the sake of unity).

We endorse this principle of unity. We've learned that peace in our lives will not be present where there is not *unity in the relationship*. This holds true especially in the marriage relationship and child rearing. That doesn't mean that we all agree with each other all the time, but it does mean that we're all civil with each other and we are striving to understand one another. Most important, we're all willing to unite around a common cause even if it was one we initially disagreed with. For the sake of unity, we must put away our demand to appear or be right—our ego and false pride must be put to bed, for the sake of unity.

Failure to unify as parents causes confusion and feelings of anxiety. Both confusion and anxiety in the home are felt by our children, and has a tendency to bring the worst out in them. If for no other reason than to bring calm in the minds and hearts of our children we should work diligently as parents, to bring about the spirit of unity in our marriage and home.

There are times when we agree to disagree, but those times should be rare. Why? Because unselfish people find ways to unite. As we grow in our relationship to that of trusting and caring, our primary interests are first and foremost to please our spouse, giving preference to his or her way above our own. With that higher nobler attitude, we're willing to put aside our idea for the sake of unifying with our spouse. This, as you can imagine, requires maturity and honesty with self and spouse.

When some of the children were still in our home, we implemented a plan to bring about more unity and order during family discussions and other family time. It was the talking stick, which is based on an old American Indian tradition, a tradition some tribes used to create order in communication. It was simply this: whoever was holding the talking stick (it was an actual stick, but it could just as well be any object) had the floor and could speak without interruption until he relinquished the talking stick to someone else, at which time that person had the right to speak without interruption and so on. This created order and order created feelings of unity; true communication most often followed.

Because true communication connects a sender and a receiver, both parties should strive for a true connection. I recall when we had many children in the home including a small baby. I would come home for lunch excited and anxious to share something with Sandi, only to find her fully engaged in the needs of one of our little babies. I would try to get my message out and she would try to listen, but no real connection was made because the needs of the child were dominating her thoughts. In my younger years, I would walk away feeling frustrated. Over time, I matured some and came to realize that she had my interests at heart but at that moment, the child's need had to take precedence.

Both sender and receiver have the responsibility to be sensitive to the other. The best thing I could do was to be patient, recognize her situation, and not lay blame but realize there would be a quiet time later when I could share my excitement, just not now. Some patience was developed and good feelings between us prevailed. Later in the day, often at bedtime, I would share my thoughts when she was able to listen without so much interrup-

tion. For me to expect her attention while she was caring for our baby, put her in an unfair position. She wanted to show respect to me but our baby was requiring immediate attention. I should have been more sensitive to her feelings, something I've tried to improve on over time. For real communication to happen, both sender and receiver need to be sensitive to the needs of the other.

This should remind us also, that communication cannot be forced. If, for instance, the husband is ready to communicate but the wife is not, the time for communication is put on hold until both are willing and able to listen intently.

We can only suppose that most married couples argue from time to time, which often comes as a result of failure to communicate clearly. An argument is the opposite of uniting. Again we state, *the goal should be to unite.* Sandi and I have learned from experience, that an argument is a fight and a fight (war or conflict) is contrary to the Spirit (a good feeling between the two of you, a feeling of peace); therefore, our goal has been to return the Spirit to our relationship as soon as possible, not an easy thing when feelings are bruised. Knowing the workings of the Spirit in that regard, we've strived to *apologize sincerely and quickly.* *Humility* and meekness are key ingredients to ensure sincere and quick apology.

Who apologizes to whom? It doesn't matter. After all, it takes two to tango; therefore, both are at fault. We've worked diligently to not measure who was the greater offender. To do so exposes more pride and runs the risk of a lengthy conflict. In the end, both apologize. Our individual interest should be to apologize sincerely and quickly no matter what our partner does.

Sandi and I learned that we had to find regular time for each other, to clear our heads and share our concerns and thoughts with each other, to get reacquainted so to speak and to have a regular date night. One fellow said as he overheard a young married couple complain they didn't have enough money to go on a weekly date, "If you can't afford a weekly date, try the cost of a divorce." The time married couples take to unite with each other through shared communication is an investment well spent.

So much of our lives is dependent upon honest, sincere communication between husband and wife and parents and children. The sooner we learn to be honest with ourselves, our spouse, and our children in communication, the sooner we build bonds that last and endure. Honest communication is dependent upon letting go of our ego and pride. So the sooner we can see our marriage as one unit comprised of two people, the sooner we unite.

Again we state how helpful these principles can be to our children, and to learn them early in their lives, ideally.

Jumpstarting Your Child's Education

No one doubts that education is essential to our children's overall success in life. The studies are many and broad. They show the advantage children have in life when they receive a solid, foundational education, followed by as much additional education as money and time will permit. But many parents feel their economic standing disqualifies their kids for that kind of educational success.

The truth is, however, we parents hold in our hot little hands the wherewithal to propel our children to far more and far better education than most parents would accept or believe. How? you might ask. The answer is simpler and easier than you might expect.

Much of it lies in this old adage: "Give a man a fish; you feed him for a day. Teach him how to fish; you feed him for a lifetime."

It's as simple and easy as this: *read* to your children often, ideally each day. Could that be any easier? Reading to them each day will, most likely, build within them a love to learn. That is the key: *to help our children learn to love to learn.* When they grow up with it from birth, they never know any different; they feel like they were born to learn—born to read. The sooner we begin reading to our children (even our newborns and infants), the sooner they begin to feel the joy of books and the joy of learning in their lives. As we make it a daily habit with our children, gradually *showing* and *telling* them *why* it's so thrilling to love to learn through books, the sooner they catch the bug for learning. That "bug for learning" is like teaching our children to fish. When they've got the "bug," they become independent learners.

Placing in our children a love for learning will certainly add a spice for life, not found in most non-learners. Any added spice for life is very welcome when the normal challenges of life beat down upon our children. And of course, our parental goal should be to position our children for success. Someone once said, "The enemy of great is good." It's not enough to prepare our kids to be like all the other kids on the block, given the fact that we hold the power to help them become the best they can be.

I recall speaking to a mother of a young son. His problem was he struggled academically. He had a learning disability that slowed him down, something akin to Attention Deficit Hyperactivity Disorder. (ADHD; this was prior to the discovery of ADD or ADHD).

He wanted to learn but was frustrated not knowing how to stay on task. He became discouraged.

The mother, very loving and caring, wanted the best for her son but knowing his continued frustration, she trained him to think a C student was okay. After all, she said, "We've had great men and women excel who were not brilliant academically." She was afraid if she encouraged him to excel like his high achieving friends, it might discourage him even more. She didn't want him to totally give up, just lower his desired bar of achievement.

She certainly meant well, and I know for a fact she adored her son. But in my opinion, she took the wrong direction in forming his educational desires. We believe we should train our kids to shoot for the highest mark, yet to find pleasure in all our progress however small—to always be striving to advance and build the mind to comprehend more and to do better. To run the risk that the child may buy into the idea that he is only average, could set his mental thermostat to C grades. What a damaging mind-set for a child, especially if he is capable of better with some help and training!

Let's assume we have one of our own children with a problem focusing his mind. Should we as parents accept that as a sign or

a fact that our son is consigned to mediocrity educationally? No, we should develop a strategy to rise to higher achievement, notwithstanding the challenge. We have him tested and examined. We find out his present level of academic potential according to the present testing systems. From there, we set a strategy of plans and goals to move him forward and upward to gradual, but sure, progress each month, quarter, and year. Along with that steady progress will result in greater confidence within our son. As we all know, we can't put a value on inner confidence.

We have a tendency to criticize the education system, particularly in America. However, even a subpar school system can do well enough to help prepare our children for their future if—that is *if*, the parents are solidly engaged in their child's education, meaning, by *reading* to them each day and by teaching them to *learn to love to learn*.

When our children were young, Sandi implemented "School Time" with them. This consisted of dedicating an area of the house where the education would take place each school day. We obtained a small table that fit perfectly for young children. Crayons, workbooks, and plenty of paper were always present.

Sandi worked with them on the alphabet—phonics for each letter in the alphabet and the beginning stages of linking words together so they could begin to make some progress. There was singing and play time, all in an attempt to keep them engaged in the learning process. Everything was well structured, most of the time, yet it only lasted about an hour each school day.

The goal was two-fold: first, to give them a head start in learning. And second but most important, to help them *learn to love to learn*. (Have we stated that phrase enough? Hopefully, we've caught the significance of that principle.) A child that is hooked on learning has learned how to fish and will be able to drink from the well of learning all his or her life. But the child who has not learned to love to learn will require some pushing and pulling throughout his school career. It is that child who has not been shown the purpose and joys of learning from his or her parents or teachers.

Hopefully, we can all see the tremendous advantage of beginning very early in the child's life. The sooner they become comfortable being read to, the sooner they become ready and willing participants. Thus, the sooner they become hooked on learning the sooner they become willing participants—wired for learning—self-propelled.

Children come to us as learning machines, ready and eager to sponge up all they can see, hear, feel, and touch. We parents can feed that desire or ignore it and let the flame die out. It begins with opening and reading the Children's books.

How much advantage will our reading to them give? Let us share with you a large study provided by The Organization for Economic Cooperation and Development or OECD. The OECD performs many duties, but one is to conduct exams as part of the Program for International Student Assessment, or PISA, which tests fifteen-year-olds on reading comprehension, math, and science. Parents of five thousand students were interviewed in the 2009 study. A substantial study I'm sure you will agree. What were their findings?

In a nutshell, the following was discovered:

When fifteen-year-olds were read to daily by their parents from their earliest years of education, compare to those who had been read to infrequently or not at all by their parents, the test scores proved dramatically different. The youth who had been read to early by their parents earned test scores twenty-five percent higher, an equivalent of over half a year of private tutoring.

The study indicated that parents reading to their children at home showed greater impact on their achievement than parents participating in PTA, back to school nights, school board meetings, or helping in the classroom.

This study, by the way, showed little to no difference between the parents' socioeconomic background. The poorer families

had as much chance for their kids' achievement as the so-called well-to-do.

Clearly, the most effective action we can take in our children's lives as it pertains to their learning to love to learn is to *read to them* and to do so early and often in their early years, continuing on to at least their first year of primary school. And the advantage of doing so brings what academic reward? Twenty-five-point increase on average equals to adding half a year of school to their learning and hours of private tutoring.

When parents add to the frequent reading to their children, habits and activities that will help them learn respect for parents and others, as well as a good work ethic (how to stick to a job to completion), you have a winning combination of habits sown within that child which will result in a life of joy, happiness, and satisfaction. The child prepared in these ways will certainly be wired for success.

The study goes on to say that when we add to daily reading to the child, frequent discussions that stimulate the child's mind, additional points are added to their child's educational progress. For instance, we can discuss with our children current events in our city, state, country, or the world. We can discuss historical lives like Abraham Lincoln, George Washington, Mahatma Gandhi, and any one of hundreds of great figures of the past. We can discuss what they learned in school that day. Each of these exercises broadens the child's mind and encourages learning and the love for learning.

Do we parents realize the power and influence within our grasp to direct and point our children in the way of learning? All mothers and fathers, no matter what their economic status may be or how unprepared and inadequate they may feel, have within their grasp the tools to advance their children to degrees in learning and education they may have never thought possible. Today, we can make a decision to make a difference in our children's lives through reading. As we read to them daily, we broaden their perspective of life—their own lives.

Imagine sitting at the kitchen table for dinner and sharing an open discussion about great leaders of the present or past. Imagine your child seeing your enthusiasm for those great leaders as you share with them events from their lives and decisions made by them. Enthusiasm truly is transferable.

We parents should take some time to prepare by learning some common facts and stories, easily found in an encyclopedia or on the Internet in our own home or at the nearest library. We can help to educate their desires in the direction we encourage and point toward, and at the same time, we will be whetting their interests in history, reading, and learning.

The teaching/learning experience can be random as well. Parents can take a five or ten minute block of time and fill it with reading to their little ones. When we need a break from the kids to get work done in the home, rather than turn the TV on to an entertaining cartoon, we try giving them children's educational channels. Selected, well-researched channels can be very helpful in priming your children for learning. They will be a support system to you, the parent reading to them.

Have you seen the amazing electronic, educational tools available to parents in our day? Some can be obtained from the Internet, others from the store. For your child's next birthday or Christmas gift, consider an educational toy.

Wiring our kids for success in life is obviously a job best performed in the home by caring, loving parents. Gone are the days where we feel helpless and incapable of giving our children more than we had. Gone are the days that we blame others for blocking our children's path to success. All the power to jumpstart our kids' success in life is within our ability as parents to change. We need only to begin.

For more information regarding the OECD PISA 2009 study, go to www.pisa.oecd.org/.

Shoot for the Heart

When dealing with our children and our spouse, we should always strive to shoot for the heart, particularly when sensitive situations are at play. Let me explain by sharing a story told to me by a mother of several children, including a teenage daughter:

> My husband and I worked hard to teach and prepare our children well to give them a sense of morality and honesty. They all turned out quite well and without much problem, but our one daughter, when she was a teenager, began to show signs of separation between her and the rest of the family including her father and me. She began hanging out with girls and boys who lived by more loose principles and standards than what she was taught. This gave us great feelings of concern.
>
> Her normal habit of dress was modest and attractive, but it slowly began to change to more immodest and sloppy dress, which shocked us. We knew something was wrong when she began speaking disrespectfully to us. She became defensive whenever we tried to offer suggestions. Added to that, she seemed to be embarrassed by our family and family size.
>
> My husband and I spoke often about what we could or should do to try to help her see how she was drifting away from the family and away from the training she had been given in her life. We worried constantly for her welfare, both bodily and spiritually.
>
> One afternoon, I felt particularly overwhelmed with concern over her, so much so that I knelt at my bedside and prayed more fervent and honest than ever before. Gone in my prayer was any flowery language or even any organized plea. My concern for her welfare was so heavy

on my mind that all I could say was, "Father, please touch my daughter's heart. Please, please."

That same afternoon, my daughter arrived home from school as usual, but she wasn't greeted by me in my typical, cheerful way. It turns out my daughter could see a change in me, in my face and disposition. She said, "Mom, what's the matter?"

I didn't answer right away. I felt to choose my words carefully, but also, tears were so close to the surface, I was a little concerned to speak. So she asked me again, "Mom, what's wrong?"

I took that opportunity to share with her the deep concern and fear that she had caused her father and me. I began to weep, so much so it was hard to continue speaking. My daughter came over to me and put her arm around me in an effort to console me. She then began to weep as well, and we both just sat there holding each other.

From that sweet and tender experience where few words were spoken and which was totally unrehearsed, my daughter came to see how much her behavior was affecting her parents and family. Best of all, she came to agree with her parents that she was moving gradually into uncharted territory, at least for her. She could see that if she persisted in that path, the goals she once believed in and cherished would likely not be fulfilled. She changed her friends and her behavior and re-set her goals and aspirations for the direction she came to know, again, that would make her life happier and more fulfilled.

This mother's story reminds us how powerful "shooting for the heart" principle can be. The kind of communication the mother had with her daughter was not the kind that spoke to the mortal, physical mind, but rather, to a different level, a higher level of the mind. Yes, our mind and brain also has a spiritual component to it, too.

We humans are dual beings; we have mortal, physical bodies which clothe the spirit that is within us (Job 32:8). Both body and

spirit make up what we call the soul of man. The human experience is working within the confines of both body and spirit. If we try to ignore one or the other, we will limit our growth and frustrate the nature of our soul (body and spirit), which is for body and spirit to work harmoniously for our individual well-being, to help each of us become the best that we can be. Maybe this is why the philosopher, Pierre Teilhard de Chardin wrote, "You are not a human being in search of a spiritual experience. You are a spiritual being immersed in a human experience" (*The Phenomenon of Man*, 1955). The spirit within a person is what is eternal. When our bodies die, our spirits live on. If we were to see our spirit, we would see ourselves as we appear now, yet without our mortal body. Our personality, our nature and mannerisms come from the real you, the real me—our spirits.

We feed our children's bodies and minds with food, hopefully nutritious foods. But what are we doing to feed their spirits? Because the spirit within our children is their real, true selves, does it not make sense that we strive more diligently to nurture their spirits? We make our greatest and most beneficial impact upon our children when we speak to their spirit—to "shoot for the heart," in every aspect of life.

I recently asked my eldest son, Sam, age forty-two, to share with me some of his most memorable thoughts from his childhood and teenage years being raised in our family. He gave me eight remembrances that impressed him the most, memories that have stayed with him his whole life. One of the key memories he shared was wrapped around an act of discipline his mother imposed on him when he was just a young boy. He said, "I don't recall all the details of the incident, but I clearly remember mother scolding me, raising her voice, and sending me to my room. Very shortly thereafter, she came to my room in tears asking for my forgiveness."

Interesting, don't you think, that after so many years of living, one of the significant memories of our son was that as a young boy, he had done something that irritated his mother, yet she was the one who humbly, tearfully, asked for his forgiveness?

Completely unintentional, Sandi impressed upon our son's heart (his spirit) many things. He learned how sensitive his mother was to his feelings. He felt much more endeared to his mother because he saw her soft, loving center. After that event, he saw his mother from new eyes, clearer eyes, more tender eyes. From that experience, he learned how human his mother was but he also learned in a powerful way, how tender her love for him was.

When we speak to our children's spirit (shoot for the heart), we're more likely to get results, but more importantly, we will be educating their desires. How so, you might ask? As we help our children become more aware of the spirit within them and that their spirits are their true selves, they begin to mature in ways they otherwise couldn't. They begin to see more purpose in life and more significance in their own choices and decisions.

When we communicate with our children, particularly during times of frustration and discipline, do we raise our voice in anger, or would we be better off speaking lovingly to their spirit core? Our experience tells us we will achieve much more with the loving, tender voice.

Have you ever had a dream that really affected your life for good? Have you ever been enlightened with encouragement, new knowledge, or wisdom? Have you ever had flashes of brilliant insights that surprised you? If you've ever experienced any of these, you can know your spirit was spoken to for a special reason by a Higher Power.

Let me share with you a more personal story, an event that happened to my mother. My father had died at his age thirty-eight in an industrial accident, leaving behind his wife (my mother) and four children ranging in age from thirteen to four. We were not a religious people, yet we believed in God and offered a blessing on our food, sometimes. Both my mother and father struggled

with some bad habits which affected our family harshly; none-theless, they were kindly, good people. Dad had been gone for two months, and mother was still mourning his death, along with the struggle to handle a young teenage daughter (who was show-ing signs of teenage rebellion), two hyperactive boys (I was the youngest hyperactive son, age seven) and a four-year-old daugh-ter. Added to my mother's stress was the Christmas season we were entering.

Mother was still crying intermittently each day and wetting her pillow by night. She missed her husband terribly, but she also worried over finances and how to manage her children and their growing problems. One particular morning, she realized she felt different, more optimistic and confident. Then she remem-bered a dream she had. This dream she related to me years after it took place.

"Your father stood at my bedside and called my name, 'Inie [her name was Elma, but Inie was his nickname for her], come with me. I want to show you something.' I, of course, was shocked because I knew he had passed away two months prior. He took me by the hand and walked me to the back door of our little home. He opened the screen door and we stepped onto the back porch. There we stood as he pointed to our back yard and beyond. He said, 'Look, Inie, look out there. Do you see how beautiful it is?' My eyes were changed, I guess, because I was able to see what he was looking at. In place of our back yard, a twelve-foot chain-link fence and a grade school beyond, I saw cascades after cascades of the most beautiful flowers, bushes, and trees I'd ever seen. I saw colors and combinations of colors I'd never seen before. It was just as he said—beautiful, no, gorgeous, more gorgeous than anything I'd ever before seen. He then assured me he was happy and not to worry."

The whole dream thrilled me as she shared it with me, but what thrilled me more was the fact that after the dream, she felt energized, more confident, and able to meet the challenges before

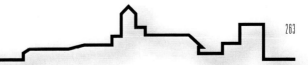

her. She felt a peace she had not felt before, or at least, not recognized. I realized as she shared the dream with me, that my father was speaking to his sweet wife's spirit—to her real self and not her physical, mortal mind, but her spirit, the part of her dual being that would be affected the most, and helped the most through her severe trial of life. My father, after his passing from this mortal life, spoke to my mother's spirit. The experience gave her a gentle, loving boost at a time in her life when she needed it the most.

When we speak to our children or our spouse and direct our words to affect their spirit, we're much more likely to make a meaningful connection, the kind of connection that brings out the best in them, in all of us. The tender, kind and loving feelings we feel when our spirit in engaged, is the kind of feeling that generates permanent change and is likely to bring two people together in ways our mortal bodies cannot accomplish.

Let's not forget the impact "shooting for the heart" has on our newborns and infants. As we hold them tenderly in our arms, we're speaking to their spirit. When we speak softly in their ears, we're speaking to their spirits. When we caress them gently, we're speaking to their spirit. All of these and more speak to their spirit the message they are safe and in good, loving hands.

Speaking from our heart to another's heart is the most direct and clearly understood language there is, as well as the most honest. If we truly desire to wire our kids and our marriage for success, we might want to feed our spirits more, that so we will be more able and ready to speak to and receive from the messages sent to us from Deity.

How do we feed our spirit within? The following are the more common and time-tested methods:

- quiet pondering and meditation
- selfless service to spouse, children, and others
- prayerful reading of the Scriptures
- sincere, honest prayer

Imagine children being nurtured with these principles and the practice of them in their lives, the impact it would have on their lives! No greater gift a parent can give their children than the habit of the principles listed above. Regular application of them solidly wires kids for success in life.

Stand for Principles

I was lying on my couch in the family room on a Friday night (it was actually very early on Saturday, 12:30 a.m.) watching television and waiting for all our teenagers to arrive home, when my son Jesse came through the back door and down to where I was lounging and said "Dad, I think I messed up, and it could get me in some trouble."

"What did you do?" I asked.

Jesse responded, "Me and some of my guy and girlfriends pulled a silly prank on some students at the college. We ran through their dormitory hallways, screaming and yelling like little kids to wake them up."

"Why did you do that?" I asked.

He said sheepishly, "One of the kids dared us, so we did it."

"What followed?" I asked.

He said, "One of the hall supervisors recognized one of the girls in our group, called her dad, and that dad called another father. Now those two fathers are demanding we go back to the dorm and apologize to the supervisor and all the students we woke up."

"Well, then, what's the problem?" I asked.

Jesse said, "I know I messed up, and I know I should apologize, but it won't feel natural to me if I'm forced to apologize. That should be on my terms and not forced, don't you agree, Dad?"

I said, "Jesse, that's completely up to you. What do you think you should do?"

"Well, I'm certainly going to apologize, and I don't want my friends to get in any more trouble with their dads, but the way those dads want to do it really gets under my skin."

"How do you mean?" I asked.

He responded, "Well, like I said, forcing someone to apologize makes no sense to me. That should be the offender's idea and not forced, right?"

"I agree, so what are you going to do about it?" I asked.

Jesse said, "All of them, including the angry dads, are going to be here for me in a matter of minutes, expecting me to get in the car and drive to the dorms and apologize."

"Are you going with them?" I asked.

"No, I don't want to, but for the girl's sake, maybe I should."

"Jesse," I said, "Do what you think is best. I trust you."

Moments later we heard a car pull up at our home followed by a ring at our door. Jesse, still unsure what to do, went out to the car, talked with the two dads for a moment and then got in the car.

As a father, this was high drama for me, so I waited up for Jesse to hear what resulted. When Jesse arrived home about an hour later, he shared with me what happened at the dorms.

He said, "When we arrived at the dorms, I was still very uneasy about being forced to apologize so I chose not to, at least under the conditions of those two fathers. There we stood in front of the supervisor and some of the students with the dads overlooking. The more hotheaded dad said, 'Okay kids, apologize!' in a direct and almost demanding voice. The girls, under the pressure of their dads, felt compelled to apologize, which they did. My guy friends also apologized. Finally, it came to me, and all eyes were on me because I had been the most vocal about the manner in which things were happening. One dad, with eyebrows furled and a gruff voice said 'Jesse, apologize.' Everything went dreadfully quiet until I said, 'Ya know, I just can't do this, not this way,' and began walking toward the car."

"So what happened next?" I asked.

"The hotheaded dad especially, became so angry he began threatening me. He was so upset I thought he might get physical. Dad, I had to work hard not to say any more for fear he would

get out of control, and I would be forced to protect myself. We all walked back to the car, and obviously, that dad was fuming with anger, and the girls were very embarrassed by it all. After they dropped me off at the house, I went directly back to the dorms, found the supervisor, and offered a sincere and honest apology. She knew I meant it and thanked me for it."

I share this because it was a tense but heartfelt experience. I'm glad that when Jesse came home initially, I didn't jump right into judgment (something I'm very capable of doing), and I'm pleased to say I kept my emotions well enough to ask him questions which allowed him to work through his emotions.

Through it all, I noticed how important it is for parents to keep their cool and not get upset and out of control. As a result Jesse and I grew a little closer that early morning. Jesse grew up some, and so did I.

I was reminded how important it is to show trust in our kids and to give them enough space to show and prove their independent decisions. When it was all over, I could see that Jesse felt good about himself and that he had made a real, grownup decision all on his own. He felt good about his decision.

It was, actually, a very innocuous event after all. No one got physically hurt, and no relationships were permanently damaged. I've thought to myself how bad things could have gone had that hotheaded dad gotten physical with my son. The hotheaded dad could have caused Jesse to defend himself even in an act of defense. Jesse, a big, strong kid then and now, could have brought great physical harm to that father and afterwards felt horrible he had beat up his girlfriend's dad, but thankfully, none of that happened. Yet through it all, Jesse was able to hold true to his own conscience and ideals.

The hotheaded dad probably felt embarrassed the following day. His daughter saw him lose control of his emotions in front of all her closest friends, a memory she will carry with her for years. The girls no doubt felt the same as Jesse regarding offending others—a heartfelt apology is much more preferred than a forced one.

How much better it would have been had the dads said to their daughters, "Sweetie, it's obvious you feel bad for what you've done. What can I do to help you?" That approach could open dialogue that could help their daughters make independent and wise decisions.

Again, Sandi and I don't claim to have all the right answers to wiring kids for success in life. We've made more than our share of mistakes, but this much we have *tried* to practice and improve upon regularly, to be patient, thoughtful, even (or especially) in times of stress, and to express confidence and love toward our kids. We can fail in many areas as parents, but if we will truly love our kids, and strive to do our best to offer wise counsel and advice at the right time, as well as learning to stay out of the way when that is the best thing to do, our kids will likely turn out pretty good. Just love them. Sacrifice for their best interests that they will not only hear the phrase, "I love you," but will recognize your efforts in their behalf. That is real, true love.

Assumed Consent and Unity of Purpose

When our family moved from Kansas to our present home, we had nine kids (the tenth would arrive a couple of years later, completing our family of ten kids). I went on the journey to this new state and city in search for a home that would fit our large family.

With a realtor's help, I looked at dozens of homes throughout the valley but with no success. Finally, on the last day of my journey, I found the home I could envision our family living in. What a relief it was. It had some acreage with it, a small barn, and a large fenced pasture. I was thrilled with the opportunity, for I could envision our kids rising to new heights and tackling this challenge and pulling together to make this a successful small farm. I could foresee the kids blossoming through this adventure through hard work and family togetherness.

Sandi lived on a chicken farm as a young child, but I had absolutely no farming background. Added to that, I had some severe back problems, making it very difficult for me to do much lifting or the like. Sandi is the pioneer type; I'm more of a city boy. I was somewhat concerned it could all fall on the shoulders of Sandi. We had always been able to count on the kids' help, yet this was asking far more of them than ever before.

When I called Sandi and told her of the home, barn, and pasture, she became very excited, which heightened my enthusiasm. We already had the kids' work ethic principle in our minds and had been applying it with the kids for years, but raising it to this higher level of commitment would be a new test for our family. I signed the home-purchase contract, and we prepared to be owners of a small farm.

Our children at that time were spread from age nineteen to toddler—stair-stepped. When we broke the news to the kids that our new residence was to be a small farm in Idaho and that we had full intention of buying a milk cow, sheep, chickens, possibly some goats, and a family cat and dog, the young kids caught only the last part—cat and dog, which excited the little children. But the older kids realized what a milk cow and chickens meant: morning and evening chores added to their existing list of household and yard duties, plus the occasional income producing jobs I found for them.

This is how it played out: Sandi and I approached the kids in a family forum setting. I (Garth) was the voice. I said, "Kids, we just bought a small farm with a barn and pasture, which means we're going to get a milk cow and chickens. We will need your daily help each early morning and late afternoon, seven days a week. Along with that, there will occasionally be additional chores to keep the farm up: mending fences, building and cleaning a hen house, hauling and stacking hay, dehorning the cow, weekly irrigation, working in the large garden, and maybe even more chores we're not even aware of yet. We have taught you how to work, and we've seen all of you work hard all your lives for which we are really appreciative. Now it's time to step it up a few notches and expect even more of ourselves, and we know of no other kids as willing and able to do that as you. You're ready for the task, right?"

How did they respond? After a few questions and a couple of concerns were raised and answered, they all showed tremendous willingness. Well, almost all. Our oldest daughter, a senior in high school, could only imagine going to school with cow manure on her shoes and dressed in overalls. We tried to calm her fears. All the other kids were either excited or simply willing to do whatever was asked of them, and Sandi and I were okay with that attitude.

Our oldest daughter, Cari, would later do some farm chores, but never did warm up to the idea of milking Toto. Our old-

est son, Sam, would be off to a church mission shortly after we arrived to our new home. Sandi and I chose not to compel Cari to do farm chores, so we increased her other work assignments, and she was fine with that.

Sam, before he left our home, volunteered to paint the house from the bright yellow, to a soft blue color. It is a big home with an unattached garage made of the same block material, so the task he volunteered for was no easy, quick job. He did remarkable, professional work for which Sandi and I were very appreciative.

Our second son, Jesse, would be the oldest son home after Sam left. It was obvious he took the responsibility with real intent. He became the go-to son for most of the larger, more time consuming chores. Dillon and Joseph were always great support, too, with never a complaint. All the kids pitched in to do their part and without complaint.

The reason we share this family story is to emphasize how we gained a common agreement, a unified decision with our family.

To begin with, Sandi and I were perfectly unified in our decision, and the kids could see and sense that fact.

Next, we paid them a sincere and honest compliment regarding their previous willingness to work for the good of the family. Along with honest and sincere compliments, we were very honest with them about what would be expected of them; we laid it all out for them to see.

And finally, we *assumed* they would unite as a family.

We've wondered how it all would have played out had we approached them defensively as though we needed to drag them into the situation. Thankfully, we assumed their consent without any hint of dishonesty.

The "assumed consent" approach to raising kids is in invaluable approach for parents to learn. If done with honor, it can bring the finest out in kids by helping them make the best and right individual and family decisions.

You see, parents sit on higher ground than their children or at least we should. Given the fact that we've lived more than twice as long as they have, our experience alone should give us greater vision and perspective as to what is best for them and for the family as a unit. Therefore, we have the God-given right and responsibility to lead and guide them into right choices.

Also, like a good athletic coach, kids are willing to follow confident, self-assured leaders, the kind that *assumes* the best in his or her players and also *assumes* they will be willing to follow his or her lead. Yes, even when the task ahead is hard, the coach, whose "been there, done that" himself, *expects* his players to fall in line with obedience and some degree of enthusiasm.

Enthusiasm (which means, God with us), is infectious and transmittable. If we, the parents, apply sincere enthusiasm for a goal or task however hard it may be, the kids are much more likely to follow our lead. They will sense your confidence and excitement, which will likely transfer to them. All of this equals *unity of purpose*.

The kids did pull together, and along the way, they learned an enhanced work ethic and much more. They learned to depend on one another and to find joy in their efforts. It was thrilling as parents to watch them follow through with their assignments and chores.

There are some special benefits to having our children work directly with animals and garden with nature. They learned that harvest comes only after planting, watering, and caring for the plant. We're confident our kids learned from Mother Nature, and were able to use their experiences to nurture patience where patience was called for. They learned you can't rush nature. Also, when harvest time comes, just like all other phases of nature, it allows a window of time to perform that labor, and when that time has ended, it is done, finished, and there's no turning back

the clock. They learned that timetables, specific processes and steps to follow as part of life, must be adhered to if you plan on having a successful harvest—a successful life.

We all learned that unity as a family brings power, power to accomplish great things. We learned that when a *clear purpose* is laid out to the kids, they are far more likely to develop motivation and endurance for the *purpose*, the *goal*. That motivation generally propelled them to completion of the goal. It was exciting for us to observe the kids perform under *deadlines* to fulfill and complete a family goal or project.

When a family cause is determined and a clear purpose laid out, parental and family unity are the results, which create motivation and urge to achieve the goal. The time we spent in laying out clear, concise family goals and projects proved to be some of the most valuable time we spent. On the other hand, the times we entered into a project or goal not fully thought out by us, the parents, generally resulted in lackluster performance. The kids would participate and do their part, but not with the same enthusiasm. A clear goal and a clear purpose for the goal made all the difference.

Unity is power, and it invites a sweet, tender influence (spirit) in the home and in relationships. Unity cannot be forced, and as such, it is imperative that we take the needed time to create a clear and concise purpose in the mind of each participant—each family member. As parents, our efforts to bring about unity in the family becomes not only quality time but also sacred time.

To emphasize our point, let us share with you an experience we had with all the grandkids on an overnighter social. For one of our activities, we placed each grandchild into one of three groups. These groups were assured that everyone would be a winner and would receive a prize. Each group had several kids in it, of all ages. The objective was to complete a list of simple tasks, one by one, until they were all complete. Each group had the same assignment. This was not a competition between each other. They were all simply to finish their tasks as a group, involving each group member young and old. Every child in each group had their own assignments, yet when the older kids finished their assignment first, they were to help the next youngest one and so on until all assignments were completed. Even though they were not competing against each other, the older kids felt the inner stress to be first and certainly, not be last to finish.

The older kids in each group were the facilitators; it was up to them to unite each group member into the common cause. It was their job, if they wanted to excel, to take the needed time to explain to the younger kids how the game worked and what they had to do to complete the process.

It was exciting for us to see each of the older grandkids from each group work patiently, with tenderness and empathy with the younger kids. After the older kids achieved their portion of the contest, they quickly went to the aid of their younger cousins to help them achieve their goal. It turned out to be one of the most synergistic examples we've ever witnessed regarding kindness, gentleness, patience, and unity. There was no browbeating in the least. It was an example of older kids coming down to the level of the younger kids in every way possible for the purpose of achieving a goal.

Likewise, when parents and kids have a common goal and a clear mental picture of what success looks like, and when all feel they are contributing toward the ultimate prize, *unity of purpose* takes hold and the result is a powerful rush of togetherness and achievement.

In order to wire kids for success in life, these kinds of lessons must be learned at some point in their lives. Ideally, these principles will be learned in their childhood when habits are more easily formed and learned.

The Dunce

The first few years in Idaho were financially challenging. While I was trying to build my business, I worked as a substitute teacher to earn extra money.

I was called upon one morning to teach a class of seventh grade kids. When I entered the classroom, I found a young college-aged woman, she was a student teacher from the local college. Legally she was unable to be a substitute as well as a student teacher, so she just observed me as I taught the kids.

The next thing I noticed when I arrived in class, besides a classroom full of noisy kids, was a four-foot-high partition separating the students from another student, a boy, sitting in the back corner. When I asked the student teacher why he was separated from the other kids by a partition and sitting by himself in the back corner, she said, "Oh, that's Joshua, he's kind of like our class dunce."

"Dunce," I asked?

"Yes," she answered, rolling her eyes, "he never participates and hardly says a word, and we've found he feels more comfortable sitting by himself in the back corner."

"Does he learn anything?" I asked.

She said, "His scores are horrible and he seems to have simply given up on learning." I could tell by her response that she didn't agree with his treatment either, but she had little to no influence to change the situation.

I immediately determined to make Joshua my goal, to bring him out of his shell and help him learn something, yet I knew I only had forty-five minutes to accomplish my goal.

As class time proceeded, I simply followed the instructions the regular teacher left for me that morning, yet I was always pondering how I could involve Joshua. Thankfully, it occurred to

me I could try to implement a principle from a marvelous book I had just finished reading entitled, *THE GAME OF WORK,* by Charles A. Coonradt. From the foreward of Coonradt's book we read the major theme of his work: "People will pay for the privilege of working harder than they will work for pay. Think about it—we call it recreation."

Coonradt encourages increased personal and business activity and production by implementing the same tools we use in many of our more popular recreation; a scorecard, a scoreboard, and a time clock. According to Coonradt, it is these that lay the foundation for our most avid enthusiasm for participation sports. He claims that as we institute these three elements into our business, whatever that may be—even teaching or individual goals, we will likely generate more enthusiasm and thus, more activity and production. So I tried it in class with the full intention of bringing Joshua out of his shell. What resulted was far more dramatic than I ever supposed.

It was a math class, so I designed three short math quizzes of ten problems each and told the kids they were being timed with the idea of each student trying to beat their best time with each of the quizzes. My thought was not so much to pit them against each other, but rather, to encourage them to compete against their individual, best time and score. Yet I knew and they knew which student would finish first, second, etc. The minute I announced the rules, Joshua's voice boomed from the back corner, "Yes!" Everyone heard and saw his enthusiasm because he literally jumped out of his chair throwing his arms like he was giving high fives to some imaginary person. I began the competition, and no sooner than I started the time clock, Joshua bore down into the work with determined focus.

Let me cut this short by saying, he not only beat his best score and time with each quiz, but he also was the first one finished in two of the three quizzes. Everyone in the classroom was shocked. The other students were obviously surprised, and the student

teacher was so alarmed she rose to her feet and began clapping for joy. You could see the thrill in his countenance, he was filled with excitement, confidence, and much joy.

After the bell rang, many of the kids in class ran over to Joshua to congratulate him. I waited my turn to talk with him. I encouraged him to make this experience a turning point in his learning experience. He said he would. The student teacher came over to me and said, "I've not seen anything like this from Joshua all year long. What happened to cause him to become so enthused and anxious to participate?"

All I could say in response was to tell her my goal to implement the fundamental principles in Coonradt's book. I reviewed the principles of the book with her and encouraged her to study it from a teacher's perspective.

The experience was so dramatic and obvious, it caused me to think upon it again and again over the years. Sandi and I have on many occasions implemented the principles in our child raising efforts, and in each case have found success.

With lots of time to ponder the whole matter, added to other principles I've learned and practiced in working with my kids, I've been reminded how anxious the spirit in man is to learn and advance, especially young children. We often allow old worn out educational principles to guide us in teaching children including our own. We've got to be willing to see outside the box so to speak.

The first thing we must never forget is the fact, as stated before, that our young children and youth are so willing to learn and be taught. This knowledge can be lost by parents and teachers especially when they receive from the child so many signals they don't want to be taught. We must ignore that message and proceed with the hope that all children, all people, want to learn and to advance in understanding. We cannot allow ourselves to be fooled by the child or person who expresses orally or with body language, "I don't want to learn, you can't teach me."

When one of our kids sends that kind of message, it's time for us parents and teachers to shift gears to another teaching method. And, of course, above all, they've got to know we care and that they can trust us.

Out of the Mouths of Babes

From our own personal history, the following is recorded from the summer of 1975.

Sandi and I, with our four little ones, who were all under the age of four, including a six month old, were in route to Mesa, Arizona, to visit Sandi's family. It was summer and the weather was unusually pleasant in our state. But the closer we got to the Phoenix valley, the weather became extremely hot, which was not a surprise to us.

We were driving in a Volkswagen bus without air-conditioning, so as you can imagine, it was a foolish trip to make through the desert with four little children. Had it not been such a sudden circumstance, we could have planned better. We didn't feel comfortable leaving our four little ones with anyone without more notice.

As we entered the desert floor, (the temperature was well above one hundred degrees), our VW engine began overheating. Thankfully, there was a rest stop nearby, so we pulled in, sat there in the bus, and wondered what to do. We were the only car at the rest stop. (Remember, there was no such thing as cell phones in those days.) I looked at the engine to see if a hose was loose but found nothing. I began to feel the weight of the situation. Not the mechanic type, I began to stress.

For those not familiar with Arizona summer desert heat, it can take the life of an unprepared adult within an hour or so, and a child can die in much shorter time. Sandi and I were feeling the stress. We had some water to drink, but even with that, we could see trouble on the horizon if we couldn't find a solution soon. We were all sweating profusely.

I'm sure the kids, especially Sam, the oldest, could feel the worry in their parents' voices. I said to Sandi, "What do you suggest we do?"

She just shrugged her shoulders. Then came the voice of our eldest son, Sam, who said, "Daddy, should we pray?"

To be honest with you, I felt a little foolish for not thinking of that myself. Sandi and I looked at each other with wonder at the wisdom and childlike faith of our son.

I said, "Sam, good idea. Would you like to pray for us?"

He began to pray the prayer of a four-year-old—pure, honest, and well, perfect. He said something like, "Heavenly Father, please fix our car."

Even before the short prayer was completed, Sandi and I heard the "putt putt putt" sound of an old car, which pulled in right next to ours. It was an older couple driving an old Volkswagen beetle. He literally came over to me and said, "Ya got a problem with your bus? Nobody knows more about VWs than me," he boldly proclaimed.

I said, "Yes, it got hot on me, and I don't know how to fix it."

He opened the back, looked in the engine for a few minutes, and said, "Oh, I see the problem." He spent another couple of minutes working on the problem, then announced, "You're as good as new." From the time he began working on the bus to when we started on the road again was no more than fifteen minutes. We thanked him for his help and off we rode to our destination, all along thrilled at what had just happened through a pure, honest prayer of a child and the quick response of a loving Father."

From our eldest daughter, Cari.

When I was about ten or eleven, I made money babysitting. On one occasion, I was asked to sit my uncle's kids,

my young cousins. They lived in the apartment below my grandmother's house.

All was going well with the kids when I heard a loud noise come from upstairs. I was afraid to go up to check because I immediately remembered my dream of the previous evening. I called upon my bravery, held to the kids' hands, and we all walked up the stairs to Grandma's.

I remember the feelings of fright; after all, every detail of my dream was happening. And then my cousin dropped his bottle, and it fell down the stairs. Oh, I thought this whole event, even the bottle tumbling down the stairs, was all in my dream.

We walked down to pick up the bottle, then back up the stairs we went. I opened the door to my grandma's house that entered into the kitchen. I immediately saw my grandmother lying on the floor. I instinctively knew she was dead. After all, I saw it the night before in my dream, every detail. I took the kids down stairs and called my mom and dad.

When Dad came, he saw me in uncontrollable tears, yet still holding to the kids. After the police and medics left with my dear grandmother's body, I told my mom, "I knew she was dead because I saw it in my dream the night before."

I can only suppose the Lord blessed me with the dream to prepare my young mind for the trauma I was to experience. I loved my grandmother dearly, and I knew she loved me. Also, I'd never seen anyone dead before. I saw the Lord's hand in it, which calmed me then and even now.

That was my first experience with death. Because of the way it all happened, the dream and all, I see death differently, which has been a blessing to me. Because of the feelings of peace that attended the whole experience, I know my Father in heaven knows me and loves me.

From Jesse our third child.

While in his high school years Jesse became kind of a go-to child particularly since his older brother, Sam, had left for college and then a church mission to Argentina. Jesse, as with all our kids, was always very helpful on our small farm, we always were able to depend on them to carry their own weight and more.

With Sandi's and my mind-set to have all the children that would come our way, we now found ourselves in our forties and nearly past child-bearing age. Our baby was Cali, age five.

We were beginning to think our family circle was complete. Sandi and I spoke of it often and felt content we had held up our end of the divine agreement. Understand, we were committed to have more, but given Sandi's age and the fact that it had been five years since our last one, naturally, we thought we were through.

Nonetheless, one beautiful spring day, Sandi informed me she thought she was expecting number ten. We were thrilled and concerned at the same time. We knew the chances of problems at her age were much higher, yet we sensed it was a special event about to happen in our home. Sandi took a pregnancy test, and sure enough, number ten was on the way. We kept this new information to ourselves, telling no one, not family, or siblings or friends.

One morning, Jesse came to the dinner table, where Sandi and I sat just the two of us, discussing matters on our mind, and he said to us both, "I had the most incredible dream last night." We asked him to share it with us.

He said, "I saw our whole family sitting right here at this table, Sam and the whole crew, all nine of us and the two of you.

But there was one more beautiful blond baby, cute as she could be, sitting in a high chair."

Tears began to fill our eyes, for we knew there was no way for Jesse to know what we knew. How could he? We had held this secret tightly to ourselves.

We revealed to Jesse the fact that his mother was expecting a baby, but until then, we had no idea whether it would be healthy or, a boy or girl, but now we knew the answer to those questions.

The following January, Cassandra Star joined our family. She then completed our family circle, and what a joy she has been. Jesse's dream came true exactly as it was given him, every detail.

From Dillon, our fifth child.

When I was about ten years old, my dad found me a paper route, which entailed delivering newspapers each day and collecting the fee each month from my customers. Whenever I went collecting, I carried along my brown Velcro wallet and stuffed all the monies in it. At the end of a collection day, my wallet was full of money, about $75 worth. A successful collection day, I thought. Halfway home, I realized I did not have my brown wallet in my back pocket. After retracing my steps and searching in places I had not even been, I began to panic. I retraced my steps again and again but still to no avail. I was becoming distraught. If I lose the money, I'll have to pay the newspaper myself, a great loss for a young boy of that age. Finally, on the road's edge, I bowed my head resting it on my handle bars and prayed. My prayer was simple and direct. "Father in heaven, please help me find my wallet." Following my prayer, I searched both sides of the street again but again to no avail. I put my head down on the handle bar of my bike again and began to walk home. It was just a few short minutes later that I literally rolled over my wallet full of collection

money in the same location I had searched multiple times before. Someone from the unseen world has always watched over me.

This is a special experience related by our eighth child, Alexis

The summer before my senior year, I had what I like to call a spiritual "aha" moment. I knew who I wanted to be and what type of adult I wanted to be, but my choice of friends was not leading me in that direction.

I watched my parents my whole life read their Scriptures daily, pray, help others, etc., and I knew how the Lord wanted me to act and live my life. I was given much—a good life, and I was taught that "where much was given, much was required." I felt more was being required of me than I had been giving. I knew what I needed to do, but it wasn't until a specific moment that summer did it hit me. I was so consciously desensitized that I had no desire to change until the Lord decided that he needed to take matters into his own hands and struck me with the most overwhelming feeling of guilt and spiritual awareness that I think I've ever had. I said out loud, "What am I doing?" From that day forward, I changed my friends, my activities, and my attitude. That spiritual "aha" moment changed my life.

When I was not quite twenty-one, home from college and living at home, one evening I was lying in bed, pondering. I had just ended a bad breakup with a boyfriend, and had just finished a challenging year at college. I was unable to sleep; my mind was racing when out of the blue, a voice in my mind said that I needed to go on a mission. A mission in the church we belong is an eighteen month commitment for young woman and two years for young men. The voice came to my mind so strongly it almost seemed audible, yet I knew it was not. I replied with an audible "no!" Once again, it replied, "You need to go on a mission."

It wasn't a suggestion or a mere thought. It was a command. The Lord wanted me on a mission for my own good and whatever good I could accomplish. I didn't need a day or a week to think about it, I knew in my heart that's what I needed to do and that's what the Lord was expecting me to do.

The next day, without telling a soul of my experience, not even my parents, I met with my bishop and filled out the paperwork. That mission changed my life, and I like to think it changed others' lives in Switzerland and France, where I was sent to serve for eighteen months. This proved to be an experience that helped solidify the very foundation for the rest of my life.

Cali, Ninth Child

It was the first week of April right before my twenty-first birthday. I had been going to college, but now I felt out of sorts, not knowing what to do with my life. My sister and best friend, Alexis, went on a mission, but I had never had the interest to go.

I was listening to a leader of our church speak on the importance of young men fulfilling their full-time mission responsibilities. He then went on to say that young women at least age twenty-one, if they were not engaged to marry, could serve if they so desired.

The moment I heard that, I began to cry uncontrollably, and in my heart, I knew I was to go on a mission. Still, I didn't like the idea and tried to brush it off. Because of what I felt, I thought I should be prayerful about it, which I did each day for several days. Each time I prayed, I had increased feelings that I should serve in that capacity, yet

I still did not want to go. More than anything, though, I wanted to do the Lord's will rather than my own.

I got to a point where I needed more evidence that it was the right thing to do, so I made an arrangement with the Lord. I asked the Lord that if he could make the answer more clear, I would go. I placed it all on an interview I was about to have with my bishop. I asked the Lord that if I'm to go, the bishop would tell me I should, and if he didn't, I wouldn't go.

While in the interview with the bishop, I told him my plight, and he said, "Cali, you are to go on a mission. That's what the Lord wants for you." I was so stunned at the clarity of his answer, which was exactly what I had requested from the Lord—clarity. I broke into tears for I knew the answer had come. Added to that, while with the bishop, the Spirit was stronger than I'd ever felt before, assuring me the decision was correct.

I sent my papers in and received a call to serve in the Cleveland, Ohio, mission as a guide at the Kirtland, Ohio, restoration site. I loved my mission. It was so good for me, and I was privileged to be of help to many people.

The Lord certainly does answer sincere prayers.

The Averdövian Society

Sandi and I have been most concerned with the kind of changes that have and are occurring in our society and around the world and the way these changes are affecting families. We are, for the most part, a secular society; God has been pushed out, and the impact of it is adversely effecting families and bringing commotion all over the earth.

We believe the family is the basic unit in society, and as the family weakens, all of society becomes weaker, more vulnerable to influences and powers that would not only erode our way of living but would have us change our religious cultures, the religious cultures that have offered our society strength for centuries.

A few years ago, it occurred to us that our children needed all the support we could give them to influence their kids, our grandkids. After all, haven't grandparents always been a factor in offering hope and encouragement to the kids? But now, with society as it is, we need to redouble our efforts. Not to take the lead, but to be another resource to our children in supporting their children.

We are not ones who believe "it takes a village to raise a child." We believe caring, loving, and unselfish parents can do the job quite well on their own. Grandparents and other extended family members, we feel, are not considered part of the "village." The main and extended family unit are the key components to raising kids in any society and in any age.

Let's get this straight. When government leaders say, "It takes a village to raise a child," they are speaking from their progressive (socialistic) mentality and not the view of the sacred, enduring family. They don't see the traditional family unit as most people do. They want to have your child raised and influenced as much by public school teachers as by parents. That formula will never return us to the noble intention of the family unit.

When the family unit breaks down as it has been in the process of doing for the past few decades, and when parents give up their divine parental role it becomes easier to look to government run programs to raise their kids, public school system, etc., as the primary nurturer of the child. We should never fall to that temptation, but rather, we should work more diligently to strengthen parents and to build the family unit. If that day ever comes when the majority of kids are nurtured primarily by a public school system or anyone other than parents, God help us as a nation.

Children have friends that influence them, coaches and teachers who encourage and teach and befriend them, and religious leaders who do likewise. But when parents nurture, love, teach, and support their children and when husband and wife grow together into a oneness relationship, the marriage becomes stronger and the children receive their best, most heartfelt nurturing and training. With that strong, united marriage and family, all other relationships become supplementary at best. Under those conditions, those other relationships could disappear and the child would grow up with moral and spiritual courage and go on to success in life. That child would be well directed in life and have confidence in his or her chosen path. Without a doubt, the family unit—meaning parents (especially), siblings, grandparents, uncles, aunts, cousins—is the single most important organization on this planet. There is no other organization suited to bring forth a strong and moral individual like the family, and for us as a society, to settle for anything less than a loving, strong family, would be more devastating than many are willing to believe. The good old fashion traditional family should be our focus, our goal.

As part of our family unit, we have organized a grandparents' club or society for the purpose of being a supplement and help to our grandkids and their parents. Our society is called The Averdövian Society. The title, Averdövian, is a made-up word

meaning, "to be the best you can be." The purpose of the club is spelled out in our mission statement and society law. We've burned the mission statement and society law into a large wooden wall hanging for all to see. It read as follows:

Mission Statement:

- To help each charter member (all grandkids) reach the measure of their creation (to be the best they can be)
- To be an example for good to charter members and to all we come in contact with from day to day
- And to have fun along the way

Society Law:
Kindness first and always.
I, Grandpa Smith, am the Grand Master Geezer.

The club or society provides additional purpose as we interact with our grandkids. We take each grandchild out for lunch on their birthday as well as other times, try to attend all their athletic events, dance recitals, and other activities as best we can. We also have a Christmas party dedicated just for the grandkids.

Most of all, we provide for each charter member (for those old enough to understand it) a goal book. This is not just any ordinary goal book. It offers reasons *why* they should set goals, it shows them *how* to set goals, and it *teaches* them *how* to include the Lord in their goals. It provides and encourages *action steps* to their goals, so they can, in an organized way, divide their goal into manageable steps, and then tackle those action steps one after another until their goal is fulfilled—satisfied. Remember the old saying "How do you eat an elephant? One bite at a time." The goal book also provides pages for them to track their progress like a *scoreboard*.

At their age twelve, we provide each grandchild their own Averdövian Society Divine Goal Book. We sit down with each one, individually, and teach them what it is and how to use it. We also give them examples of those who have achieved greatness by writing down goals and following them to completion. We encourage them to look into their own futures and to remind them they can choose who they wish to be and what path in life they choose to follow. In other words, we try to motivate and commit them to become an avid goal-setter, in an effort to help them "become the best they can be," or to be an Averdövian-type person. We remind them they were born to succeed, born to greatness. We remind them they have God-given gifts and it is their responsibility to find their gifts and talents and make them great through application and practice, and then we proceed to teach and show them how to find their natural gifts and talents.

This divine goal process encourages them to at least try to look into their futures, to "write their journal in advance" as best they possibly can.

Grandparents don't need a club or society to stay active in supporting and encouraging their grandkids. However, when we grandparents begin to see our role from a broader perspective, that of being a supplement and resource to our children in raising their children in *coaching, encouraging, training*, and *leading* their kids to be the best they can be, some kind of structure can be helpful. It occurred to us that a society club would add some pizzazz to it. This approach can particularly be helpful to those grandparents with more limited financial resources.

We have some friends who are financially well off. They adore their kids and grandkids, and so every opportunity they have (and they create those opportunities as often as possible), they hop on a plane or drive to see them. They regularly find occasion to babysit their grandkids and give their kids valuable time off for a few days or a week. During holidays and birthdays they pay special attention to each grandchild. They nurture their grandkids just as the kids' parents would. They teach them, love them, and encourage them just as their parents do.

Grandparents are already wired through the bonds of love and family to give freely to their kids and grandkids; therefore, the natural feelings of love and appreciation are already intact, with some effort on our part. With that accepting bond already in place, maybe we could help our grandkids learn to read, learn their multiplication tables, and much more.

One grandmother we know noticed her four-year-old grandson had an interest in trains. She immediately went out and purchased a Thomas the Train set. He treasures it, plays with it every day, and has become a sort of specialist of trains. If your pocket book is leaner, consider used trains—less expensive sets.

One set of grandparents we know found that a granddaughter was struggling in grade school and that she had an attention deficit problem (ADHD). She struggled to focus her mind, thus making learning harder to achieve. They coordinated with the parents and helped set in place a program through the summer months to help her gain confidence through better learning skills.

Another way grandparents can be of great service to their kids and grandkids is to be a resource for parenting ideas and helps in parenting. They can provide for their kids ideas, books, articles, forums, lectures, and a host of other helpful tools to support, educate, and encourage as they strive to become better parents themselves.

Wiring kids for success in life is primarily the parent's job. Grandparents and other extended family, however, can be another set of hands and hearts that parents can trust, to help mold and nurture as a supplement to their parents. When grandparents coordinate with parents to find what resources and support would be most helpful, a *strategy* and *plan* can be established. From that strategy will flow *purpose* and *adrenalin* to the grandparents to fulfill a common goal. The sky's the limit to what can be done to bless our grandkids lives, and when we bless theirs we bless our own kids as well.

Time passes too quickly to let our grandparent influence go unused. Any grandparent can love their grandkids, but a wise grandparent will help stretch them, inspire them, and encourage them to become better in whatever their dreams and aspirations are to help wire them for success in life.

Life:
The Importance of a Why

Husband, wife, and family traumas appear to be on the rise throughout America and the world. That's not surprising given the fact that nearly half of all marriages breakup, and with the family divided, children internalize the pain which most often negatively affects their lives for many years to come, sometimes a lifetime. It's common for parents to become so heavy laden in their own struggles they forget that their little children have a tendency to blame themselves for their parents' mistakes that results in divorce or other trauma, but it's often the case.

As we know, little children do not have the wherewithal or vocabulary to express their inward pains, so they suffer within. Sooner or later those pent-up pains and anguish show themselves in behavior they otherwise would not have acted out. What a shame. They often find themselves quick to anger and with feelings of self-doubt; such internal agonies are a daily occurrence for most who suffer from such losses.

Divorce is probably the biggest culprit, yet there are dozens or hundreds of life events that can influence a child in the wrong way causing a skewed view of life. What can we parents do to help our little ones take the hard knocks of life without blaming themselves and weakening their chances for success in life?

Prevention is the obvious answer, and whatever we have control over to protect our family and children we should strive to do. Divorces happen, but for the kids' sake we should do all in our power to prevent it. Unfortunately, a child's emotional state can cause them to see their life different than what is real—what is true. Yet we parents must—we must—do everything possible to prevent such a tragedy from happening. But how?

This chapter is about wiring our kids against any and all the hard times of life, that when they do occur, and they often do, they survive, and not only survive, but learn to gain strength through life's struggles. After all, overcoming life's challenges is a key purpose of life. So then, how do we prepare our kids—strengthen them—so tough times don't prevent them from becoming all they are capable of becoming? Much academic research and many books have been devoted to answers to this question. Let us give you our simple answers.

We have observed over the years, some actions parents can take to largely inoculate their little ones from feeling the most severe brunt of family trauma. The following are a few of our suggestions.

First, let us address the matter of little children, the ones who are incapable of expressing their fears and doubts but who are old enough to know trauma has hit the family. When a painful event occurs, causing deep hurt to all the family, we must realize the child's needs with careful, heartfelt, and continuous attention. Granted, the parent(s) may be suffering too, but as we've got to train our minds to realize the unseen and unheard cries of our little ones. By addressing their emotional needs first we may well be healing ourselves.

When such losses happen in the lives of our little ones, we should hold them close multiple times daily, search for those opportunities. Give them reason to *see* and *feel* hope and *security*. This is done through words of comfort we parents and siblings speak and soft and gentle touches we give them, as well as the feelings we send through the expressions on our face. After a family trauma, we've got to get a grip on ourselves for the kids' sake as quickly as possible. Let's never forget that our little ones (those old enough to sense a trauma) hurt as much as we do but are incapable of offering expressions for help and consolation. Therefore, as best we can under the circumstances, our attention

should be to our little ones emotional welfare and making the assumption they are hurting as severely as we are, possibly worse.

Next, to those younger children as well as our older children, when trauma hits the family, discovering a satisfactory "why" can offer tremendous solace. As stated in our chapter on goals, a solid "why" can satisfy almost any "what." There are events that occur where we find it hard to find a "why," a reason for the loss. This is where religious faith becomes a strength.

In the chapter "Wired for Success: How To," we shared with you a severe trauma that happened in my family at my tender age of seven. The death of my thirty-eight-year-old father. This was not the first trauma for us young Smith children as dad was an alcoholic, which brought all the typical problems with that kind of struggle.

My mother was quite overwhelmed with his passing and the caring of her four children ages thirteen, eight, seven, and three, with the family income almost totally shut off. All but our baby sister was in pained shock, and we all showed our shock in different ways. My eldest sister became angry and lashed out at life, so to speak, by hanging out with friends more than family—friends, I might add, who were not a healthy influence on her. His passing was the likely cause of her low self-image, which likely gave her justification in her mind in the many poor decisions she made, along with the painful consequences of those decisions.

My brother, fifteen months my senior, knew of Dad's death even before it was announced—a premonition, I guess. He suffered the worst in my opinion. He and Dad were best of friends. He turned inward, closing up like a clam for several months; he never did fully heal from his pain and carried the regrets with him to an early death at age sixty-two. His inward pain was never addressed, aiding in the breakup of three marriages and the effects of those divorces on his four children and, for the most part, a lonely and pain-filled life.

I, on the other hand, suffered in a different way. I blamed God. Yes, a seven-year-old blaming God may seem somewhat strange, but that was how it was. I wasn't angry with God. I simply concluded he must not be such a good guy if he would allow this curse to come to our family. So you see, in my little seven-year-old mind, I was trying to make sense of all this, and I did it by concluding a falsehood, but that was the best I could do at that time.

For me to blame God meant I must have believed in him. So yes, I did believe he existed, but I knew nothing of him only that people prayed to him, including our family at meal times.

Kids take trauma harder than parents do, I'm convinced of that, and for that reason the bulk of our attention should be to them and their needs when trauma hits. So guiding our little ones through the maze of pain by giving them a solid "why" (the reason for the trauma, or at least a clear path to heal and become stronger rather than weaker) to the "what" (the "what" is the trauma, usually the loss of a loved one, divorce, or a range of other so-called tragedies) is the wisest thing we can do as parents. In my case, thanks to an astute and thoughtful mother, I came out of the trauma stronger rather than weaker.

Thanks to my mother's foresight, I was able to place my dad's death in a nice little compartment in my mind, a compartment that was okay for me. It allowed me to move on without blaming God. Did I still struggle? Yes, mostly in the area of self-image and self-worth and all the entanglements that go with them.

The "why" for me was because God said so, my dad was supposed to die, and that was good enough for my untrained seven-year-old mind. With my mother's help, I was able to conclude that God was nice and loving, and since my mother addressed him "Father in heaven," I also concluded he must be my father too. That thought alone did more to give me peace of mind than anything else she could have said or done. The ideas that he was my Father would prove to be a key connecting dot later in my life.

She gave me a truth that expelled a falsehood, which soothed my mind and heart in many ways.

The interesting thing to me is that my mother was not a student of religion, not in the least, nor was she an active member of the church our family belonged to. Yet she shared with me a fundamental belief in God. She couldn't explain anything about him—his character, nature, or powers, but she simply knew he existed and that he was our father. The little bit she knew, she gave to me, and it made all the difference.

Believe it or not but I'm certain it's true, we are all wired to believe in God. All we must do is give that wiring a little oxygen so to speak. We need to apply ourselves to that prewired condition and then be sensitive to your feelings. As we all know, young children, even seven-year-olds, are very believing, very trusting, especially when we feed the gift with encouragement as my mother did for me.

It would be many years for me to apply myself to that belief, but when I added to the knowledge my mother introduced to me, my life changed for the good and would never be the same again.

Because troubling events come to all of us and because the rain falls on both the good and not so good in the selfsame way, we should prepare ourselves that we can guide our children through the trouble, that we might wire them for success in life by turning trauma into blessings.

Life truly is a journey. Let's help our children see a meaningful "why" to events, thus giving them hope and purpose.

Traditions Build Family Memories

From our daughter, Cali, we received this Christmas memory:

Every child is excited for Christmas. At our house Christmas morning, waiting was the hard part. We always had to wait until Toto (the family Jersey milk cow) was milked and all other animals fed and watered. It was the worst when Joe had to milk Christmas morning because he would go slowly just to irritate us three younger sisters. Finally, after Toto was milked and the other animals fed and watered, milk strained and put in the refrigerator, we would all jump in Mom and Dad's bed. We would all kneel around the bed while holding hands and offer a morning family prayer. And then, Mom would line us up youngest to oldest, open the bedroom door, and allow us to run into the living room to open our gifts.

Mom would have all the Christmas stockings out on different sections of the living room furniture. After the excitement of the small gifts in our Christmas stockings, we opened our gifts, but not just randomly; Mom and Dad had a list and an order to follow. You see, all our gifts were numbered under the tree rather than named. This way nosy kids would never know which gift was theirs, very smart.

One of the kids was assigned to read the numbers and who they belonged to, one by one, slowly, allowing each child to open his or her gift before the next one was opened. After one gift was opened and everyone joined in his or her excitement, we would go to the next gift, and so on until all the gifts were opened.

One year, Mom accidentally lost her gift list, so when we opened the numbered gifts, she didn't know who the gift belonged to. She tried to go by memory but that didn't work very well. After a present was opened by someone, she would say, "Oh, that gift actually goes to —— Sorry." It was hilarious.

This chapter is about traditions and how personal and family traditions can create happy memories. Christmas time at our home reflects many of our traditions.

Our Christmas morning would begin exactly like any other morning, caring for the animals. At about 5:30 a.m., two of the kids would milk Toto and feed and water all our other animals— sheep, chickens, cat, and dog. This didn't have to take too much time, depending on the milkers.

We had the daily and evening tradition of family and personal prayer. For us, it was (and still is) a wonderful experience to kneel together with the kids (and now grandkids included when they are present). We would kneel in a circle, all holding hands.

Sandi has a Christmas hobby that has now become a family Christmas tradition—to collect and display Christmas nativity scenes, all different sizes, shapes, and looks but all addressing the same theme. But of all the traditions we as parents tried to live by each Christmas, it was to have everyone together, feel each other's love and support, and most of all, feel the love of our Savior.

One Christmas after we had just moved from Kansas to our new home in Idaho, family income was very lean. So for Christmas we chose not to purchase any gifts, but rather we chose to give of ourselves to each and every family member. It turned out to be our most memorable Christmas of all. Each child was invited to give a gift of self to each sibling, but the gift given had to be a valued possession they themselves owned, made, or a service.

One child, Dillon, had a favorite ball cap. He knew his younger brother, Joseph, loved that cap and wanted one just like it, so he gave that cap to him. That was touching because we all knew

how much Dillon liked his favorite ball cap. Tears were close to the surface already, but then Jesse (the oldest son home at the time) gave his favorite ball cap to Dillon. Dillon, who esteemed his older brother, Jesse, with great love and always tried to model himself after him, was overwhelmed with the gift from his mentor brother. We all just sat there and cried tears of love and joy. The feelings of sacrifice were evident. We were reminded how even small acts of service and sacrifice could mean so much to both giver and receiver.

Tender feelings continued as Lyric gave to her older brother, Jesse, a pair of volleyball shorts. It happened like this: Jesse had been creating some frustration, in weeks past, by using (without permission) his younger sisters long, baggy, athletic shorts for his high school basketball practices. So, for Lyric's special gift, she gave Jesse her shorts. This was a sacrifice for Lyric because she really liked them. But she knew how much Jesse loved the feel of those baggy and long cotton shorts. We were all emotionally touched by this.

One of our daughters, Lexi, age six at the time (and one of our best milkers) took a shoebox and decorated it with Christmas festive colors. On small slips of paper she wrote different projects or family chores she would volunteer to do for each family member. Christmas morning, she asked each family member to reach in the box and pull out a slip of paper with the promise of doing that project or chore for them. Some of the promises included taking their turn to milk, do their daily washing of dishes, cleaning their room, etc.

Each child in their order gave of themselves to every family member that memorable Christmas morning. With each selfless gift, tears flowed, for we all knew how much sacrifice each child had given for the sake of each family member. It was a spirit-filled Christmas morning, never to be forgotten.

Now that all the kids are married with children of their own, we still make Christmas and Thanksgiving a time to get together. For

Christmas, we all meet together at one of our homes where Sandi and all the daughters and daughters-in-law create a scrumptious meal. We all sing Christmas songs. And some brave souls performed a musical number for our entertainment. Afterwards we pull out our Christmas candles, one for each person. This is like a special ceremony for each of us. Sandi or I usually begin by lighting our candle then choosing a member of the family to make mention of him or her. After that person is celebrated, Sandi or I lights his or her candle. He or she then chooses someone they would like to celebrate by saying why he or she makes her happy or why she impresses her, then lights her candle and so on until all candles are lit. That experience always seems to end in tears shed by all. Kindnesses and tender thoughts have been shared and all have been recognized. It has been a beautiful way to bring the family together in feelings of love and appreciation.

The holiday season is a wonderful time because it encourages so many traditions. But of course, traditions are always appropriate and good for any and all times of the year. We've noticed, however, that traditions, to be memorable, will invite *unity* and *togetherness* within the family. You need not have a large family like ours. It can be a mother and daughter, a father and son, a grandparent and grandchild, or simply you yourself. If your tradition brings peace and love to the heart, it is a tradition worth continuing.

One set of parents and grandparents we know have the wonderful tradition to carve time out of their schedules and budget, to leave their comfy home and travel to wherever their married children are (and they have six married children) where they volunteer several days of child care while the busy and heavy-laden parents go on a much-needed vacation without the kids, knowing that their little ones will be well cared for by loving grandparents, maybe even spoiled before they return.

This kind of tradition builds love in every direction. But of course not all parents can sacrifice in that way. There are some

creative things all can afford to do that will invite a wonderful feeling between you and the receiver. Maybe your tradition will not involve children or grandchildren, for maybe you have neither. Your traditions will be appreciated and enjoyed as you apply your wonderful talents and gifts to help another.

Dictionary.com gives us this definition of tradition: "a continuing pattern of culture beliefs or practices."

Traditions, at their best, will *strengthen* and *encourage* you and will likely add meaning and purpose to your life. They will be the kind of thing that will most likely be a pleasure for you to do and will be an honor for your posterity to continue well after you've passed. Many traditions will not only make your life better but will also enhance the lives of others. Meaningful traditions will also foster pleasant memories.

Besides Christmas and Thanksgiving, we've tried to form other traditions to bring the family together or to simply create memories. Another tradition Sandi had in our home when most or all the kids were still at home did not connect to any particular holiday but would occur each and every regular school day. When the kids began arriving home from school, Sandi would have a fun treat for them, usually homemade cookies, homemade bread with homemade butter and jam or something of the like. They were given the treat while they would sit around the kitchen table talking about their day. After the treat, they were each handed a 3 × 5 card with their afternoon chore list on it. The understanding was after their school home work was completed, they were not to do anything else (play with friends, call friends on the phone, television) until the work was completed in full. Homework first, followed by chores. The little treat beforehand seemed to take the edge off the tasks that followed.

Memorial Day is an American holiday where families remember and pay respects for those who died while in the service of their country. It has since been extended to honor all family members who have passed away.

When we moved to Idaho, we didn't have any family grave to decorate. So we decided to adopt a grave. We went to one of our city cemeteries and chose a little grave site that appeared to be forgotten—the headstone old and chipped and with writing on the headstone almost illegible. You could hardly determine whose grave it was, but we finally found the name: Allen Ray Stone. Allen Ray Stone has become our family member we honor each Memorial Day. It gives us another reason to get together. Afterward, we all meet at our favorite restaurant for lunch.

Family Home Evening is a family tradition we've held each Monday evening ever since we were first married. This tradition is highly encouraged by our church. The purpose is to get all family members together without interruptions, for one evening, generally Monday. For that evening, we enjoy each other's company and have a short lesson (whatever the parents feel is appropriate at the time), sing a few songs, kneel in family prayer all holding hands in a circle, then end with a fun dessert. With little children the lesson lasts only a few minutes. There is always music and dessert. For the music, each of the kids, in order, would play they're latest piece they learned from their piano teacher. Each child would have a moment to add any thoughts on his or her mind. Sandi would pull out the family calendar and go over every family members upcoming week, we would then coordinate activities as best as possible with the hope that no event would fall through the cracks.

The little kids loved Family Home Evening (FHE). The teen-agers became slightly bored, but that was much of the challenge, to create meaningful and helpful Family Home Evenings that would meet the needs of all family members, not an easy task but very much worth the effort. It required some creativity, some-thing I was not so good at.

We've tried to raise our kids to be patriotic and to love our country and what it stands for. We've tried to instill in them a deep respect for our Founding Fathers. In this light, each Fourth

of July, we have encouraged family togetherness in honor of our country and those who sacrificed so much to bring it forth.

Birthdays have provided another reason for us all to get together. On one of our kid's birthdays, they were privileged to choose the family dinner, even down to the dessert. Typical parties were held with all the fun that it brought for young kids. We still do this, but now we celebrate once per month for all whose birthday is in that respective month. The whole Smith clan gathers under one roof where we sing, pray, share gifts, and just visit while all the grandkids run in and out of the house playing with their cousins.

These are just a few of our family traditions. What traditions have you established in your life or within your family? Is there another tradition you would like to begin or an old one you would like to begin anew? If the tradition *unites* you with others, it's worth the effort to begin or maintain. Does your tradition draw you closer to another? If so, it too is worth the time and effort you put forth to keep it alive.

As parents, we want to do all we can to help build meaningful memories for our children. When we tie unity to the purpose of any tradition we have, we begin to see how helpful family traditions can become as we strive to wire our kids for success in life.

Renewing the Mind

I was not wired for success as a child, and as a result I've had significant challenges in my life I've struggled with and tried to overcome. I don't blame my parents for my struggles, after all, they did the best they knew how. As I've stated in an earlier chapter, without the inspired help and direction of my mother at a crucial time in my childhood, I may have never found my way.

The purpose of this chapter is to share with you a discovery I've found that has been a boon to me particularly in times of discouragement and frustration.

As a result of my struggles and challenges earlier in my life, particularly, I've had to find ways and means to get back on track and to move forward in the face of discouragement, fear, and frustration for my sake and for the family. Over the years, these times have been frequent, to say the least. And when they do occur, it's as though my mind shuts down; and in my mind, the future looks bleak, and then fear follows.

Over time, I've noticed a special but basic fundamental secret that has been like a key, a key to unlock the door of the human mind and to create an open mind, free from doubt and fear, which has allowed me to get back on track to progress and right-mindedness.

This is what I've done to get back on track. I find a task or a job that needs to be done, particularly one I've procrastinated and put off, and get off my duff that instant and strive to complete the task with as much enthusiasm as possible.

Yup, that's it! This is the simple little secret many people do not know: *activity* and getting up and *doing* is, without question, a key that unlocks the mind to progress. It allows the human mind to break through the blockade of mental garbage and fear thus allowing us to see with clearer minds and with feelings of hope and action. It becomes a hope builder. For many who are filled with much fear and doubt, this becomes a significant leap of faith.

Why is it an important secret to learn? Because thousands or millions of us though wired for success, have a tendency as a result of fear and doubt to rewire our thoughts for failure. These parental mental battles go on amidst our duty and responsibility to prepare our little ones for life. And more importantly, we don't want to pass on to them our failures, so we must learn to either eliminate or make short order of those times of mental disability for the kids' sake. We want our kids to see a face of success and hope, not a face of doubt and fear.

Don't get me wrong, our kids will eventually see all or most of our weaknesses, and they will even see in our eyes and on our faces the look of fear and doubt. But we parents must strive to put on our face the look of hope and optimism, as often as possible.

So in a nutshell, the key that opens the door to a clearer mind and feelings of hope is to force ourselves off the bed of discouragement, doubt, and fear and find a task and get after it with as much enthusiasm as we can muster up under the circumstances. Honestly, I assure you, this simple little step will begin to retread the mind.

There is another point I'd like to share: prayer. My prayer goes something like this: "Father, I'm in a pickle. I'm stuck and can't seem to get unstuck by myself. Please give me the energy and strength to begin some activity that I might help myself."

Prayer plus a push to activity regenerates the mind and the resolve, allowing us to go to the next step upward and onward. There is absolutely no reason for any of us to stay stuck. Between our God and our God-given minds, we've been given the tools to overcome any and all obstacles that lie before us.

Each day, as we strive to wire our kids for success and to give them a better start than what we had, we must learn these simple little keys to keep us on task for our kids' sake, our marriage's

sake, and our own sakes. We were born for success and our kids likewise. We can do this.

This seems a good place to share with you that our remarkable ten kids were raised with the language of hope, faith, personal effort, and goals, and all this came from a father who struggled more than I dare share with you, but it was very severe. Granted, you might think the kids did well because of their mother. You would be right. Sandi's primary role was to *nurture* the little ones with tender loving care and *show* and *tell* all the kids how to be industrious and stay on task daily.

When we moved from Kansas to Idaho, we moved to an area totally unfamiliar to us. I started a business from scratch, working both day and night. Most of the stress from child-raising was on Sandi. The pressure I felt was to provide financially, something I've never been very skilled at doing. Don't get me wrong, we always had plenty of food and clothing—enough and to spare. We always had excellent credit, yet with just a few exceptions, we were never financially wealthy nor even on the fringes of wealth. For the first few years in Idaho, times were tough for us. I can say without hesitation, that I was not gifted with the vision and understanding of business, but we were wealthy in different ways.

Sandi, on the other hand, was wired for many things, one of which was to be a modern-day pioneer. She was and is very sweet, sensitive, and feminine, yet she had the determination and inner resolve to do the task before her and without complaint and to do the tasks now, no procrastination. She could have survived well in any era under any challenging circumstances. This made her well equipped to give birth to and nurture ten kids.

My primary role in the kids' development was that of the teacher and motivator. I was the one with the duty of training and developing them early in their lives, trusting that early development would bring great and noble fruit later in their lives. Sandi and I worked well together; she was strongest in the area of my weaknesses, and I was strongest in the area of her weaknesses.

I share this with you because I want you to sense how ordinary we were and are, how unprepared we were to raise a house full of kids and give them the good start and the tools to become achievers in their lives in whatever they chose to do.

It seems clear to us that anyone can follow the traditional basic, fundamental parenting guidelines and find success in raising kids. You don't have to be superhuman or extra gifted. You simply need a solid resolve to learn and follow time-tested systems of child raising, systems that have been known to us always, yet we've allowed liberal and over-tolerant educators to rewrite the guidebooks on how to raise amazing children. So we say, stay with the old traditions, the traditions that have never failed us. And we encourage you young parents to largely ignore most of the more modern ideas of how to nurture, discipline and love your kids.

Large Family Blessings and Blues

Thoughts from Sam, our Eldest

I don't remember the time I wasn't expected to work, in the house or the yard or a shoppers guide or newspaper route. Later on, it was cleaning buildings, and then for me, it was a commercial painter. Work wasn't so much of a chore for that's all I knew. It just came with the territory.

I remember as a young boy, probably about age eight or ten, my friends and I stole a box of chocolates from a girl in our Sunday school class. We laughed about it and thought it so funny. But when wind of it got to Mom and Dad, all the silliness ended, and it turned into serious business. Dad spoke to me about the seriousness of stealing and treating others with respect. He told me I had offended him and Mom and especially the Lord. And then Mom and Dad asked me to apologize, which seemed like a good idea since I then had a new perspective of what I'd done wrong. So I went to the phone to call her, but Mom told me I had to do it in person. I also had to take money out of my hard-earned money to pay her back. Mom and Dad didn't care much that other kids were in on the heist too; their only concern was that their boy learns from the situation. Going through so much humiliation simply because of a box of chocolates made me realize a life of crime was not for me. I learned my lesson.

I think I was about age seven when I started my paper route. My route was on the other side of town, and the papers needed to be rolled and prepared by about 5:30

a.m. each morning, rain or shine, but snow was the biggest obstacle. For Christmas, I received a nice bike light to attach to my bike. Riding in the dark at that early hour and at my age seven, getting that light caused me to feel like I'd found the Mother Lode. I'm sure Mom and Dad worried over me at that young age out in the dark, but I trusted them, and in the end, it all worked out. Having learned how to work and be responsible at such an early age has made life much easier for me as I've compared myself to others who never received such early training.

We Smith kids laugh at the tradition in our home and that one certain gift we all received on our twelfth birthday was a clothes basket. From that age forward, washing our own clothes was our own responsibility. If we ran out of clean underwear, we had no one else to blame but ourselves. We all learned to carry it all in stride.

In our household, college expenses were our own responsibility. We were all taught to get as much education as possible, but we were also reminded the expense would be on us. We were encouraged to earn scholarships as best we could. As I recall, the only Smith kids to earn any meaningful scholarships were two of my brainy sisters, Lyric and Hilary. We knew, though, that if we ever got in a serious bind, we could always call home for help, but we were raised to try to work things out ourselves first as best we could. When I went off to college (the college I chose was Brigham Young University, Provo, Utah), I realized I would have to find a part-time job. The only one I could find was janitorial work. I had to be on the job each morning at 4:00 a.m., which meant I had to wake up before that, get ready and be there on time. I knew that job well because I had cleaned buildings for years as a teenager, jobs my dad found for me. There were times I would be out with friends until early morning hours (you know, college kids), and on those days, I'd leave my friends and go straight to work. I would work from 4:00 till 8:00 a.m. The loss of sleep wore on me, so I searched for another job. I found one at the college medical center. That was a perfect job for a college student. I loved it, and the pay was good. In my sophomore and junior years, however, I landed a job with the Missionary Training Center (mission training for new, young men and woman preparing to go on their missions) teaching Spanish, something I'd learned serving a full-time mission for the church in Argentina for two years. Oh, and by the way, my mission expense was on my shoulders too, same with all the Smith kids who would go to college or on missions (all the boys and two of my sisters served missions). Some of our mission expense was picked up by an uncle of my mother, Joe Hundley. A total mission expense for two years was at or about $10,000, so we had to save for all these expenses as best we could.

Growing up in this family was interesting. As I compared my life to many of my high school and college buddies, I realized the Smith kids' home life was far more structural (household jobs) and considerably more was expected of us than most other kids I knew. But looking back, I would have it no other way.

I was not fearful of leaving home for college and mission. I was excited to get on with what I saw as steps to reach and the life I wanted. I remember being excited to get to college. Once there, the huge task at hand was almost overwhelming. I knew my parents had prepared me to work hard and set goals. It was very humbling to be on my own in the big, competitive world. I looked forward to each Sunday, which was the day we decided I would call home. To hear my parents' voices and to share with them the accomplishments of the week rejuvenated me and reminded me of the goals I had set as a young boy at home, goals I still tried to stay focused upon.

Cari's Memories—Second Child

I recall when tensions were high among us kids and anger flared, Dad would lighten the mood by taking the main culprit (on some occasions that would be me), wrestle me to the ground, and begin tickling me causing laughter. The other kids would just watch and laugh, wondering if they were the next to get the same treatment. It always had a tendency to change the mood, causing us kids to forget what we were arguing about.

Cari on Grandparents

I really appreciate that, as grandparents, you and Mom still see the importance of *teaching* your grandkids, not *spoiling* them. As a parent, it's great to know I don't have to reprogram my kids when they come home from an extended stay at your home.

I remember times friends or even a stranger would ask if I received enough attention while growing up in such a large family. The look on their faces when they learned I came from a family of ten kids usually told me they were thinking something to the effect, "How can someone not feel some form of neglect when the parent/child ratio was 1:5?" I'm sure I never received the sort of attention an only child would receive, and I don't think I would even care for that much attention. I do know that I never felt neglected and always felt loved and cared for. As a young child, Dad would take each of us children, one at a time, out to lunch a couple times a year. He would pick us up from school, take us to get a burger, talk about our lives—friends, concerns, sports—then take us back to school. My friends were always jealous of me.

I recall my mom taking as much time as needed to teach me things like cleaning my room and doing my schoolwork. But her biggest sacrifice of time for me came when I had their first grandchild, Saydi. Mom had planned to fly down close to the due date, but as nature sometimes does, Saydi came eight days early. I called Mom as soon as I got to the hospital so she could make new plans. With six children still at home, the youngest, Cassi, age three, and a backed-up well in the pump house (that happened regularly), she changed her flight and left that morning. Unfortunately, Mom missed the birth by an hour, but she stayed for the following week. What she did in that week taught me so much about service and selflessness. Before I had even gotten home from the hospital, she had dinner prepared and had scrubbed down my kitchen. Over the course of that week, she washed walls, rescreened many of the windows in the house where screens were torn or missing, put together a portable closet kit that we had purchased, made dinner on nights when the ladies from our church didn't, and all this while letting me rest. She did plenty of baby-holding too.

Even today with twenty-eight grandchildren to add to the equation, I don't feel at all neglected of my parents' attention. The grandchildren don't either—at least the three that are mine. Dad takes each grandchild out for ice cream on their birthday. Mom and Dad come to every possible sporting event they can. Believe me when I say that that keeps them busy!

Bottom line, there has always been enough love to go around in the Smith home.

Jesse's Memories - Family Night

When I was a child, my parents went to great lengths to dedicate one evening a week to being together as a family and teaching us more about God. I know they went to great lengths, because I am now a parent of young children and I struggle to muster the energy just to sit with them one night a week, let alone come up with all of the activities and lessons my parents did for me and my siblings.

During a certain phase of our family's development, I suppose my parents noticed that anger and short tempers were becoming a problem in the home, so they used the family night venue as an opportunity to address the issue. My mom called us into the living room for family night; we noticed that dad was not there. "Where's dad?" "Dad's not here! We can't start without Dad," we complained. "Calm down," my mom said, "we're going to start without him tonight." Although we were puzzled by his absence, my mom began to teach us a lesson about how we need to be "slow to anger," and that a "soft answer turneth away wrath" (or something like that). As we were all sprawled on the couch and the floor, probably paying closer attention to distractions, like a sister's foot in my face, than to my mom's lesson, my father burst into the living room roaring and flexing his muscles. He was painted green from head to toe; he was not wearing a shirt, but thank heavens was wearing an old pair of pajama bottoms that he had cut just below the knee. We all screamed for our lives and clung to whomever we were close to. I remember Sam was sitting on the armrest of the couch, and was so shocked that he flipped backward onto the floor. We all loved watching The Incredible Hulk series on TV as a family, so we understood the reference my parents were attempting to make; and the metaphor to short tempers was not wasted on us, despite our youth. I don't think anyone was permanently scarred by the incident, but it had the intended impact. After the terrorization, we had a good laugh. My parents made a chart with a picture of the Incredible Hulk, on which we marked the progress of controlling our tempers; and when I say "my parents," I mean, my mom made the chart. Regardless of how effective the chart was, meeting the Incredible Hulk in that way cannot be erased from my memory.

But rarely did my parents put on such theatrics. Family night was mostly made up of gospel lesson, followed by dessert. A regular occurrence on family night was memorizing scripture passages. My parents had a list of scriptures that we were expected to memorize, and my mom taught a method of linking a particular scripture to something quirky or memorable.

For instance, when I was about six or seven, while in Sunday school class, the teacher asked me to come to the front of the class to answer a question (probably because I was doing something to disrupt the class). She asked me, "Jesse, what commandments were on the stone tablets that God gave to Moses?" "Ok..." I said with a sigh, "here goes.

"One – One God. Thou shalt have no other gods before me.

"Two – Zoo. Zoos have statues, and statues are graven images, so... Thou shalt not make unto thee any graven image.

"Three – Tree. Trees have leaves and a leaf has veins. Thou shalt not take the name of the Lord thy God in vain.

"Four – Fort. Forts have holes in them because soldiers shoot cannonballs at them. Remember the Sabbath day, to keep it holy."

"Wait a mintue," my teacher interrupted with amazement. "You mean to say that you know all the Ten Commandments?" I guess she only wanted me to say

"God gave Moses the Ten Commandments," and leave it at that. Well, that was easy; why didn't she say so?

I know that some of the memorization techniques are a little quirky, but that seemed to be the key to children memorizing a litany of scriptures, that otherwise would've been impossible.

My parents also used family night to instill in each of us a sense of patriotism and honor for our Founding Fathers. We would recite the Pledge of Allegiance every family night, followed by the Preamble to the U.S. Constitution, accompanied with hand gestures, which are even more quirky than the scripture memorizing techniques (e.g., flapping our arms like an eagle at the end of the Preamble when we say "...of the United State of America."). I saw the same amazement in my elementary school teachers' faces that I saw in my Sunday school teacher, when I, of all the students in the class and arguably the most unruly and easily distracted kid in the class, cold jump up and recite the Preamble to the Constitution at the drop of a hat.

Looking back, I can say with certainty that my parents' use of a weekly family night aided, if not was principal cause for, my understanding of life and mortality, being spiritually minded and having a love for my country and honoring those who have sacrificed so much for my freedom and blessings. Thanks mom and dad.

Lyric's Memories—Fourth Child

When I was at college, all my friends were buying roller blades. I was using my own money for school plus scholarships, so I felt I could buy a pair. The only problem was my paycheck from my part-time job had not arrived, so I used a credit card. When Mom got word I had purchased roller blades with a credit card, she scolded me telling me not to get in that kind of habit. "Wait and pay cash," she said. A few days later, Mom and Dad sent me a check for $150 to pay off the credit card debt.

Dillon's Blues and Blessings—Fifth Child

When we first moved from Kansas to Idaho, I was in seventh grade with no friends. Most of the kids in my grade had been friends for years, and they were slow to allow me into their circle of friendship.

When they learned I was a Mormon, came from a large family, and milked a cow each day, they began to make fun of me. Granted, at age twelve, most boys are quite immature, yet I was settled enough in my mind to allow their barbs to simply roll off me without having much effect on me. I'd hoped for friends and longed for them, but I was doing fine. I guess you could say I was, for that age, comfortable in my own skin.

Our first few years in Idaho, we had to skimp financially, which was hard for me because most of the kids I knew in school came from well-to-do families. I didn't dwell on it much, but from time to time, I did feel some jealousy.

I must add, though, all of these types of challenges and more would prove to form my character. Being required to have a job at such a young age, along with many responsibilities on the small farm and around the house, as well as church service I accepted to do including scouting (all the Smith boys earned their Eagle Scout Award), all helped to make me who I am. I thank the Lord daily for the experiences of my childhood and youth. Dad and Mom expected a lot of me and all the Smith kids, and I feel fortunate to have been a part of those character building experiences.

Hilary's Blues—Sixth Child

I was about three, and Mom was pregnant with Alexis and on bed rest. It was Christmas time, so Mom made a list of gifts to purchase for each child and asked Dad to purchase them—big mistake—ha.

Dad, not as much into details as Mom, went for all the gifts and did a pretty good job, but he all but forgot about me. So Christmas morning, I ended up with a small box of crayons and a coloring book. Dad, realizing the error, took a general family gift, a gum ball machine, and gave it to me in his effort to cover the oversight. I felt bad at first, but felt good about the gum ball machine. It all worked out.

I have fond memories of Lyric and I milking Toto in the early morning hours. Lyric and I would sing "The Star Spangled Banner" a capella. We weren't too good, but I think Toto enjoyed it.

Our little farm created many memories. On one occasion, Mom took a bummer lamb (a lamb separated from its mother for any one of many reasons. In this case, the lamb was not well mentally). We often wondered why Mom took the lamb, a softy I guess.

In an effort to try to save the little lamb, she even had a small pen in our kitchen for a short time so she could keep a closer eye in him. Yeah, the kitchen, it seemed weird to us kids too, but Mom really felt to help that little lamb. Not many weeks later, he died.

All of us Smith kids were raised with clear-cut principles. That benefited me greatly when I was in high school. I was a pretty good basketball player and made the varsity team as a sophomore. We were a good, competitive team with lots of good seniors. We were invited to play in a tournament in Alaska, quite an honor. While there, some of the senior girls while in their motel rooms pulled out a large bottle of whiskey and began drinking it. One of the mothers of the players provided the drink—crazy, wouldn't you agree?

I and one other player were also invited to participate in the drinking party, but we both refused. In fact, we tried to persuade them not to do such a stupid thing.

It turned out the girls were discovered by one of the coaches. They were disqualified from playing in several of the regular season games. That left me and a couple of other younger players to fill in for the experienced seniors. It worked out well for me, allowing me to gain some valuable experience. In fact, those games were the best games I'd played all year. Most importantly though, it allowed me to see firsthand the importance of the things I'd been taught at home, a valuable lesson I'll never forget.

We had more fun toys when we lived in Kansas, but when we moved to Idaho, Dad's income went down for the first few years especially. We didn't have fancy video games or anything of the like, so we learned to entertain ourselves. On Sundays, when we couldn't go outside to play, we would often have sock wars. We'd move the furniture in the family room to form two forts. We would then gather all our socks and roll them into balls, choose side. Then the battles were on.

We also had to share more stuff. We had a pair of white, leather roller skates. Since more than one person wanted to skate at one time, we shared. Each person took one skate and would push with the other foot, kind of like a skate board. Eventually, it got to where I preferred just one skate.

Joseph's Blues—Seventh Child

Our son Joseph who, as a young boy, was playing in the dirt with a friend beyond our fenced pasture in a neighboring lot. Sandi told me to call the kids in for supper. I stepped out the back door and yelled, "Soups on!"

Joseph, when he heard the announcement, immediately jumped to his feet, took a big leap to clear the barbed wired fence. He cleared the fence but a thread of his back pant leg was caught in the fence and caused him to fall to the ground.

Once he untangled himself, rather than run to dinner, he climbed back over the fence to continue playing with his friend. His friend said, "Aren't you going to supper?"

Joseph replied, "It's too late."

Our kids took supper time very serious, and although there was enough to spare for food, you'd think, at times, they'd not eaten a meal in days.

Our son, Jesse, for instance, a teenager at the time, took meal time very seriously, like it was his last meal. When he was a teenager, he was drinking one and a half to two quarts of Toto's good whole milk each and every meal. Looking into his face at meal time, you just knew he thoroughly enjoyed not only Toto's milk but the family meal. Following family prayer and blessing on the food, food frenzy took place right before our eyes. Don't get us wrong, there was order and politeness, but they certainly took their meal times very seriously.

A Memory From Joseph

I recall as a grade school boy, I hit a particularly difficult time academically, which frustrated me. Also, Mom and Dad felt I wasn't getting the right influence at school.

They arranged with the principal of the school to keep me home half of every school day for a period of time. That time period turned out to be very helpful to me as a child. Through the experience, I was able to differentiate between the influence and spirit at school and that of my home. It was a remarkable experience for me, being so young, to identify differences in the Spirit, to see, or rather, to feel the difference between a calm, peaceful environment compared to one of something less than peaceful. For one of such a young age, it was a tremendous eye-opener and one that would help form the rest of my life.

I never recall Mom and Dad arguing, at least not in our presence, or raising their voices at each other. That has helped me see the kind of spouse and parent I wish to be.

We always had family dinners together. I have wonderful memories of Mom and Dad sitting next to each other at our large oak dining room table, with all the other kids filling in the rest of the chairs.

As an undergrad college student entering into my junior year and with sights set on dental school, I needed my summers to make the amount of money to carry me through the following school year. I had contracted with a friend to be a door-to-door salesman in Tucson, Arizona. I was told the company would pay for my expenses. All I had to do was sell. I learned I was not a particularly good salesman. Added to that, the company did not cover my expenses. I came home broke and with high credit card debt.

I was facing my toughest semester: organic chemistry, cell biology, and calculus, twenty credit hours total, and too many credit hours to take on a part-time job, just to name a few. To qualify for dental school, I would need a 4.0 or close to it, a job on top of school could jeopardize that. Added to that, my credit card monthly payments were due, and I didn't have the money to pay them. I was getting discouraged even depressed; my goals were not going as planned. I decided I would skip school for a while and work even though that would considerably slow down my entrance into dental school, something I'd hoped I wouldn't have to do.

I hadn't told Mom or Dad about my plight and didn't want to worry them. They must have noticed my concern on my face because one morning at the breakfast table, Mom and Dad informed me they had paid off the credit card debt by phone and that they wanted me to simply focus all my energies on college.

I think often of that morning at the breakfast table and the thoughtfulness of my dear parents. I'm grateful they were observant enough to determine my concerns and needs. What they did for me did more to bolster my focus and determination than they probably realized. I redoubled my efforts, got back on my chosen path and goals, graduated from college, entered dental school, and am now a practicing dentist.

Alexis' Memories—Eighth Child

Throughout my life, I have compared my life to back when I was eight years old. Yep, eight years old. I had such self-control and did everything I should be doing, and in return, I was filled with such a strong, constant spirit. I read my Scriptures daily, wrote in my journal daily, thought of others, saved my money, ate healthy, and shared the gospel with my friends and even teachers. Even as an adult, if I'm not feeling the spirit as a constant companion, I will remember back to when I knew I had the spirit so strong and try to remember the things I was doing to receive it.

Growing up in this family was the perfect recipe for a good imagination, for me at least. We had plenty of land with chores to do and animals to care for. That kept me outside much of the time except in the winter, cold season of the year. We didn't have lots of money for extracurricular activities when we first arrived in Idaho, and even if we did, I'm confident Dad and Mom would not have used it to spoil us. Also, we were allowed very little TV time. I used to daydream while milking Toto of how I could make a small corner of the corral into the most beautiful playhouse. I dreamed of making a clubhouse out of it and only members of my club would be invited to the lavish dinner parties, or so I imagined. I grew more and more excited about the layout of my playhouse until one morning, I ran out to the corral to see a new baby calf had taken it over. I was very disappointed.

So I shifted my daydreams to the space between the tall raspberry patch and our apple tree. I thought to myself how perfect it would be for the play house. Cali and I designed it perfectly, and we actually pulled it off and had many wonderful days of play there. Not many days later, however, earwigs overtook it and dashed our fun. So I shifted to other dreams; I was always dreaming.

Not until I became a mom did I realize how much work and time it took for my parents to discipline and implement certain family traditions and habits into the family and kids' lives, including spiritual habits. I only have two kids rather than ten, but I know that it is much easier to give in to whining and crying rather than sticking to my guns. And to get the whole family together for morning and evening prayer seems virtually impossible, not to mention planning a kid friendly Family Home Evening every Monday night. I had such a great example of how a child should be raised. Even though it is harder and takes more time, I have hope that if I do the things my parents did my kids will turn out great.

Cali's Blues—Ninth Child

I played volleyball as a freshman in high school and loved it. I was looking forward to playing my sophomore year. However, I got a C grade in one of my classes which violated the family B or better rule. As a result, I was not able to play my sophomore year, which devastated me. I was so angry at first, but I realized I had to try harder academically. Mom and Dad were so strict regarding that rule, but it did, finally, cause me to want to be better in school.

Growing up in our home meant you had lots of chores to do, often before school began and certainly after the school day ended. When we got home from school, the first thing we all had to do was finish our school homework. After that, Mom would select chores for each of us to do from her Chores Card File. And then, after chores were completed, we could watch one television show—yeah, just one! We chose that one show wisely. If we wanted to watch a real cool show like *The Mickey Mouse Club* or *Saved by the Bell*, we had to get our chores done extra fast because they began at 4:00 p.m., just one hour after school ended; it was torturous. In the end, it was good for us. I'm trying to figure out exactly how, but I'm sure it was—ha.

Cassi's Blues—Tenth Child

As a sophomore and junior in high school, I felt so rushed to get to school; I would leave my clothes in piles on my bed. Mom noticed the piles and gave me a couple of mild scoldings. I suppose I didn't take her counsel too seriously, because I continued to leave my clothes on my bed.

Finally, Mother took action. She took all the clothes that were on the bed and the floor and hid them from me. Each day she would examine my room; and if it passed inspection, she would give back to me one article of clothing. When Christmas came around, she returned all remaining articles as a Christmas gift.

This whole process was quite painful. You see, we Smith kids, when we came to a certain age of responsibility, were expected to save our own money for clothes and other things we desired. The clothes she took from me were clothes I'd purchased with my own hard-earned money.

Needless to say, I began putting my clothes away in their proper places.

Cassi's Memory

Each Smith kid had chores to do, whether it is during the school year or the summer months. Mother was the one to dish out assignments, and I assure you, she could always find something for us to do.

One day in the late fall, she gave me the assignment to sweep off our driveway. We have a large driveway, so this was not a quick job. Added to that, we had a huge pine tree that hung over part of the driveway, which dropped its pine cones all over the concrete.

I got the broom out and began to work. It took me about an hour to finish. Mom inspected the work and determined it wasn't quality work. She said, "Cassi, no halfway measures. If you're going to do a job, do it right the first time." So I was expected to redo the whole job again—another hour job. This was a common occurrence with all the kids until we learned to do our jobs right the first time. Quality work was important to her.

Was I mad? Yes, well, kind of, but I learned a good lesson, something I plan to pass on to my kids.

Sandi's First Auction

In the summer of 1989, we moved our family of nine children from Kansas to Idaho on a little two-acre farm. It was complete with a barn, pasture, garden site, and chicken coop area. Having been raised on a chicken farm part of my childhood, I had a lifetime dream of raising my children on a farm surrounded by animals.

Not long after arriving, we purchased a ewe we named Dorothy (Wizard of Oz/ Kansas connection) and a flock of laying hens. Our next project was to acquire a milk cow. Since I had milked a cow as a young child, I knew the amount of work it took and, therefore, the lessons to be learned for our children. Garth and I talked about it and determined the amount of money that we could spend, but no more. We had a wonderful neighbor who became not only our mentor farm hand but also our children's surrogate grandpa. His name was John. John told me that for a family milk cow, we should get a Jersey since they were a smaller breed, and produced less milk, so as not to overwhelm us. He had pointed out a few Jersey cows in the area, so I knew that they were brown. Obviously, I'd milked a cow as a child but really knew nothing about them.

After reading in the newspaper about a cow auction to be held in the neighboring state of Oregon, I determined that since Garth was busy getting his business up and running, and I was the "expert," I would go to the sale to purchase our cow. The advertisement had read that "dinner would be provided." Since it was a place where cattle were raised, I just assumed it would be a sit-down steak dinner, of course. I had never been to an auction before, even though I was raised on a farm. The only auctions I had ever seen were on TV, where people sat in a beautiful room, dressed nicely, and bid on fine pieces of art. The morning of the auction arrived. I knew it would take me about forty-five minutes to get there. Cali was our little toddler at the time, so I dressed both of us up in our Sunday's best. I even remember which dress I chose—a pale peach dress that I thought looked good with my coloring and tan heels. I asked Garth if I could take his nice car rather than our fifteen-passenger van; I wanted to make an impression.

Following the directions in the newspaper, I came to the end of the paved road and had to continue on a dirt road. This should have been my first clue and would have been a good time to turn back. But knowing we needed a good brown Jersey milk cow, I continued. Finally arriving at the sale, all I saw were lines and lines of dirty old pickup trucks with trailers attached, and cow poop running down all sides. Clue number two! The only women I saw were a couple of old cowboy type in dusty jeans and boots, and absolutely no children present. The rest were men in all their wrangler worst and dusty, poopy boots. Clue number three!

I had traveled so far I decided to stay and look around. As I started up the gravel road, I noticed an old chuck wagon selling hotdogs. Clue number four! There was my steak dinner.

Obviously, there had been a little miscommunication in my mind, but I was determined to get a family cow. The auctioneer was on a loud speaker, I was sure could be heard a mile away. I don't know how he noticed me, but as I was walking up to look at the cows, I heard in his shrill voice, echoing through the air, "Hey, little miss, what are you looking for?" As everyone turned their eyes toward me, I realized he was asking me. Clue number five! I did the only thing a reasonable person would do in that situation: I said, "I need a brown cow." The laughter erupted from everyone. Now I had done it. I was the auctioneer's personal attraction. For the rest of my time there, I was just answering questions shouted to me from his speakers with a volume control set on extra loud.

As different brown cows entered the arena, I was told to bid on them. Finally, I told the auctioneer that I did not know what the bid was up to because I could not understand him. When it was over my price range, I would just shake my head and say that it was too much.

Before long, a brown heifer was paraded into the corral. I was called to attention by the auctioneer telling me that this was a little brown cow like I wanted. I looked at the cow and could only see short little stubs for teats. (I did not know that a heifer's udder grows after she has her first calf, and this one had not had a calf yet.) I called back to the auctioneer, "The handles are too short." They say that laughter is the best medicine. Well, I was the best medicine for a whole lot of people that day!

As inconspicuously as I could, I started to work my way around the arena closer to the side where my car was parked. I knew I needed to get out of there.

Walking behind people, I heard the same, familiar shrill voice say, "Hey, little lady, do I have a cow for you?" Knowing I should just turn and run, my curiosity got the better of me, and I headed back to the arena. I looked through the fencing and saw the oldest milk cow yet alive with handles almost dragging on the ground. When I say that you could put two hands on each one lengthwise, I am not kidding. The audience roared with delight, and I picked Cali up in my arms and walked as quickly as you can in heels on gravel to the car and drove home.

The story does not end with that humiliation. I drove home, deciding not to tell anyone what had happened that day. As far as anyone would know, I couldn't find a suitable family cow, and the steak dinner was tough!

A few hours later, our oldest daughter, Cari, had bummed a ride home from school with a farm boy that lived down the road. I was in the yard washing the dirt off Garth's car when he jumped out of the old truck laughing. I asked him what was so funny. He said that his uncle was at a dairy auction in Oregon that morning and started to relate what his uncle had told him about this lady that showed up to the auction wanting a brown cow with long handles. This kid was laughing and hooting around like that was the funniest thing in the world. He said that it was the talk of the area.

I decided not to respond and lowered my head to keep scrubbing off all that dirt and grime on the car wheels!

A Tender Word Soothes the Mind

Some years ago, a sweet young lady and mother of two little boys came to my office. After she sat down, she broke into tears. After a moment to regain her composure, I asked her how she felt I could help her. She proceeded to tell me how insensitive her husband was of her weight, how he would make comments about her weight that would cut to the core. She told me how some of his comments were even in the presence of others. She explained how at times he used awful sarcasm pointed toward her regarding her weight.

She told me how much she wanted to please him. She had tried hard to lose weight, but obviously not enough to make him happy. She felt so humiliated, yet pained that her body had become such an issue in their marriage. I encouraged her to continue faithful in the marriage and to be patient, that maybe over time, he would become more sensitive to her feelings. I also encouraged her to share all her feelings with her husband in the hopes he could realize how much he was hurting her with his comments.

Compare the above story with this true husband-wife relationship:

Like the story above, a young woman, mother of two little children—a boy and a girl—came to me and asked for a few minutes of my time. She shared with me her frustration in losing weight, and I immediately thought, "Oh boy, here we go again, another disgruntled mother." But immediately, she put a beautiful smile on her face and began talking about her husband. She told me how much she wanted to please him yet how hard it was to lose weight and that she was concerned he was not pleased with her size. She also said he knew her concerns about her weight as it related to their relationship.

She recounted that one day, he approached her, held her hands in his, looked her straight in the eyes and told her she satisfied him perfectly well in every way. She said he then proceeded to tell her the thing that turned him on and made him weak in the knees (yeah, she said that) was her beautiful smile and her sweet countenance. She told me, "For him to tell me those sweet things has caused such feelings of confidence and assurance, and my love for him has grown leaps and bounds." She went on to say how much more determined she was to lose weight now that "I don't feel such pressure. I feel so grateful to have him as my husband."

This sweet little wife and mother simply wanted to share with me how amazing her husband was; she was so excited she had to tell someone, and I'm glad I was the one.

I share this contrast of stories because I've come to know through these experiences and more of my own experiences with my wife, that our dear wives carry a heavy load as wives and mothers. I've come to learn that the life of a wife and mother of little children, particularly, is the hardest job on earth, without question. And that the most significant thing we can do for our wife is love her, simply love her unconditionally.

One wise man said to me years ago, "Choose your love and love your choice." Over the years, I've come to learn more about the significance of what he said. I've had plenty of years to observe how monumental the work my wife does on a daily basis is, and that would apply to nearly all mothers. The best thing we can do as husbands and fathers is love our wives with all our heart and with all our minds. As we do this day in day out, we will always remain safely couched in our marriage promises and likely create a marriage and family legacy.

As it applies to our children, there is nothing more important to their development than having the knowledge their father loves and cherishes their mother, his wife. Ah, the stuff those legacies are made of.

The Courage to Endure

Many today are fleeing from their marriage promises and covenants as well as their parenting responsibilities. Think of the growing number of dads and moms who abandon their spouses and children. Painful to us all are the reports of moms and dads who tragically take their own lives, or the lives of their offspring or both. Who knows why people do what they do, but we feel we can all agree, when adults come under more stress than they are prepared to handle, danger lurks. And, of course, health issues come into play in many instances. But for the rest of us whose mental health is in check, much is expected of us as married couples and especially as parents. After all in this life, we're all on the front lines of the battle, and the sooner we come to realize that fact the sooner we can help our children learn it, too, and to become prepared for the battles of life that come from within and without.

A successful life including marriage and parenting requires courage. Life is a test. All of us, each and every one, find themselves alive and in a mortal, physical setting and for most, not knowing what this experience is all about or how to proceed only from the training from their parents or knowledge they've learned on our own, and often that knowledge and experience is flawed.

This life requires courage of each one of us. To reach deep inside ourselves and find that inner strength to do as our inner core encourages, requires a high level of courage. And then to continue that course to a successful marriage and family, defines the highest levels of courage.

The *courage* to do according to our own heart and conscience, is a habit we must bring back to the marriage, family, and to teach our kids to do the same, is a courage many feel is outdated. For many today, this speaks of being old fashioned and not in tune with modern child raising methods. Some think and teach that to encourage a child to listen to his or her heart, is to weaken them and to encourage them to build a crutch for living. We've found exactly the opposite to be true.

The words courage and heart are closely related as stated in an earlier chapter of this book. The root of the word courage is the Latin *cor*, which speaks of the heart, and the inner strength and resolve to endure through trials small and large. It tends to point to one's courage to face his or her most bitter inner struggles—*to expose and face one's most fierce mental battles*. A thrilling thought, don't you agree, that as we face and even expose for all to see, our most feared inner doubts and fears, is the essence of real courage. That doesn't mean we are encouraged to expose all our dirty laundry for the world to see. It does mean, however, that when we learn to face our doubts and fears, we will discover a new level of peace.

That by sharing our demons with certain individuals—exposing them to be seen, a new maturity will be reached. The courage we need, then, is to face our demons straight on with a willingness to allow certain individuals to see them.

How then, can we expect to win the most common battles of everyday life if we're unwilling to face our greatest most personal fears and doubts? To be sure, the more prepared we are for life's challenges the more likely we are to be victorious over all our life challenges and battles. Ever more reason to ready our children for life.

Searching for and discovering our inner doubts and fears must come first if we are to achieve success in this life, morally speaking particularly. We're only as strong as our weakest link; therefore, we can also expect that our greatest achievements will come by conquering our inner demons.

I knew a man from my childhood who prepared himself in every conceivable way, or at least it appeared that way. But it turned out that he failed to address his most feared inner strug-

gles. He was a great athlete and earned a college degree with that talent. He was highly intelligent and so his resume appeared stellar. He was chosen among hundreds of applicants to be the financial advisor for a large American city. Yet, because he had not previously faced his Achilles Heel with courage and determination, when he was faced with a severe challenge, he chose wrong, and as a result, his reputation was ruined. It was only through the good graces of his superiors that he was prevented from going to prison.

Parents will do their children well to discover their inner demons and help them conquer. It's not an easy thing to do, but as parents, we should do our best for their sake. Teaching them to be "comfortable in their own skin" is a good place to start (read the chapter of the same title in this book).

For instance, do you have a child who lacks confidence? We should strive to help him address that issue and conquer it while he is still in your immediate care. This same thing can be applied to any inner demon. The hard part is coaching the child to acknowledge it, to face it and begin the work to make that weakness a strength. Imagine the confidence that comes to a child (and ourselves) as we conquer such a threatening obstacle.

Courage then is best described as facing our most fierce threats. For one to be comfortable in their own skin, it seems logical that we find the energy and resolve to face those things that we're working so hard to hide from everyone else, those inner hidden, feared secrets that prevent us from becoming the best we can possibly be.

James Thurber, the American cartoonist best known for his contributions to *The New Yorker* magazine, said the following:

"All men should strive to learn before they die what they are running from, and to, and why."

Imagine if each one of us were to pose these questions to ourselves regularly, and then take the time to evaluate our most sincere and honest answers, the impact such a query would have on each of us. Then imagine training our children to make the same habit.

The answers to Thurber's questions from each of us could bring about the kind of internal honesty that brings about lasting change. No longer will we, as parents, be held hostage by our secret struggles, struggles that prevent our progress and fill us with fear of change. With this kind of honesty, our children will be raised with confidence in their abilities and genuine hope for their futures and their ability to face life with courage and confidence.

Just by identifying and addressing our greatest fears does not, in itself, resolve our problems. Once identified and faced, we can work on them, though it may take months or years to totally absolve ourselves of them. To finally face them, though, will bring a confidence and peace to your life previously unfelt.

Again we state, one of the most important things we can do for ourselves and our children, is to muster up the courage to face those issues head on with the resolve to rid ourselves of them, hopefully sooner than later. It could take time, so we should be patient yet resolute in our courage.

By simply addressing those demons can stimulate feelings of encouragement for many. As we work the Thurber questions, the question we should ask ourselves is this: "How do I determine what I'm running from and to and why?"

Most of us will know immediately what we're running from; our conscience will bring it to our quick attention once we ask the question of ourselves. For many, however, the harder question is, "What am I running to, and why?"

One way to help ourselves identify the answer to these questions is to scan our thoughts to determine where most of our daily thoughts are placed. After all, "we move in the direction of our most current, dominate thoughts." With this in mind, an honest-minded person can review her most dominate daily thoughts and come up with an accurate answer.

Are our thoughts moving us in the direction of the unselfish or selfish, the honest or dishonest, things of a spiritual nature or carnal? Do we have the tendency to sabotage ourselves or are we honest with ourselves? What of our most hidden secrets, are we being truly honest with ourselves or ignoring our weaknesses? Self-honesty is a must if we're to identify our demons and work on them. A failure to be honest with ourselves is, in itself, at the root of our demons.

Life is a wonderful journey, or is intended to be so. So, let's position ourselves and our children for the best chance of success we can muster up. Wiring our kids for success pretty much demands it, wouldn't you agree?

Where it all started; Garth and Sandi dating.

We're still dating. This one was in the Switzerland Alps.

Our daughters (left-right): Cassi, Cali, Alexis, Hilary, Lyric and Cari.

Our sons (left to right): Jesse, Joseph, Sam and Dillon.

Smith kids (not including newborn Cali) in Kansas.

Our whole family (less Sam, who was off to college). Toto, our milk cow and loyal pet, was so gentle.

The whole family, including spouses, at McCall, Idaho.

Joseph and Rachel's wedding; glorious evening.

The End (Result)

Well, this is the last chapter; the end of the book. We hope you've enjoyed it and more importantly, we hope it has offered some encouragement and support to your noble decision to be an enduring husband and wife and parent.

We have learned from our own experience, that marriage and parenting, if it is enduring, is the hardest work there is to do, yet the most fulfilling. We've learned that we become our best selves as we strive to be the best spouse and the best parent possible. As we work through these wonderful burdens (marriage and parenting), we can't help but believe they are not nor were they ever intended to be the end after we leave this frail existence.

I (Garth) recently had a business dealing with an eighty-year-old couple. They raised a wonderful family and endured over fifty years of marriage. They were remarkably connected to each other in love and kindness. We could say they were one, not two people. They had the most endearing feelings for each other, their kids, and grandkids.

We were together long enough to discuss many varied subjects, and we all came to realize how alike we were in our views. Finally, we got to the discussion of love of family. The Misses said she felt family was the most important organization on earth and then expressed how much she loved her family. We all came to the same conclusion, that tender feelings of marriage and family are so deeply woven within mankind, that it is hard to imagine life after death without them. She said, "How can heaven be heaven without my sweetheart husband, my precious children and grandchildren?" She answered her own questions, "I think it cannot. Families", she said, "must go beyond the grave, at least I hope it does."

We agree with her, families are intended to last beyond the grave, how could it be otherwise? Every fiber of a happy husband, wife, and children points to this being the ultimate happiness now and forever. They shared with me some background of each of their three children, all grown and with their own families. Each child had achieved good educations and was well defined in their chosen fields of endeavor. Each child was, as we would say, comfortable in their own skin.

We spoke of how it was that their children turned out so well, and they responded, "Well, we just applied the good old fashioned patterns of raising kids—we taught them to be happy, work hard and easily forgive others, including themselves."

It reminded me that when we really apply our best effort to our marriage and our kids, good things always result. Surely there are always challenges to overcome, heartache to endure and misunderstandings to forgive. But when we look back, we generally find the struggle was not only worth the effort, but that we discover much of our joys in life come from working through our struggles with our spouse. After all, if life were a smooth path all the time, monotony would overwhelm us.

We've come to believe that we are never alone, not in the smooth paths of life and certainly not during the rocky, rough paths. We always have divine help whether we want it or not. The truth is, our Father in heaven has a plan designed that meets the needs of each and every one of us; it is often referred to as The Plan of Happiness, and it extends beyond this life. All we need to do is learn to be accepting of his influence by striving to see His hand in all things.

Sandi and Garth

Me, Garth, with Sandi and all the Kids filed behind. Taken about 1990.

Sam, our eldest, with his wife, Hollie, and their six children.

Cari, our second child, with her husband, Justin, and their three children.

Jesse, our third child, with his wife, Becky, and their four children.

Lyric, our fourth child, with her husband, Steve, and their three children.

Dillon, fifth child, with his wife, Nicole, and two of their three children. Daughter Lucy is a newborn not shown.

Hilary, sixth child, with her husband, Andrew, and their two children.

Joseph, seventh child, with his wife, Rachel, and their son, Whitaker. They are expecting baby Elias any day.

Alexis, eighth child, and her husband, Quinn, and their two children.

Cali, ninth child, and her husband,
Ryan, with their two children.

Cassi, tenth child, and her husband, Brenan, and their two children.

All the Smith girls about 1991.